The

International

Traveler's

GUIDE TO

Doing Business
in Latin America

TERRI MORRISON AND
WAYNE A. CONAWAY

MACMILLAN SPECTRUM
MACMILLAN • USA

Macmillan General Reference
A Simon & Schuster Macmillan Company
1633 Broadway
New York, NY 10019

Manufactured in the United States of America

10   9   8   7   6   5   4   3   2   1

ISBN: 0-02-861755-X

Book design by Kevin Hanek

Dedication

To Alex and Nica, around whom our worlds revolve.
Blessed are the pure of heart . . .

To Stella F. Conaway and Wayne E. Conaway.
For four decades of love, understanding, and support.
The peacemakers . . .

and Many Thanks...

*To Virginia Stokes Brubaker. Linchpin of a wonderful family—
CEO—steadfast friend. Thank you Gin,
for always believing the best of us!*

To Jennifer Lickey. Thank you, again, for the time and space.

*To Jane E. Dorchester. Thank you for keeping
Wayne from going ballistic.*

*To Joyce and Terri Hayden. Capable, witty,
intelligent and caring players.*

And to Liam! Whose timing was impeccable!

*To Robert E. Lee (the lawyer, not the General). The epitome
of integrity, grit, and southern graciousness. Thank you for
your complete attention and generous aid!*

To Bernadette Verdi for her creative designs.

To Richard Staron, who believed in and edited our first book:
KISS, BOW OR SHAKE HANDS:
HOW TO DO BUSINESS IN SIXTY COUNTRIES;
and who conceived of this new series:
THE INTERNATIONAL TRAVELER'S GUIDE TO DOING BUSINESS.
An honest judge, a keen sense of value, and an open mind.

Civilization is the encouragement of differences
—the more diverse a system, the more stable it is.

− MAHATMA GANDHI

Contents

APPENDIXES

Foreword

By John H. Ostdick, Editor-in-Chief
American Way, the magazine of American Airlines

We often pepper discussions of the evolving world markets with contradictory imagery.

> Global issues.
> Global reach.
> Global culture.
> A shrinking world.

Of course, we realize the world hasn't lost any mass in the past twenty years; the reach of our technology is merely catching up with modern expectations, making us re-examine how we interact with others a half a planet away.

The technological catapult is also rearranging daily planners on desks from Pittsburgh to Tokyo. Doing business in Buenos Aires—or Milan, Warsaw, Moscow, Beijing, or Seoul, for that matter—is no longer the exclusive domain of multinational corporations. The independent parts producer in Dayton, Ohio, struggling to survive five years ago, may have found an emerging customer base within these global circles and is now grappling with the need to move smoothly around them.

How? You don't have to be a Bill Gates to realize making connections is tantamount, for both David and Goliath, and that the most critical currency in making savvy business decisions is often of a cultural ilk. Information, that old business bedrock, is still the foundation for forging any alliance. Despite the changes in immediacy wrought by our ongoing technological shrink-wrap, existing historical and cultural nuances still shade behavioral norms within international markets.

A writing colleague once told me the ultimate test of an intruder, which a writer generally is in any new environment, is the ability to not only understand the language of a specific place or culture, but further to assimilate the nuances of the language, place, and culture well enough to tell an acceptable joke therein. That ability was what allowed him as an outsider to cross a familiarity threshold and absorb the essence of the people and place he was writing about. I couldn't argue with him then nor do I now, although realistically most of us do not become that fluent in our secondary languages.

Understanding a culture, however, becomes even more critical in a business venture when mere color choice for a presentation board can yield apocalyptic results. At the very least, the well-equipped decision-maker—or savvy traveler, for that matter—needs to understand what basic gaffes, in and of themselves irreversible impressions, to avoid in specific countries.

A sizable number of globe-trotting corporate decision-makers and entrepreneurs are among the more than 91 million who board American Airlines planes each year. As editor of the magazine serving this readership base, I had been searching for a reliable source for culturally implicit information who could also present it in an entertaining and comprehensive manner. Terri Morrison and Wayne A. Conaway are such resources, and *American Way* readers have responded enthusiastically to their work.

With this book series, Terri and Wayne take another quantum leap in the process of making far-flung communication less daunting and more successful. Certainly this book, or the entire series for that matter, is no panacea for those of you flying through international business markets at warp speed. In the yin and yang of global philosophy, however, it's just good business to be studied in what awaits behind each door you wish to open. This material can get you over that threshold. The rest is up to you.

INTRODUCTION

New Prospects in the New World

by Terri Morrison and Wayne A. Conaway

W hen you go to Europe or Asia, and you're asked where your headquarters is, do you say "America"? The word America means both a country (the USA) and an entire hemisphere. And if you're only doing business in the United States of America, you're only doing business in about a third of the American Hemisphere. Almost two-thirds of the population of this hemisphere is in Latin America.

The United States of America and Canada are often considered to be "mature markets." The populations of these two countries are well-served in most areas; they are exposed to a blizzard of advertising and have already established their buying patterns.

Much of Latin America, however, is only now entering the global economy. Even though the European influence in Latin America is older than in the USA or Canada (since Europeans first colonized Central and South America), the broadening of an economically-active middle class is a more recent phenomenon. Month by month, thousands more potential Latin customers enter the global market.

Like many terms, "Latin America" has different meanings to different people. Is it everything south of the USA? Does it include the Spanish-speaking Caribbean?

For the purposes of this book, we have decided to cover every continental Latin nation. This excludes such Hispanic Caribbean locales as Cuba and the Dominican Republic. It also excludes the three non-Latin colonies and former colonies in South America: Guyana (the former British Guiana), Surinam (the former Dutch Guiana), and French Guiana. So why have we have included Belize (the former British Honduras) in this book? Only because you cannot cover the history of Central America's Mosquito Coast without explaining the British presence. To explain Guatemala and Honduras, you must explain Belize. (On the other hand, it is quite possible to explain Venezuela and Brazil without ever mentioning Guyana, Surinam, and French Guiana.)

We have made one other "exception" to our list of Latin American countries. Although most English-speakers would consider Brazil to be part of Latin America, the Brazilians themselves do not. They take pains to point out that their heritage is Portuguese, not Spanish. But a book on Latin America would hardly be complete without South America's largest and most populous nation, so Brazil has been included.

The layout of this book, and this series, follows a common interrogative pattern: "Who, What, When, Where, Why, and How?" As in our previous books, *Kiss, Bow or Shake Hands: How to Do Business in Sixty Countries* and *Dun & Bradstreet's Guide to Doing Business Around the World,* we felt that a consistent template for each country would make the work a more valuable resource for our readers.

The International Traveler's Guide series is meant as a sophisticated briefing for the busy executive. Global nomads will find data here . . . from a country's greatest authors and artists to its chronology and largest corporations. Each chapter starts with a Cultural I.Q. Quiz (which, if you get a perfect score, skip to the next country) . . . and ends with helpful and interesting Web sites to support the data and keep you current!

As with our previous books, we would like to invite your comments. The study of intercultural communications represents a lifelong interest for the authors, and we appreciate your input—whether your experience confirms or diverges from the data in this book. You may want to visit our Web site at http://www.getcustoms.com and send your feedback to e-mail 74774.1206 @compuserve.com, or telephone: (610) 353-9894 / fax: (610) 353-6994— or write to us at:

> Getting Through Customs
> Box 136
> Newtown Square, PA 19073

> *Si fueris Romae, Romano vivito more;*
> *Si fueris alibi, vivito sicut ibi.*
> *(If you are at Rome, live in the Roman style;*
> *If you are elsewhere, live as they live elsewhere.)*
> – ST. AMBROSE (C. 340-397)

Argentina

WHAT'S YOUR CULTURAL I.Q.?

1. TRUE or FALSE? The first European expedition to Argentina was led by Ferdinand Magellan.

    ANSWER: False. Spanish explorer Juan Diáz de Solis beat Magellan to Argentina by four years. Neither expedition left a permanent settlement.

2. Which of the following is Argentina's oldest, continuously occupied city?

    a. Buenos Aires

    b. Rosario

    c. Santiago del Estero

    d. Tucumán

    ANSWER: c. Established in 1553, Santiago del Estero has the longest unbroken history. Buenos Aires was established first, in 1536, but that settlement was abandoned due to attacks from the local Querandí Amerindians. Buenos Aires was reoccupied in 1580.

3. TRUE or FALSE? Generally speaking, the Spanish had more success conquering the highly organized

Amerindians of the Andean foothills than they did conquering the nomadic tribes of Patagonia.

ANSWER: True. The tribes in the Andean foothills tended to be centralized agriculturists that maintained complex irrigation systems. This agricultural infrastructure made them vulnerable to conquest. If they fled from an invader, they lost their irrigated fields and risked starvation. On the other hand, the nomadic hunter-gatherer groups of Patagonia could run from any forces too powerful for them to fight. The last of the Patagonian tribes were not conquered until the year 1880.

4. Which of the following is commemorated as Independence Day in Argentina?

<blockquote>
a. 25 May 1810

b. 9 July 1816

c. 3 February 1852

d. All three dates

e. a. and b.
</blockquote>

ANSWER: e. Argentina has two Independence Days. The first, 25 May 1810, was the date that Buenos Aires declared its autonomy from Spain. Independence for the entire country was not declared until 9 July 1816, in the northwest Argentine town of Tucumán. (The other date, 3 February 1852, was the day that Argentina's first dictator, Juan Manuel de Rosas, was deposed.)

5. The dictators who led Argentina during the Second World War were pro-Fascists and sympathetic to the Axis Powers. TRUE or FALSE? Argentina never entered World War II on either side.

ANSWER: False. Although the Argentine leaders were sympathetic to the Axis powers, pressure from the USA forced Argentina to break relations with the Axis in 1944. Just before the end of the war, Argentina formally entered on the Allied side.

6. Juan Domingo Perón founded a political dynasty. Which of the following peronistas did NOT serve as president of Argentina?

a. Juan Domingo Perón

b. His second wife, Eva (Evita) Perón

c. His third wife, Isabel Perón

d. Carlos Saúl Menem

ANSWER: b. Despite her fame, Eva Perón never was president—she died while her husband was in office. Isabel succeeded to the presidency after her husband died in office in 1974. Carlos Saúl Menem, elected president in 1989, is a member of the Justicialista Party—the modern-day Peronist Party.

7. The tango is both the national dance and national obsession of Argentina. TRUE or FALSE? In 1954, a tango artist named Astor Piazzolla so outraged some Argentine tango fans that he received death threats.

ANSWER: True. For years, Astor Piazzolla had been one of Argentina's top tango musicians, leading tango bands with his bandoneón (a type of accordion). In 1954, Piazzolla came out with a radically different New Tango, which broke decades of tango conventions. This brought him many fans—and violent opposition from tango traditionalists.

8. All of the following men were authors. Which of them was NOT born in Argentina?

   a. Che Guevara

   b. Manuel Puig

   c. Jacobo Timmerman

   d. Pablo Neruda

   ANSWER: d. Pablo Neruda, the Nobel-prize winning poet, was from Chile. Of the others, revolutionary Che Guevara (real name: Ernesto Guevara Serna) fought with Fidel Castro in Cuba and authored the phrase "guerrilla warfare". (The nickname "Che" is often given to Argentines by other Latin Americans.) Manuel Puig, author of *Kiss of the Spider Woman,* was also Argentine, although he chose to live most of his life in Brazil. Journalist Jacobo Timmerman's works include *Prisoner Without a Name, Cell Without a Number.*

9. Argentina is South America's largest Spanish-speaking nation (only Portuguese-speaking Brazil is larger than Argentina). TRUE or FALSE? The Argentines speak a classical version of Spanish, similar to that spoken around Madrid in Spain.

   ANSWER: False. Actually, due to the large number of Italian immigrants, Argentine Spanish is a unique mixture of Spanish and Italian.

10. Argentina is a nation of immigrants. The ancestors of Argentine president Carlos Saúl Menem (first elected in 1989) came from what country?

    a. Syria

    b. Japan

    c. Italy

d. Germany

e. Austria

ANSWER: a. Menem's parents immigrated to Argentina from Syria.

QUOTATIONS ABOUT ARGENTINA

"(Argentina) is a simple colonial society created in the most rapacious and decadent phase of imperialism."
—V.S. Naipaul

(Paul Theroux speculates that Naipaul's dislike for Argentina stems from Naipaul's vegetarianism. Argentines consume huge amounts of meat—many eat beef twice per day.)

" . . . gloom was part of the Argentine temper; it was not a dramatic blackness but rather a dampness of soul, the hangdog melancholy immigrants feel on rainy afternoons far from home."

—From *The Old Patagonian Express* by Paul Theroux.

"A hundred and fifty-three Welsh colonists landed here (Port Madryn) off the brig Mimosa *in 1865. They were poor people in search of a New Wales, refugees from cramped coal-mining valleys, from a failed independence movement, and from Parliament's ban on Welsh in schools. Their leaders had combed the earth for a stretch of open country uncontaminated by Englishmen. They chose Patagonia for its absolute remoteness and foul climate; they did not want to get rich.*
　　"The Argentine Government gave them land along the Chubut River. From Madryn it was a march of forty miles over the thorn desert. And when they did reach the

valley, they had the impression that God, and not the Government, had given them the land."

—From Bruce Chatwin's *In Patagonia*. The Welsh were only one of many immigrant groups to come to Argentina.

> *"Sometime in the early sixties, in the Argentine comic book* El Tony, *there appeared a new and startling series,* El Eternauta, *signed by a certain Héctor G. Oesterheld. In the first installment,* El Eternauta—*a wonderful word that combined 'cosmonaut' with 'eternity' and conjured up the image of a time traveller through the infinity of the ages—arrived one day in a vaguely mythical Buenos Aires during a freak snowstorm. The reason for his quest was vague; more important than the plot were El Eternauta's melancholic reflections on Argentina and its people . . . .*
>
> *"A decade and a half later, on 27 April 1977, the 50-year old Oesterheld was abducted by the Argentine military . . . . Osterheld was not seen again, one of the 30,000 'disappeared' during the military dictatorship.*
>
> *"It isn't clear what threat Oesterheld represented to the military regime. Nothing in his comic strips—of which* El Eternauta *remained the most famous—overtly protests military abuses, denounces government corruption or encourages subversion in any obvious political sense. It is as if the military censors, with keener eyes than those of the common reader, discovered in Osterheld's science-fiction romances and tales of adventure a hidden accusation, a reminder of the sanctity of individual freedom or a wordless call to arms."*

—From the essay "Dangerous Subjects" by Alberto Manguel and Craig Stephenson.

"There are two things of which I am proud: My love for my country and my hatred for the oligarchy."
—Evita Perón

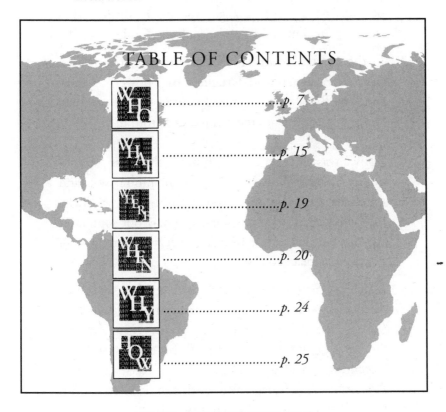

TABLE OF CONTENTS

THE ARGENTINES

HOW TO TELL ARGENTINA AND THE ARGENTINES FROM THEIR NEIGHBORS

1. Argentina is big. It's the second largest nation in South America, smaller only than Brazil.

2. The Andes Mountains run down the western side of South America (the left-hand side as you look at it on a

map). Argentina runs from the Andes to the Atlantic Ocean (except in the north, which we'll get to next). Argentina's perennial rival, Chile, lies on the other side of the Andes. Argentina got the better deal—it has almost four times as much land area as Chile.

3. In the north, Argentina borders three small countries: Bolivia, Paraguay, and Uruguay. Big, powerful countries like Brazil and Argentina tend to gobble up small countries, so why are these three still around?

    • Bolivia was where the Spanish made their last stand in South America. Bolivia was where the money was, and the Spanish tried to hold on to it. Maybe it was lucky for Bolivia that its mines started to play out soon after the Spanish left. Also, Bolivia is very mountainous— not an easy place to invade.

    • Much of Paraguay did get gobbled up by Argentina, during something called the War of the Triple Alliance (1865–70). Paraguay took on Brazil, Uruguay, and Argentina, and lost about a third of its territory. Argentina gained some of the Chaco desert. (This was Argentina's last foreign war until the 1982 war with Great Britain over the Falkland Islands.)

    • As for Uruguay, both Argentina and Brazil wanted it. Rather than go to war over it, they allowed Uruguay to exist as a buffer nation.

4. Although the Spanish did not find the gold and silver they sought in Argentina, the country has abundant resources, especially in the agricultural arena. The perennial Argentine complaint is that their country has been "blessed by resources and cursed by politics."

5. Argentina was populated by immigrants from all over the world. Although the ethnicity of the country is predominantly Latin, other influences are part of the culture. A very British reserve, complete with a formality of dress and manner, is characteristic of many Argentines.

6. Like other nations in South America's Southern Cone (which includes Chile and Uruguay), Argentina suffered through a brutal military dictatorship in the late 1970s. All these regimes kidnapped, tortured, and killed their opponents. However, the Argentine military seemed to be unique in one horrific technique: They drugged citizens and shoved them out of airplanes over water.

LITERATURE

Argentina has given the world a number of top-class writers. However, Argentina's share of the international publishing industry is in decline. As late as the 1920s, Argentina produced 80% of all the books printed in South America! Since then, the publishing industries in Chile and Brazil have boomed, decreasing Argentina's share.

Argentina's most noted authors include:

Jorge Luis Borges (1899–1986) remains the most famous 20th-century Argentine writer. His output was as impressive as his reputation; he wrote fiction, essays, and reams of poetry. His *Ficciones* is considered a classic of Spanish literature.

Julio Cortázar (1914–84) was a contemporary of Borges. His metaphysical novel *Hopscotch* was the most important Argentine novel of the 1960s.

Esteban Echeverría (1805–51) came of age during the dictatorship of Juan Manuel de Rosas, who ruled Argentina with an iron fist from 1835 to 1852. Echeverría's *El Matadero* is the story of a young man slain by Rosas' enforcers. Echeverría was also the founder of the May Society, a socialist political group.

Ricardo Güiraldes (1886–1927) wrote the quintessential Argentine male coming-of-age novel, *Don Segundo Sombra.* The book follows a boy in his attempts to become a full-fledged gaucho.

José Hernández (1834–86) was the Argentine "Poet of the Pampas." His epic poem *Martín Fierro* is said to explain the Argentine soul better than any other work. Hernández lived among the gauchos, so he knew his subject matter intimately—unlike some later writers. It is interesting that so many Argentines chose this as their favorite work, since the title character of *Martín Fierro* is an honest gaucho forced to become an outlaw after wealthy city-dwellers legally appropriate his land.

Manuel Puig (1932–90) was not the first homosexual to find life difficult in Argentina, so he moved to the more relaxed locale of Rio de Janero in Brazil. Best known in the US as the author of *Kiss of the Spider Woman,* his works include *Cursed Be the Reader of These Pages* and *The Buenos Aires Affair.*

Domingo Faustino Sarmiento (1811–88) is unique among Argentine opposition writers, since he actually achieved a position of political power. Another enemy of the Rosas dictatorship, he wrote the seminal work *Facundo: Life in the Argentine Republic in the Days of the Tyrants.* While in exile in the US, he was chosen as president of Argentina. He served as president from 1868 to 1874, and built so many schools that Argentina achieved nearly total literacy by the start of the 20th century.

Jacobo Timmerman is a newspaper publisher, author, and theorist. *Prisoner Without a Name, Cell Without a Number* is his best-selling account of his imprisonment during the dictatorship of Lt. General Jorge Rafael Videla. He has written about the dictatorship of neighboring Chile as well, in *Chile: Death in the South.*

INVITATION TO THE DANCE

First, the tango is not Argentina's only indigenous style of dance. Gaucho dancing is a form of folk dance associated with rural Argentina. But the tango is arguably Argentina's greatest artistic gift to the world.

Second, the tango is not just a dance. Tango also refers to a style of music. Tango dancing is done to tango music, but there is a lot of tango music that is not suitable for dancing. Some tango music even has lyrics, although the dancing is usually done to instrumental tango music.

Third, many Argentines are crazy about the tango.

The traditional tango evolved out of the slums of Buenos Aries, where Spanish, Italian, German, and Jewish immigrants lived in close quarters. These diverse musical heritages were combined with African rhythms. Since Argentina never imported slaves, it has few blacks. Nevertheless, the tango has antecedents in West Indian dances such as habanera and milonga—which, in turn, have African roots. Just as jazz in the USA was first played in the bordellos of New Orleans, the tango was associated with the bordellos of Buenos Aires. And, like jazz, the tango needed decades to attain respectability. (Unlike jazz, the tango's central instrument was not the piano but the bandoneón, a deep-toned German variant of the accordion.)

During Argentina's boom era (1910–30), Argentina embraced the tango as a native art form. By the 1920s, the tango became popular around the world. Hollywood musicals featured the tango, further spreading its fame. As Argentina's fortunes waned during the Great Depression, tango music became fixed in style.

Like a fly in amber, the tango remained frozen until a bandoneón player named Astor Piazzolla returned to Buenos Aries in 1938. After making his way to the top of the tango world, he suddenly broke tango out of its ossified state in 1954. Piazzolla's New Tango was nothing short of revolutionary. As *Boston Globe* columnist Fernando Gonzalez put it:

"He stretched old song-form conventions and eventually dismissed them entirely. He retained tango's romanticism while rejecting its tendencies to nostalgia and bouts of moribund self-pity. He revised the harmonic language to include Ravel and Messiaen and Schoenberg and Bartok—and then he added a walking bass. He incorporated three-part fugues and jazz-style improvisation and powered it all with an improbable blend of traditional tango pulse and Stravinskian rhythms. He outraged the tango world.... Tango was part music, part religion and there was no room for heretics."

Today, *Tangueros* (tango aficionados) are divided into two camps: traditionalists and Piazzolla fans. In general, traditionalists are older Argentines, who grew up with the old-style tango.

LIGHTS! CAMERA! ACTION!

 Since 1933 (when Argentina's first film, *Tango,* was produced), Argentina has had one of the strongest film industries in South America. The country has produced a number of important films. They also provide a good (albeit skewed) introduction to Argentine life. The following films are listed by order of their time setting:

1. **Camila** Set in 1847, Camila is the wife of a wealthy politician. When she has an affair with her priest, the two lovers find both the church and state united against them. Based on a true story (1984, directed by Maria Luisa Bemberg).

2. **Miss Mary** Set amid the turbulence of Argentina in the late 1930s, the English nanny (portrayed by Julie Christie) of an important political family inadvertently implicates her employer in a scandal (1986, directed by Maria Luisa Bemberg).

3. **Details of a Duel** An examination of Argentine machismo in a Andean town in the 1950s. Two

unlikely warriors—a butcher and a schoolteacher—are manipulated by their fellow townspeople into fighting a duel to the death. An instructive comedy of small-town life in a rarely seen region of Argentina (1989, directed by Sergio Cabera).

4. **Funny Dirty Little War** A clever anti-war satire of conflict in a small Argentine town in the 1950s. The townspeople divide into opposing factions, and the formerly peaceful town becomes a battlefield. The film is instructive because both factions identify themselves as Peronist, until one side brands the other as Communist. *Unforgettable moment:* The cropdusting plane that bombards the town, first with pesticide, then with manure (1983, directed by Hector Olivera).

5. **Veronico Cruz** Set in the Argentine pampas during the Falkland Islands War, a young boy's life is forever changed when soldiers are stationed in his small town, polarizing the citizens (1987, directed by Miguel Pereira).

6. **The Official Story** A middle-class housewife in the 1980s is content to ignore Argentina's political strife—until she realizes that her beloved adopted daughter is the child of political dissidents murdered by her government. This picture won the 1995 Academy Award for Best Foreign Film. *Unforgettable moment:* The parents of "los desaprecidos" (the disappeared ones, slain by the government and buried in unmarked graves), bearing pictures of their missing children and grandchildren, hoping that someone will recognize one of their offspring from the photos (1985, directed by Luis Puenzo).

7. **Time for Revenge** An absorbing drama of class conflict in 1980s Buenos Aires. To expose the unsafe working conditions at a demolition site, a worker rigs an industrial accident. His plans go awry when a fellow

worker is killed in the accident (1983, directed by Adolfe Aristarain).

8. **Man Facing Southeast** The oft-examined theme of a sane person in a madhouse is given a new twist when a mysterious man appears at an asylum, claiming to be an alien from another planet. His doctor in this contemporary Buenos Aires asylum soon suspects that the stranger might be telling the truth. *Unforgettable moment:* An uncaring asylum employee drags a coffin down a flight of steps, with the nude corpses of the inmates (buried two to a coffin!) bouncing out at each jolt (1987, directed by Elisio Subiela).

9. **Times to Come** A surreal science-fiction nightmare about Buenos Aires in the near future. A visitor to the city is accidentally shot by an out-of-control policeman. A bad situation gets worse as officials try to hide the incident, while the policeman himself is stalked by a harasser. The title comes from the pessimistic Argentine saying, "It'll even be worse in times to come." *Unforgettable moment:* The victim, the policeman, and his harasser—all following each other through the paper-strewn corridors of a deserted futuristic hospital (1981, directed by Gustavo Mosquera).

Taking Movie Dollars Out of Argentina

During the reign of Juan Perón, US movie companies were prohibited from taking the profits from their films out of Argentina. Stuck with Argentine currency they couldn't take home, some Hollywood studios used the cash to film in Argentina. One such movie was Taras Bulba *(1962), in which Argentina doubled for medieval Poland!*

LANGUAGE

Although the official language is Spanish, a very distinct dialect of Spanish is spoken in Argentina. There were so many immigrants from Italy that Argentine Spanish absorbed many Italian words. In addition, there are many Argentine slang words (collectively known as *lunfardo*) derived from many sources, including the Amerindian language Guaraní. If you speak classical Spanish (Castilian) you will be able to make yourself understood, but you may have trouble understanding Argentine speech.

Linguists have categorized 25 different languages spoken in modern Argentina—*Ethnologue: Languages of the World,* 12th Edition from their Web site at (http://www.sil.org/ethnologue/ethnologue.html).

BUSINESS IN ARGENTINA

BUSINESS SUCCESS IN ARGENTINA

Caveat: While many options are open to foreign firms wishing to do business in Argentina, most firms create a separate subsidiary incorporated in Argentina. This minimizes the firm's liability. Should a foreign firm simply open a branch in Argentina, all of the firm's assets (not just those in Argentina) may be subject to potential liability.

In addition to establishing a subsidiary, franchises and joint ventures are available for foreign companies who wish to do business in Argentina. The services of a competent Argentine lawyer are necessary for either type of agreement. The obligations of each party must be spelled out in detail.

continues

Since the enactment of the 1989 privatization decree, Argentina has become a world leader in privatizing national industries, services, and utilities. Most major public sector companies have been privatized since then. The "Buy Argentina" program was also suspended in that year. Since then, only 10% of the goods and services sold to the Argentine government are of Argentine origin.

Advertising is done primarily in print, notably newspapers. However, both television and radio have been successful for some products and services.

LEGAL AFFAIRS IN ARGENTINA

 The effects of Argentina's "Dirty War" will haunt Argentines for at least another generation. The continued presence in Argentine society of former torturers and death squad members is an ongoing source of anguish for many people. Yet the Due Obedience Law (signed by former President Raúl Alfonsín) grants amnesty to most lower-ranked officers as long as they were following the orders of their superiors.

As for the military leaders who gave the orders, they were tried and convicted in 1985 and 1986. They were subsequently pardoned by President Carlos Saúl Menem in 1989.

The government considers the issue closed. Consequently, survivors of the "Dirty War" who seek redress now go to courts outside Argentina, where the amnesty is not recognized. In September of 1996, a federal judge in Spain opened a case against 97 former and active members of the Argentine military. But the Argentine government is unlikely to extradite these men, so they will remain safe as long as they do not travel outside Argentina.

Like most countries, Argentina also has many antiquated laws still on the books. The country's complex laws on dueling may offer some insight into the Argentine character. The very existence of laws on dueling demonstrate the importance of protecting one's honor in Argentina. But the formalities of the duel are important to Argentines (as they are in so many areas of life).

Killing an opponent in a duel can result in a punishment of five to 25 years. However, if the formalities of the duel were properly arranged by a second (that is, a designated assistant), and the opponent was offered the choice of weapons, then the penalty is only three to ten years—even if the opponent was slain.

On the other hand, a second who does not arrange the duel properly (which includes taking action to minimize injury to the duelists) is himself subject to punishment of one to four years.

LEADING BUSINESSES IN ARGENTINA

The following businesses are some of the largest employers in Argentina:

Baby King S R L
Santiago.
Recreational vehicle dealers. 32,605 employees.

Electronica Ion S R L
Buenos Aires.
Electrical work. 29,494 employees.

Empresa Nacional de Correos y Telegrafos (ENCOTEL)
Buenos Aires.
Telegraph and communications. 30,000 employees.

Empresa Nacional de Correos y Telegrafos SA
Buenos Aires.
Telegraph and communications. 25,000 employees.

Ferrocarriles Metropolitanos SA
Buenos Aires.
Railroad. 15,000 employees.

Gas del Estado S E
Buenos Aires.
Natural gas transmission. 10,545 employees.
El Hogar Obrero Coop de Cons Edif y Cred Ltda
Buenos Aires.
Department stores. 10,960 employees.
Telecom Argentina Stet-France Telecom SA
Buenos Aires.
Telephones. 15,343 employees.
Telefonica de Argentina Sociedad Anonima
Buenos Aires.
Telephones. 16,836 employees.
Vallo Ricardo Sociedad de Hecho
Pinamar.
Paint, glass, and wallpaper. 10,176 employees.
YPF Sociedad Anonima
Buenos Aires.
Petroleum and natural gas. 7,090 employees.

The following are some of the largest newspaper publishers in Argentina:

Arte Grafico Editorial Argentino SA
Buenos Aires.
1,300 employees.
Editorial Diario la Capital SA
Rosario.
450 employees.
Editorial Sarimento Sociedad Anonima
Buenos Aires.
600 employees.
Sociedad Anonima la Nacion
Buenos Aires.
1,000 employees.

ARGENTINE GEOGRAPHY

ARGENTINA

FLAG AND MAP OF ARGENTINA

The Argentine flag has two light-blue horizontal stripes separated by a single horizontal white stripe. A sun symbol, known as the Sun of May, may appear in the center of the white stripe. The Sun of May represents the sunlight which shone through the clouds on the independence demonstrators on 25 May 1810. The flag of neighboring Uruguay was inspired by the design of the Argentine flag.

Size: 1,073,518 square miles

Population: 34,297,742

Argentina is one of the major countries of the Southern Cone of South America. Argentina is a charter member of the Mercosur Customs Trade Union. The other Mercosur members are Brazil,

Paraguay, Uruguay, and most recently Chile. Collectively, Mercosur represents a population of: 213,611,000.

Is There Anything There Besides Buenos Aires?

Buenos Aires, the "Paris of the Americas," dominates Argentina's political and cultural life as much as, well, Paris dominates France. Buenos Aires is the capital, the largest city, the industrial and economic center, and the cultural heart of Argentina.

Nevertheless, there is more to Argentina than Buenos Aires— even though many foreign businesspeople never have the need to step outside its city limits. Some must-see areas include Patagonia, Iguazú, and Tierra del Fuego.

ARGENTINE HISTORY

Until 1516: Several nomadic hunting-and-gathering tribes roam the Argentine plains. At the fringes of the plains, Amerindian groups adopt more specialized patterns. In the Andean foothills, the Comechingones and Diaguita peoples build irrigation canals to support agriculture. Coastal tribes like the Yahgan harvest seafood. None of Argentina's native peoples are city-builders like the Inca, so there are few physical remains of their civilizations.

1516: While searching for a route to the Pacific, Spanish explorer Juan Díaz de Solís becomes the first European known to have set foot on Argentine soil. He is soon killed by the local Amerindians.

1536: Buenos Aires, the first Spanish settlement in Argentina, is founded by Pedro de Mendoza. Like most early explorers, he was hoping to find precious metals. But no gold or silver is found, and the local Querandí tribe is so hostile that Buenos Aires is abandoned after five years. Most of the Spanish move upriver to Asunción in Paraguay.

1553: Failing to colonize Argentina from the sea, the Spanish come overland from Peru. The town of Santiago del Estero is established in northwest Argentina. It will become the oldest continuously occupied European settlement in Argentina. Other interior settlements soon follow. The Spanish discover that the centralized, agricultural Indians of this area are more easily enslaved than the nomadic, warlike tribes of the south. No precious metals are discovered in Argentina, but these northwest settlements become important agricultural and ranching areas supporting the mining industries of Bolivia.

1580: Buenos Aires is reoccupied by the Spanish.

1600: An expedition led by Magellan (Ferdinañode Magalhañes) spends the winter in Southern Argentina before passing around the tip of South America and circumnavigating the globe. Six years later, another circumnavigator, Sebastian Cabot, also sets up a temporary base in Argentina. No permanent settlement is established by either explorer.

1713: British ships are licensed to bring African slaves to Buenos Aires. British interest in South America focuses on Argentina.

1776: Spain establishes the Viceroyalty of Río de la Plata, with Buenos Aires as capital. This Viceroyalty includes Argentina as well as Uruguay and Paraguay. Bolivian silver is shipped via Buenos Aires to Spain, and the city grows in size and importance.

1806: Great Britain occupies Buenos Aires, but is driven off by the Spanish. The same thing happens in 1807. Spain's inability to keep the British from invading fuels support for independence in Argentina.

1810: On 25 May, residents of Buenos Aires declare their autonomy. The British immediately begin trading directly with the residents of Buenos Aires, bringing prosperity.

1816: Independence for all Argentina is declared on July 9th at the northwestern town of Tucumán. Faced with rebellions throughout Latin America, Spain concentrates on retaining its wealthiest colonies. Mineral-poor Argentina is not a priority, and relatively little fighting takes place on Argentine soil. However, independence does not bring unity to Argentina.

1819: The congress of Tucumán presents a constitution for Argentina. Unwilling to yield to a central authority, all the Argentine provinces reject the new constitution. Local strongmen, the caudillos, rule various parts of Argentina.

1826: Buenos Aires intellectual Bernardino Rivadavia becomes president of the United Provinces of the Río de la Plata. Provincial caudillos force him to resign within a year. Conflict between these forces erupts into civil war.

1835: The governor of Buenos Aries, Juan Manuel de Rosas, assumes power over all of Argentina. He creates a national police force, the mazorca, which ruthlessly enforces his will. He rules as dictator until he is overthrown in 1852.

1853: A new constitution is enacted, cementing the authority of the office of the presidency but granting a decree of autonomy to the provinces. This constitution is still in use today.

1862: Bartolomé Mitre is elected president. A series of elected presidencies follow, with peaceful transfers of power. Argentina encourages immigration and foreign investment.

1865–70: Argentina, Uruguay, and Brazil go to war against Paraguay in the War of the Triple Alliance. The three allies win this lopsided war, and Argentina annexes some Paraguayan territory.

1879–80: The last of the Patagonia's warlike Amerindians are defeated, an event recorded in Argentine history as the "conquest of the desert." Argentine agriculture booms, and new refrigeration technology enables frozen Argentine beef to be shipped to Europe.

1890: The new middle-class Radical movement (Unión Cívica Radical) gains strength. Radical revolts break out in 1890, 1895, and 1905.

1916: The Radical Party candidate, Hipólito Yrigoyen is elected president of Argentina. Radical presidents serve for the next fourteen years.

1930: Argentine exports fade with the worldwide depression. Serving a second term as president, Yrigoyen is ousted in a coup led by General José Uriburu. As president, Uriburu is the first pro-Fascist leader of Argentina.

1940–45: Argentina's pro-Fascist leaders give tacit support to the Axis side in World War II. Pressure from the US forces Argentina to break relations with the Axis powers in 1944. Belatedly, Argentina declares war on the Axis in March 1945. The Argentine minister of war at this time is Juan Domingo Perón.

1946: With the military out of favor, Juan Perón runs as the Labor Party candidate for president. He wins, and remains in power for nine years. His second wife, Eva Perón, builds up an extraordinary personal cult, which helps to support her husband's dictatorship. Although Eva died of cancer in 1952, she remains an Argentine legend.

1955: The first Perón presidency ends in a military coup. Juan Perón flees to Spain. Political stability continues to elude Argentina, and several coups take place over the next 17 years.

1972: Juan Perón returns from exile. His support wins the 1973 presidential election for the Peronista candidate, Héctor J. Cámpora. Within months, Perón assumes the presidency himself, and makes his third wife vice-president.

1974: Juan Domingo Perón dies in office. His wife, Maria Estela Martínez de Perón (known as Isabel) becomes president. Under the ill-qualified Isabel, Argentina descends into chaos. Violence erupts at both ends of the political spectrum, from left-wing guerrillas to anti-Communist death squads.

1976: A military coup ousts Isabel Perón, and a new government led by Lt. General Jorge Rafael Videla takes power. To restore stability, the Guerra Sucia ("Dirty War") begins, in which the military arrest and kill thousands of Argentine citizens. Left-wing guerrillas, as well as Communists and Peronistas, are targeted. At least 9,000 Argentineans "disappear"—after being arrested or abducted.

1982: As the military regime begins to falter, the military tries to bolster its popularity by invading and occupying the British-owned

Falkland Islands. Argentina has claimed these offshore islands (which the Argentines call the Malvinas Islands) for over a century. But the Argentines underestimate Great Britain's resolve. Argentina's armed forces are defeated by the UK after a 74-day war. Completely discredited, the Argentine military calls for elections.

1983: Radical party candidate Raúl Alfonsín is elected president. Argentina returns to civilian leadership.

1989: With inflation reaching as high as 196.6% per month, the Radical Party loses power in the 1989 elections. Justicialista (Peronista) party candidate Carlos Saúl Menem is elected president. The son of Syrian immigrants, Menem had been imprisoned during the "Dirty War." He successfully stabilizes the economy and begins a privatization program. Menem is reelected to the presidency in 1995.

1994: A bomb at the Jewish Cultural Center in Buenos Aries kills 86 people. This is the single worst anti-Semitic incident in Argentine history.

1997: A newsman, Jose Luis Cabezas, is murdered in January while investigating corruption. The justice minister, Elias Jassan, is forced to resign after he is caught lying about his relationship to the businessman Cabezas was investigating.

ARGENTINE BEHAVIOR

Who is this "Che" that everybody talks about?

Argentines use the phoneme "Che!" in lots of situations. In the broadest sense, it is a demand for attention. In a restaurant, Argentines call for their waiter by shouting "Che"—which is no more polite than shouting "Yo, Ace!" in a New York City diner. But "Che" is sometimes spoken when no one else is around to hear, they way North Americans might exclaim "Whew!"

Argentines use "Che!" so frequently that it has become a nickname used by other Latin Americans for any Argentine national. That's how Ernesto Guevara Serna got the name Che Guevara when he joined Castro's army in 1953.

What is mate and why does everyone drink it?

Mate (pronounced "mah-tay") is a drink prepared from the yerba mate leaf (*Ilex paraguayensis*), and is also known as Paraguayan tea. Argentines of every social and economic class drink it. It is not alcoholic, but, like coffee and tea, it contains caffeine.

Do Argentines dress formally?

"Buenos Aires . . . was the first place I'd ever visited where I always felt underdressed: When I went to a tearoom, my first afternoon in town, at three o'clock on a weekday, every single male in the place—but me—was wearing a tie."

—Travel writer Pico Iyer

Yes, Argentines dress up—constantly. Buenos Aires must be one of the most formal cities on the planet. Everyone who can afford it (and many who can't) dress in fine, conservative clothes. The styles are often European, but usually a few years behind the latest trend. During the dictatorship, men were arrested for wearing shorts on the streets of Buenos Aires, and women were often harassed for wearing pants instead of a skirt.

Despite the Falkland Islands War, Argentines seem enamored of British style. They wear conservative clothing, and adopt a polite but distant behavior. Argentina is, without a doubt, the most un-Latin country in Latin America.

HOW CAN I FIND MORE INFORMATION ABOUT ARGENTINA?

Here are a few resources to start with:

Getting Through Customs' Web site at **http://www. getcustoms.com** tracks current holidays in Argentina. They also post Cultural I.Q. Quizzes, gift-giving guidelines, a demo of the PASSPORT database, and further international information. Telephone: (610) 353-9894; fax (610) 353-6994.

Embassy of the Argentine Republic
1600 New Hampshire Avenue, NW
Washington, DC 20009
Telephone: (202) 939-6400; fax: (202) 332-3171
Their Web site links to other diplomatic facilities world-
wide: **http://www.ar/cwash/homepage/**.

Argentina National Tourist Council
12 W. 56th Street
New York, NY 10019
Telephone: (212) 603-0443
They maintain a Web site at **http://www.turismo.gov.ar/**.

El Sur del Sur— a comprehensive Web site with general
information about Argentina. **http://www.surdelsur.com**

The International Academy at Santa Barbara at
http://www.iasb.org/cwl publishes Current World
Leaders, an excellent resource for data on political leaders
and parties in Argentina. Telephone (800) 530-2682 or
(805) 965-5010 for subscription information.

The Bureau of Consular Affairs at **http://travel.state.gov**
can give you detailed information on obtaining passports,
visa requirements, and consular affairs bulletins.

The Center for Disease Control at **http://www.cdc.gov/**
provides valuable medical information, as well as information on any outbreaks of virulent infections in Argentina.

Like all Web sites, the preceding Internet addresses are subject to
change, and there is no guarantee that they will continue to provide
the data we list here.

Belize

WHAT'S YOUR CULTURAL I.Q.?

1. TRUE or FALSE? Punta is a popular style of music and dance in Belize.

   ANSWER: True. Punta is an unusual dance because the feet remain stationary. Instead, the rest of the body (especially the hips) moves.

2. The first Europeans to establish permanent settlements on Belize were from:

   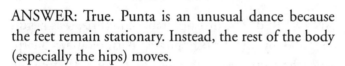

   a. Spain

   b. England

   c. Holland

   d. France

   ANSWER: b. The Spanish claimed Belize but never bothered to settle it. It was an Englishman, Peter Wallace, who established the first European settlement in Belize in 1638.

3. TRUE or FALSE? Most of the first European settlers in Belize were pirates or privateers.

   ANSWER: True. Belize, the one area of Central America free of Spanish settlements, had long been a haven for the pirates and privateers who preyed on Spanish shipping. This piracy went into decline in the 17th century (in part because the British revoked the charters of its privateers), leading some pirates to settle down.

4. Which of the following became Belize's first industry?

   a. Fishing

   b. Slave trading

   c. Exporting nitrate fertilizer

   d. Logging

   e. All of the above

   ANSWER: d. The first profitable enterprise was begun in 1660 by the British pirate, Bartholomew Sharp, when he began exporting logs to Europe. (Before the advent of synthetic dyes, logwood was a valuable source of dyes for textiles.) Belize has no marketable nitrate deposits, and local Mayans were too few and elusive to be profitably enslaved. Black slaves were imported later, for the timber industry.

5. TRUE or FALSE? Even though they never colonized Belize, the Spanish tried to drive the British settlers out of the country.

   ANSWER: True. The Spanish did expel the British settlers, not once but three times, in 1754, 1759, and 1765. Each time the British returned after the Spanish forces left.

6. After the Spanish colonies gained independence from Spain, the main threat to Belize came from neighboring Guatemala, which claimed Belize's territory. The United Kingdom signed a treaty with Guatemala, but

failed to live up to one important provision of the treaty. What clause of the treaty did the UK violate?

a. A prohibition against commercial agriculture in Belize

b. Making Spanish the official language of Belize

c. Building a road from Belize City to Guatemala City

ANSWER: c. The UK promised to build a road through the jungle, and never did. There was a prohibition against agriculture in Belize, but that was in the 1783 Treaty of Paris with Spain (the Spanish correctly feared that agriculture—unlike logging—would result in permanent settlement). Since the British never built the road, Guatemala continued to claim Belize's territory, and the UK had to station troops in Belize.

7. TRUE or FALSE? The USA was happy to see the UK make Belize into the Colony of British Honduras in 1862.

ANSWER: False. However, the US was too busy fighting the US Civil War to invoke the Monroe Doctrine and oppose the British by force.

8. British Honduras finally became the independent nation of Belize in what year?

a. 1884

b. 1931

c. 1950

d. 1964

e. 1981

ANSWER: e. Each of these years represents an important event in Belize's history, but independence did not come until 1981.

9. TRUE or FALSE? Tourism now generates more income in Belize than the country's traditional base of agriculture, forestry, and fishing.

ANSWER: False. While tourism is growing, the traditional triad of agriculture, forestry, and fishing remains Belize's main industry.

10. For a country founded by British pirates, Belize has a remarkably peaceful history. The country's different ethnic groups have managed to coexist in relative harmony. Which of the following groups do NOT make up at least 5% of Belize's population?

a. Whites

b. Creoles (persons of mixed white and black ancestry)

c. Garifunas (persons of mixed white and Carib Indian ancestry)

d. Mestizos (persons of mixed white and Amerindian ancestry)

e. Amerindians

ANSWER: a. Whites make up 3.9% of Belize's population. While the mestizos now make up the largest group, it is the urban Creoles who essentially run Belize. Note that although the Creoles speak English, the Creole dialect is difficult (if not impossible) for most English-speakers to understand!

QUOTATIONS ABOUT BELIZE

"*. . . this all but empty British territory . . . incongruous in Latin America: Mexico the industrial giant to the north, Guatemala of the high mountains, the political assassinations, the temperate flowers and fruit, with Spanish and Mayan antiquities, to the west and south.*

"The Empire here was never grand. It began as a seventeenth-century coastal intrusion on the Spanish American Empire. The territory doubled its size in the last century. But it was acknowledged as an intrusion and was never settled; it never became a land of plantations. The first interlopers came with their Negroes to cut logwood; their successors went further inland to cut mahogany. The mahogany forests have all been cut down . . . in the last ten years, some thousands of Mennonites, a Bible-reading German-American sect, who have transformed many square miles of tropical bush, bought at fifteen shillings an acre, into the landscape of pioneer America. The descendants of the Negro log-cutters, now two-thirds of the population, and confirmed lovers of city life, live in the overcrowded coastal capital, Belize City."

—From V.S. Naipaul's *The Overcrowded Barracoon.*

"If the world had any ends British Honduras would certainly be one of them. It is not on the way from anywhere to anywhere else. It has no strategic value. It is all but uninhabited . . . Why then do we bother to keep this strange little fragment of the Empire? Certainly not from motives of self-interest. Hardly one Englishman in fifty thousand derives any profit from the Britishness of British Honduras. British Honduras goes on being British because it has been British."

—From *Beyond the Mexique Bay* by Aldous Huxley.

"A severe hurricane early in the twentieth century, and several smaller storms since that time had helped to give parts of the town the appearance of a temporary camp. But this was misleading, for Belizeans loved their town which lay below the level of the sea and only through force

of circumstances, moved to other parts of the country. It was a town, not unlike small towns everywhere perhaps, where each person, within his neighbourhood, was an individual with well known characteristics. Anonymity, though not unheard of, was rare. Indeed, a Belizean without a known legend was the most talked about character of all.

"It was a relatively tolerant town where at least six races with their roots in other districts of the country, in Africa, the West Indies, Central America, Europe, North America, Asia, and other places, lived in a kind of harmony. In three centuries, miscegenation, like logwood, had produced all shades of black and brown, not grey or purple or violet, but certainly there were a few people in town known as red ibos. Creole, regarded as a language to be proud of by most people in the country, served as a means of communication among the races. Still, in the town and in the country, as people will do everywhere, each race held varying degrees of prejudice concerning the others."

—From the award-winning novel *Beka Lamb* by Belizean writer Zee Edgell.

"Ricardo did not known that he was born to girdle trees.

"When he asked to go to high school, his father said: I'm sorry to disappoint you, son, but I don't have the money to send you. You'll have to become a chiclero like me.

"At first the boy felt very sad, but he became strong. Nimbly he ascended the dark-greened cliffs of trees. He could tap eight or a dozen of them a day.

"Now he loved to work. School was far on the road behind him. He loved the jungle whose veins he opened."

—From the collection *Thirteen Stories and Thirteen Epitaphs* by William T. Vollmann.

TABLE OF CONTENTS

THE BELIZEANS

The bulk of Belize's population is of mixed ancestry. Spanish-Indian mestizos make up 43.6% of Belizeans. Blacks and black-white mulattos (collectively known as Creoles in Belize) account for 29.8%, Amerindian (primarily Maya) for 11.0%, Garifuna (mixed black-Carib Indian ancestry) for 6.7%, whites for 3.9%, and East Indians for 3.5%. The remaining 1.5% includes Chinese, Lebanese, and others.

The Garifunas are also known as Garinagus or Black Caribs. While their genetic heritage comes mostly from Africa, their culture and language is primarily Amerindian. Some friction exists between the Garifunas and the more populous Creoles.

HOW TO TELL BELIZE AND THE BELIZEANS FROM THEIR
NEIGHBORS

Belize is the youngest nation in Central America. Until 1981 it was
a colony called British Honduras. Guatemala did not relinquish
claims to Belize's territory until 1992. Belize is the second-smallest
country in Central America.

1. Belize is the only English-speaking nation in Central
   America. (This doesn't mean that most native speakers
   of English can *understand* the heavily inflected Creole
   dialect. But it is English.)

2. Belize borders Mexico to the north and Guatemala to
   the west and south.

3. Belize's Amerindians, mestizos, and whites are much
   like their counterparts in other parts of Central America
   (although Belize's whites hold less of the country's
   wealth than in neighboring countries). Even Belize's
   Garifunas are similar to many black-Indian zambo
   groups in neighboring countries. But Belize's Creoles
   are unique on the American mainland. From their
   open, easygoing manner to their distinctive version of
   English, the Creoles make Belize a unique nation.

LITERATURE

Belize has not yet produced many world-renowned writers. One
Belizean writer who is known to have been published outside the
country is:

Zee Edgell (1940–) is a Belize-born writer of Creole descent.
She started her writing career as a journalist in 1959 in Jamaica.
Later she moved to the United States and volunteered for the

US Peace Corps, which took her to Afghanistan and Bangladesh. Her first novel, *Beka Lamb,* examines the transition of Belize from British colony to independent nation. Published in 1982, it was one of two books awarded the 1982 British Fawcett Society Book Prize, which is given to "works of fiction which contribute to an understanding of women's position in society today." Her second novel, *In Times Like These,* was published in 1991. It focuses on the conflict between Belize and Guatemala (which claimed Belize's territory). Edgell has taught in the English department at Kent State University in Ohio.

LANGUAGE

The official language of Belize is English. However, the dialect of English spoken by most of the Creole population is unintelligible to most foreigners. While the speech patterns sound familiar, the overall speech is not understood by outside English-speakers.

Linguists have categorized nine different languages spoken in modern Belize—*Ethnologue: Languages of the World,* 12th Edition from their Web site at (http://www.sil.org/ethnologue/ethnologue. html).

BUSINESS IN BELIZE

Aside from tourism, lumber, and agriculture, there is not a lot of business in Belize. Agriculture is the largest of these, with substantial production of sugarcane, oranges, grapefruits, corn, and bananas.

> *"The peculiar essence of Belizean politics was never clearer: For twenty years under (Prime Minister) Price's quasi-socialist, paternalistic first administration the economy had stagnated to the point where it was entirely dependent*

on foreign aid. By all accounts, the new president, Esquivel, had turned things around. Things were brighter economically in Belize than ever before. But Esquivel rode in one limousine too many, with one too many well-dressed foreign dignitary. He didn't drive a beat-up Land Rover out into the smaller villages the way Price used to. He didn't have open house at his home on Sundays. He lost to a 'Belize for Belizeans' platform . . . quite a shock to the United States. 'They totally voted the man, not the issue,' an amazed U.S. embassy spokesman told us."

—From *Fever Coast Log* by Gordon Chaplin.

Belize does have some mining interests, but only in limestone, sand, and gravel. Manufacturing is concentrated in areas related to the country's agriculture: Sugarcane is Belize's largest agricultural crop, so sugar and molasses production make up its largest manufacturing sector.

Energy remains at a premium in Belize. The country has no oil or coal resources.

BUSINESS SUCCESS IN BELIZE

The government of Belize welcomes foreign investment, and supports the establishment of partnerships and joint ventures. Unfortunately, the potential market in Belize is too small to guarantee a return on most foreign investments, except perhaps in the growing tourist-related industries.

The only franchises currently in Belize are Coca-Cola and Pepsi.

Most foreign businesses use a local distributor or agent to sell their products or services. The majority of Belizean importers also provide their own distribution network to get the products to local retailers.

Advertising in Belize is done primarily through newspapers, radio, and television. Note that newspapers are associated with specific political parties, and are generally read only by supporters of those specific parties. Radio can also be politicized, since the most popular local programs are call-in shows on which politics are discussed. Advertising on televised sporting events offers one of the best venues for reaching all political persuasions, but not all Belizeans own televisions.

LEGAL AFFAIRS IN BELIZE

Belize has become known as a banking haven. On 20 January 1995, the Supreme Court of Belize upheld the right to privacy in banking by rejecting the demands of the Securities and Exchange Commission of the United States of America. The US SEC had demanded records from Swiss Trade and Commerce Trust, Ltd. of Belize.

Belize offers citizenship to most anyone for $50,000 US (plus processing fees). The money is considered a "special contribution to the economy of Belize," and is payable in two installments: $25,000 before applying, and $25,000 after acceptance of the application. Dual citizenships are acceptable to Belize, so an applicant can retain his or her original passport while holding a Belizean passport as well. There is no residency requirement—you don't even need to visit Belize to get a Belizean citizenship!

The Belize Passport Consultants & Co. suggests the following reasons for having a second passport:

- Political instability in your country of origin makes travel on your current passport difficult.

- Your assets are the target of litigation or you are overburdened by taxation.

- Your basic human right of travel is restricted.

- You are not allowed to work or settle in another country.

- Your assets, freedom of movement, and even your life are threatened by your country's political situation.

- You are subject to persecution for your religious or political beliefs and for pursuing certain harmless activities.

Sales of Belizean passports have been brisk to the Hong Kong Chinese due to the takeover of the colony by the People's Republic of China in 1997.

LEADING BUSINESSES IN BELIZE

Except for the government, Belize has only one sizable employer:
   Belize Telecommunications Ltd.
   Belize City.
   358 employees.
The following are the newspapers with the largest circulation in Belize. Each of Belize's newspapers supports a different political party. All of them are weekly papers and have a limited circulation:
   The Belize Times Press
   Belize City.
   The Reporter
   Belize City.
   The People's Pulse
   Belize City.
   San Pedro Sun
   Ambergris Caye.

BELIZE GEOGRAPHY

BELIZE

• Belmopan

BELIZE

FLAG AND MAP OF BELIZE

When Belize achieved independence in 1981, the flag for the new country evolved out of the flag of Belize's majority party, the People's United Party. Small red stripes were added at the top and bottom to represent the opposition party, the United Democratic Party. Fifty green laurel leaves circle the central shield; these commemorate the start of the Belize independence movement in 1950. Two men adorn the seal: a Creole sailor and a mestizo lumberman. Underneath them is the motto *Sub Umbra Floreo* (I Flourish in the Shade). The origin of the motto is unknown, although Belize is certainly hot enough to cause its inhabitants to seek shade whenever possible.

Size: 8,867 square miles
Population: 214,061

Fever Coast or Mosquito Coast?

Both of these terms refer to part of the Central American coastline on the Caribbean. The term "Fever Coast" is generally used

continues

for the coasts of Belize, Guatemala, and Honduras. "Mosquito Coast" is technically a larger area: from Belize all the way down to Panama. Either way, Belize is considered to mark the northern end.

Belize is the second smallest nation in Central America. It is slightly larger than El Salvador. With only 205,000 people, it is also the least-populated country in Central America.

BELIZEAN HISTORY

Until 1520: Belize is part of the Mayan Empire. They build impressive cities, but many are abandoned before Columbus comes to the New World.

1520s: Belize is claimed by Spain. Spanish conquistador Hernán Cortés may have crossed Belize during this time. But the Spanish find no use for Belize and fail to establish any permanent settlements.

Early 1600s: The enormous wealth of Spain's American colonies draws pirates and privateers. English privateers find the Bay of Honduras a profitable locale for attacking Spanish ships traveling between Mexico and Panama. Belize, unoccupied by the Spanish, has a convenient coast for resupply.

1638: British pirate Peter Wallace establishes the first European settlement in Belize, near the mouth of the Belize River.

1660: Another British pirate, Bartholomew Sharp, begins regular timber exports from Belize. He ships valuable logwood, which provides dyes for textiles. His success brings other British loggers to Belize. The white loggers become known as the Baymen.

1700–10: The first black slaves are brought to Belize for the timber-cutting industry. The slaves soon outnumber the whites, and interbreeding results in Belize's Creole population.

1754: The Spanish drive out the Baymen. They free the slaves who remain. But the Spanish do not stay, and the Baymen soon return.

1759: The Spanish again drive out the Baymen. Once again, the Baymen return as soon as the Spanish leave.

1765: The beginnings of local government take root when the Baymen establish Burnaby's Code. Synthetic dyes make logwood obsolete, so mahogany becomes Belize's most important export.

1779: The Spanish drive away the Baymen for the third and final time. Again they return.

1783: The Treaty of Paris confirms Great Britain's right to conduct logging in Belize, but prohibits the establishment of agriculture.

1853: Belize establishes a local legislative assembly.

1859: Britain and Guatemala sign a treaty to secure Belize's borders. However, since the British never fulfill their promise to build a road from Belize City to Guatemala City, Guatemala continues to claim Belize's territory. Consequently, Britain has to keep troops in Belize to protect it from Guatemala.

1862: While the USA is embroiled in the Civil War (and unable to enforce the Monroe Doctrine), Belize formally becomes the British colony of British Honduras, ruled by a lieutenant governor who is subordinate to the governor of Jamaica.

1871: At its own request, the British Honduras assembly is abolished. British Honduras now becomes a Crown Colony, without internal autonomy.

1884: The post of British Honduras' highest official, the lieutenant governor, is raised to governor (and is no longer subordinate to the governor of Jamaica).

1931: A major hurricane devastates Belize City.

1950s: An independence movement is established.

1964: British Honduras' internal autonomy is returned. A new Constitution is instituted. George Price becomes prime minister for the first time.

1981: British Honduras becomes the independent nation of Belize. George Price remains prime minister.

1992: Guatemala finally relinquishes its claim to Belize's territory.

BELIZEAN BEHAVIOR

What is the truly remarkable thing about Belize?

Belize is a country founded by pirates—yet it is one of the most peaceful countries in Central America. Unlike its neighbors, Belize has not suffered even a single coup, uprising, or guerilla war. Belize does not even have an army; it depends on British troops stationed there to protect its sovereignty (mostly against territorial aggression from Guatemala).

Why are Belizeans the way they are?

Isolated behind its barrier reef, Belize has been (and continues to be) ignored for the most part by outside forces. The trend is especially noticeable in the fairly quiet state of race relations. The Creoles have formed the backbone of Belizean urban society for centuries.

> *"When Colonel George Arthur arrived in British Honduras to become Lieutenant Governor in 1814, he reported that he was 'astounded and dismayed by the prominent position of colored people in Society.' But by the time his eight-year term was up, he had come to consider the Creoles as the most stable members of the population."*
>
> —From *Fever Coast Log* by Gordon Chaplin.

Ultimately, what has surely allowed Belize to remain unbothered by the outside world is the fact that it has no major resources. Timber cutting brought only temporary prosperity. Today, limited tourism is bringing some income to Belize, but it is dependent upon foreign aid.

How do Belizeans dress?

Belize is hot, hot, hot. Even the prime minister rarely dons a jacket or tie. Attire is casual.

HOW CAN I FIND MORE INFORMATION ABOUT BELIZE?

Here are a few resources to start with:

Getting Through Customs' Web site at **http://www. getcustoms.com** tracks current holidays in Belize. They also post Cultural I.Q. Quizzes, gift-giving guidelines, a demo of the PASSPORT database, and further international information. Telephone: (610) 353-9894; fax (610) 353-6994.

Embassy of Belize
2535 Massachusetts Avenue, NW
Washington, DC 20008
Telephone: (202) 332-9636

Belize Tourist Board
421 Seventh Avenue
New York, NY 10001
Telephone: (800) 624-0686
Fax: (212) 563-6033

Belize by Naturalight—Virtual tour of Belize, including hotels, tour operators, businesses, publications, and more. **http://www.belizenet.com/**.

The International Academy at **Santa Barbara** at **http://www.iasb.org/cwl** publishes Current World Leaders, an excellent resource for data on political leaders and parties in Belize. Telephone: (800) 530-2682 or (805) 965-5010 for subscription information.

The Bureau of Consular Affairs at **http://travel.state.gov** can give you detailed information on obtaining passports, visa requirements, and consular affairs bulletins.

The Center for Disease Control at **http://www.cdc.gov/** provides valuable medical information, as well as information on any outbreaks of virulent infections in Belize.

Like all Web sites, the preceding Internet addresses are subject to change, and there is no guarantee that they will continue to provide the data we list here.

Bolivia

WHAT'S YOUR CULTURAL I.Q.?

1. TRUE or FALSE? Landlocked Bolivia maintains a navy.

   ANSWER: True. Bolivia still hopes to get back its coastline, lost to Chile in the 1879–83 War of the Pacific. The Bolivian Navy currently patrols Lake Titicaca.

2. Bolivia fought one other major war. What was this war called?

   > a. The Chaco War
   >
   > b. The Chico War
   >
   > c. The Mate War

   ANSWER: a. The Chaco War of 1932–35 was fought with Paraguay over the control of the Chaco Desert.

3. TRUE or FALSE? Since winning its independence from Spain, Bolivia has never won a war.

   ANSWER: True. Although the Chaco War was something of a draw, outside arbitration took most of the Chaco away from Bolivia.

4. "As rich as Potosí" became a popular expression once the Potosí mines opened in 1545. What mineral were the mines famous for?

   a. Gold

   b. Silver

   c. Platinum

   ANSWER: b. For two hundred years, the silver from the mines made Potosí the richest city in the New World.

5. TRUE or FALSE? Now that the original mines have played out, mining at Potosí has ceased.

   ANSWER: False. The silver is now gone, but Potosí now produces great amounts of tin.

6. Bolivia has had bad rulers, but none more outrageous than General Mariano Melgarejo, who is known as the caudillo bárbaro. Which of these did NOT occur under his reign?

   a. Bolivia lost land to Chile

   b. Bolivia lost land to Brazil

   c. Melgarejo had the British ambassador stripped, tied to a donkey, and run out of town

   d. Melgarejo tried to march his army all the way to Europe, so he could assist the French during the Franco-Prussian War

   ANSWER: c. This is a widely told story, but it cannot be true, since Britain had pulled its ambassador out of Bolivia back in 1853, long before Melgarejo became dictator in 1865. The two countries did not resume relations until 1910.

7. TRUE or FALSE? The 1952 Miner's Strike led to a radical change of government in Bolivia.

   ANSWER: True. The miner's revolt led to the accession of Victor Paz Estenssoro of the National Revolutionary Movement (MNR). As President, Paz nationalized the mines and redistributed land to the peasants.

8. The short regime (1980-81) of General Luis García Meza is remarkable for which of the following:

   a. Meza's involvement in the cocaine business

   b. The redistribution of land to the peasants

   c. The completion, after 150 years, of the La Paz cathedral

   ANSWER: a. Meza's narco-regime did nothing for land reform and had no legitimacy; Meza came to power in a coup and was himself ousted by a coup. And the La Paz cathedral is still unfinished.

9. Bolivia is known for opening itself to foreign religious communities who want to set up farming colonies (such as the Mennonites). TRUE or FALSE? A religious farming community was founded in Bolivia by a man who would later become Governor of Oklahoma and run for President of the USA.

   ANSWER: True. William "Alfalfa Bill" Murray set up a short-lived farming community in the arid Chaco, which failed within two years. He returned to his native Oklahoma, became Governor in 1931, and ran for President during the Great Depression, promising the American people "Bread, butter, bacon, beans."

10. Bolivia is so remote that it often makes international headlines only when a famous foreigner dies there. Which of the following people did NOT die in Bolivia?

    a. Butch Cassidy and the Sundance Kid, American outlaws

    b. Che Guevara, Communist guerrilla

    c. Klaus Barbie, Nazi war criminal

ANSWER: c. Butch and Sundance seem to have died in Bolivia in 1911, and Che Guevara was killed there in 1967. Former SS Colonel Klaus Barbie lived in Bolivia (under his own name) for some 30 years, but he was eventually repatriated to France, where he was tried, imprisoned, and eventually died.

QUOTATIONS ABOUT BOLIVIA

"Since independence in 1825, Bolivia has had sixteen constitutions and nearly 250 governments, each lasting an average of ten months. At times it boasted several governments, while at others it had none at all. In 1849 the American ambassador had to wait three months before an administration materialized to which he could present his credentials."

—From *In Bolivia* by Eric Lawlor.

"La Paz is situated in a canyon, and one comes upon it very suddenly: the plateau terminates abruptly, and there is the city, flowing down the steep slope below. From its highest point to its outskirts, on the floor of the canyon,

there is a fall of nearly two thousand feet. It is a pretty, light, airy city, and its setting is enhanced by the towering snowfields of Mount Illimani, rising beyond out of the clouds which shroud its base."

—From *The Cloud Forest: A Chronicle of the South American Wilderness* by novelist and travel writer Peter Matthiessen.

"The pueblo of Tarabuco is red: from the Indians, their ponchos, the steaming cauldrons of chicken and peppers. It was the day of the weekly fair. On sale were utensils, food, trinkets, quena pipes and coca leaves. Every Indian in these altitudes takes the drug.

"The drug-takers carry a leather pouch and a small gourd. The pouch contains the supply of leaves, the gourd pulverised unslaked lime. A few leaves, the stalks having been carefully picked off, are masticated into a small ball. At this stage a very slight admixture of the powdered lime is made; this draws out the taste, and the saliva flows. Part of the saliva is expectorated, part swallowed. If you don't do it properly, you burn your lips. The flavour is slightly bitter and aromatic, like poor green tea. Habitués have bad breath, pale lips and gums, greenish stumpy teeth, and an ugly black mark at the angles of the mouth. One far gone will have an unsteady gait, yellow skin, dim and sunken eyes with purple rings, quivering lips, and general apathy.

"Unharmful in small doses, it may even be beneficial. Chewing it, one can go without food for days, and this is one reason why it is chewed so much."

—From *Summer at High Altitude* by Gordon Meyer. The Bolivian village of Tarabuco is in the Andes near Sucre.

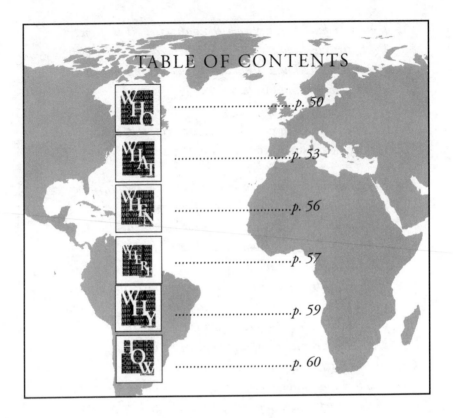

TABLE OF CONTENTS

THE BOLIVIANS

Full-blood Indians (Quechua and Aymara) account for over half of the Bolivian populace. About 30% are mestizo (of mixed Indian and European heritage) and 15% are of European descent. While Protestantism has been making some gains, about 95% of the people are Roman Catholics. Catholicism is the official religion, but freedom of worship is guaranteed by law.

LITERATURE

Few Bolivian writers have been translated into English. The development of writers has been hampered by Bolivia's low level of literacy. After years of effort to improve education, the country's literacy rate has reached 79.5%.

Alcides Arguedas (1879–1946) was a landowner who nevertheless wrote sympathetically of the plight of the Bolivian Amerindians, His 1909 novel, *Pueblo enfermo,* examined Bolivia's social stratification. His best-known novel, *Raza de bronce,* was published in 1919. It focuses on conflict between Amerindians and landowners near Lake Titicaca. Arguedas' work has not yet been translated into English.

Renato Prada Oropeza (1937–) is the only Bolivian author to have a novel translated into English. His novel *Los fundadores del alba* (1969, translated in 1971 as *The Breach*), examines the turmoil of Bolivia's impoverished citizens.

LIGHTS! CAMERA! ACTION!

Bolivia has a modest local movie industry, but few of its films have been shown outside Latin America. Some of these Bolivian films have had great local impact. When Bolivian locales are called for in a foreign film (such as *Butch Cassidy and the Sundance Kid*), non-Bolivian locations are often used. The following films are illuminative of Bolivia and the Bolivians:

1. **Blood of the Condor (Yawar Mallku)** has an unusual distinction: it created such a furor that the US Peace Corps was expelled from Bolivia. The film centers on an Amerindian named Ignacio, who is frustrated by his wife's inability to have children. Ignacio discovers a plot by US members of the "Progress Corps," who are secretly sterilizing Bolivia's native peoples! (The people respond by castrating the Americans.) This paranoid indictment of US cultural imperialism nevertheless contains rare footage of indigenous life, as much of it was shot on location in the Andean community of

Kaata. Initially banned by the Bolivian government, it became one of the most popular movies ever made in the country (1969, directed by Jorge Sanjines).

2. **Chuquiago** was one of the most expensive and successful films ever made in Bolivia by Bolivians. The film was seen by so many Bolivians that it recouped its $85,000 US budget entirely within Bolivia itself. Divided into four sequences, it depicts the lives of several Bolivians, from poor Aymara-speaking Indians to wealthy Spanish-speaking landowners. *Unforgettable moment:* Johnny, an Aymara, tries to pass for a member of the upper classes by speaking Spanish, studying English, and putting light powder on his dark face to disguise his heritage (1978, directed by Antonio Eguino).

3. **Exposure** a small, moody revenge film based in Brazil and Bolivia. Peter Coyote portrays an American photographer in Rio de Janeiro who becomes involved with gangsters after he takes incriminating pictures of a street killing. After he and his girlfriend are attacked, he embarks on a cross-continental trip of revenge to find his attackers. His travels include a long bus ride through desolate Bolivian countryside. *Unforgettable moment:* Preparing for his revenge, Peter Coyote studies knife fighting under the tutelage of Tchady Kerenko (1991, directed by Walter Salles).

4. **Hotel Terminus—The Life and Times of Klaus Barbie** The third film in director Marcel Ophuls' cinematic trilogy on the Second World War. Nazi war criminal Klaus Barbie, known as "The Butcher of Lyons," lived peacefully in Bolivia for some 30 years. This $4^{1}/2$-hour documentary spans three continents and 70 years as it traces Barbie's crimes, the manhunt,

and his eventual arrest and imprisonment (1988, directed by Marcel Ophuls).

5. **Sierra Maestra** is an Italian documentary focusing on French writer Regis Debray, who was a member of Che Guevara's doomed guerrillas in Bolivia. The film follows Debray's arrest and imprisonment in Bolivia. Che Guevara's actions in Bolivia captured the attention of people around the world, and to this day he remains a cultural icon to radicals (1969, directed by Ansano Giannarelli).

LANGUAGE

The Bolivians speak a conservative, almost archaic form of Spanish. Unlike the rest of Latin America, where the second-person plural (vosotros) is replaced by the third-person plural (ustedes), the Bolivians continue to use the second-person plural.

Linguists have categorized 38 different languages spoken in modern Bolivia—*Ethnologue: Languages of the World,* 12th Edition from their Web site at (http://www.sil.org/ethnologue/ethnologue. html).

BUSINESS IN BOLIVIA

THE BOLIVIAN ECONOMY

Despite its mineral wealth, Bolivia has the lowest per-capita income of any country in South America. Almost half of Bolivia's 6.5 million population is involved in agriculture. Mining now occupies only some 3% of the work force. A full two-thirds of the population live in rural areas.

Bolivia is cooperating with the US in combating the cocaine trade. Efforts are also being made to diversify the economy, so that Bolivia's stability is not tied to the world price of the tin it exports. Prospects seem good that exploration will yield exportable amounts of oil; Bolivia already exports natural gas to Argentina. A major project currently underway is the construction of a natural-gas pipeline to the Bolivian-Brazilian border, which will supply a Bolivian power plant designed to sell electricity to Brazil.

BUSINESS SUCCESS IN BOLIVIA

Caveat: Bolivia's economy has been subject to hyperinflation, which reached 24,000% a year in 1985. Severe austerity programs have since brought some stability to the economy.

Most foreign firms wishing to conduct business in Bolivia set up either a local subsidiary or a local branch. This local presence allows them to provide better service to customers—an important consideration in distant, isolated Bolivia.

Joint venture legislation is covered under the Investment Law and the Supreme Decree 22526 of 13 June 1990. The regulations require the foreign business partner to possess documentation verifying the legal status of the partner's business in his or her home country. It is not necessary for the foreign partner to obtain a Bolivian business license in advance.

There is no regulation specifically covering franchises in Bolivia.

Due to illiteracy in Bolivia, radio and television advertising is often more effective than newspaper ads. Another venue is movie theaters, which traditionally show advertisements before the feature presentation.

LEGAL AFFAIRS IN BOLIVIA

Even while incarcerated, affluent Bolivians are better off than poor Bolivians. Prisoners in Bolivia must pay for their incarceration. Those unable to pay receive the minimum accommodations: no medical care, barely enough food to sustain life, and a cell that is 3" by 4" by 6"—so small that the prisoner has to sleep standing up, and a tall prisoner cannot stand at all.

Prison fees have a wide range, starting at $20 US per week for a slight improvement in accommodations, up to a reported $5,000 US per week for top-of-the-line treatment.

As in other Latin American countries, the Bolivian legal code presumes that a person is guilty until proven innocent. Only the affluent can afford bail, and detainees are sometimes held for many months before they come to trial.

LEADING NEWSPAPERS IN BOLIVIA

The following are some of the largest newspapers in Bolivia. All are dailies.

Presencia
La Paz.
El Diario
La Paz.
Ultima Hora
La Paz.
Hoy
La Paz.
El Mundo
Santa Cruz.
Los Tiempos
Cochabamba.

BOLIVIAN HISTORY

Until 1538: Bolivia is part of the powerful Inca Empire, which is centered in nearby Peru.

1538: After defeating the Inca in Peru, Francisco Pizarro conquers the remaining Incan outposts in Bolivia. Bolivia becomes known as Upper Peru.

1545: Silver is discovered at Potosí. Bolivia soon becomes Spain's most valuable colony.

1809: The first uprising against Spain is led by Pedro Domingo Murillo. It fails. Spain is determined to retain Bolivia's wealth.

1825: After years of fighting, Bolivia finally achieves independence from Spain. The country is named for Venezuelan revolutionary leader Simón Bolívar, who defeated the main Spanish army in Peru.

1826–28: Bolívar's deputy, Antonio José de Sucre, becomes Bolivia's first president. The country's first constitution is adopted. De Sucre is overthrown just two years later, which sets a pattern for future political instability.

1837–39: Bolivia and Peru confederate and fight Chile. Chile wins and the confederation is broken up. Chile occupies the valuable coastal nitrate deposits claimed by both Peru and Bolivia.

1865–71: General Mariano Melgarejo, the caudillo bárbaro, seizes power. Sometimes known as the "Caligula of Bolivia," his indifference towards running the country results in Bolivia losing land to both Chile and Brazil. One of his most notorious escapades involves a drunken attempt in 1870 to march his army from Bolivia to Europe, to fight alongside the French during the Franco-Prussian War.

1879–83: The War of the Pacific again unites Peru and Bolivia against Chile. Chile wins again, and annexes Bolivia's seacoast.

1903: Bolivia is persuaded to cede territory to Brazil.

1952: A miner's revolt leads to Victor Paz Estenssoro of the National Revolutionary Movement (MNR) taking power. As president, Paz nationalizes the mines and redistributes land to the peasants.

1981: The narco-regime of General Luis García Meza is overthrown.

1982: Democratic government is restored to Bolivia. The president is Gonzalo Sánchez de Lozada Bustamente.

BOLIVIAN GEOGRAPHY

FLAG AND MAP OF BOLIVIA

The Bolivian flag has been changed several times, with the size and order (but not the colors) of the three stripes switched around. The red represents the bravery of Bolivia's military; the yellow represents Bolivia's wealth (an odd choice, since Bolivia's mineral wealth was in silver, not gold); and the green stands for Bolivia's agricultural bounty.

Size: 424,164 square miles

Population: 7,896,254

Bolivians often blame their country's problems on their loss of their coastline to Chile. Despite this loss, Bolivian trade goods do reach the coast.

Unlike most of its neighbors, Bolivia is not currently a member of the Mercosur Customs Trade Union (which consists of Argentina,

Chile, Brazil, Paraguay, and Uruguay). Brazil actively seeks to bring Bolivia into its sphere of influence.

HOW TO TELL BOLIVIA AND THE BOLIVIANS FROM THEIR NEIGHBORS

Bolivia and its inhabitants exhibit several distinctive characteristics that set them apart. These include:

1. If the country has a coastline, it's not Bolivia. (Bolivia is one of two landlocked nations in South America. Paraguay is the other one.) Bolivia lost its coastline in a war with Chile in 1879–83. But landlocked Bolivia still maintains a small navy on Lake Titicaca, just in case it ever gets its coast back!

2. If the country has rotating capital cities, it's Bolivia. Alone in the Americas, Bolivia has a winter capital, La Paz, and a summer capital, Sucre.

3. If the country went from South America's richest nation to one of its poorest, it's Bolivia. Mining made Bolivia into Spain's wealthiest colony, but the silver mines ran out centuries ago. Now Bolivia has one of the lowest per-capita incomes in Latin America.

4. The majority of the people are of mixed Spanish-Amerindian descent, which in Bolivia are called *cholos* rather than mestizos. Many Bolivians speak an Amerindian language in addition to Spanish (in Colonial Bolivia, the Amerindians were prohibited from learning Spanish!). These Amerindian languages are usually Quechua or Aymará—as opposed to Paraguayans, whose major Amerindian language is Guaraní.

5. If foreigners know it chiefly as "the place where some-
   body died," it's Bolivia. American outlaws Butch
   Cassidy and the Sundance Kid are believed to have
   died in a shootout with Bolivian authorities in 1911.
   And the revolutionary guerrilla leader Che Guevara
   was shot and killed in Bolivia in 1967.

BOLIVIAN BEHAVIOR

Why are Bolivians the way they are?

The lost glory of Colonial Bolivia is remembered wistfully by its
people. It's hard to exaggerate the magnitude of Bolivia's former
wealth. Its silver mines yearly outproduced the entire silver stock of
pre-1492 Europe!

Bolivian geography has also had an effect on the character of its
people. Since losing its coastline, Bolivia has been isolated from the
outside world. Bolivia's varied terrain makes unity within the country difficult.

How do Bolivians dress?

Dress varies in different regions. In general, dress is conservative.
In the high altitudes, cooler weather encourages the use of heavier,
formal clothing, but in lowland Sucre, dress is more casual.

HAZARDS IN BOLIVIA

The following are some factors travelers to Bolivia should be
aware of.

- *Altitude sickness.* In the Andes, altitude sickness presents a problem in areas over 6,000 feet above sea level.

There is no effective predictor of who will succumb and who won't. People of different ages, sexes, and health are struck down.

The best way to avoid altitude sickness is to acclimate yourself to the altitude. Once you get to 6,000 feet, you should ideally spend at least two nights at that altitude, repeating this acclimation period at each increase of 3,000 feet.

- *Earthquakes.* Bolivia is subject to earthquakes. However, Bolivia is not quite as prone to earthquakes as the neighboring countries of Chile and Peru.

- *Tobacco.* Many Bolivians smoke heavily, and it can be difficult to escape from cigarette smoke. Although smoke-free areas in restaurants and hotels are being established, enforcement is lax.

HOW CAN I FIND MORE INFORMATION ABOUT BOLIVIA?

Here are a few resources to start with:

Getting Through Customs' Web site at **http://www. getcustoms.com** tracks current holidays in Bolivia. They also post Cultural I.Q. Quizzes, gift-giving guidelines, a demo of the PASSPORT database, and further international information. Telephone: (610) 353-9894; fax (610) 353-6994.

Embassy of Bolivia
3014 Massachusetts Avenue, NW
Washington, DC 20008
Telephone: (202) 483-4410; telex 440049; fax (202) 328-3712

Secretaria Nacional de Turismo
Ed. Mariscal Ballivian Piso 18
La Paz, Bolivia
Telephone: 591-358.213 / 367.463
Fax: 591-2-374.630

BoliviaWeb—Premier source of information on the
Republic of Bolivia.
http://www.boliviaweb.com.

The International Academy at Santa Barbara at
http://www.iasb.org/cwl publishes Current World
Leaders, an excellent resource for data on political leaders
and parties in Bolivia. Telephone (800) 530-2682 or
(805) 965-5010 for subscription information.

The Bureau of Consular Affairs at **http://travel.state.gov**
can give you detailed information on obtaining passports,
visa requirements, and consular affairs bulletins.

The Center for Disease Control at **http://www.cdc.gov/**
provides valuable medical information, as well as information on outbreaks of virulent infections in Bolivia.

Like all Web sites, the preceding Internet addresses are subject to
change, and there is no guarantee that they will continue to provide
the data we list here.

Brazil

WHAT'S YOUR CULTURAL I.Q.?

1. The discovery of Brazil is credited to Portuguese explorer Pedro Cabral, who landed near present-day Porto Seguro on 22 April 1500. TRUE or FALSE? Cabral was lost; he was supposed to be headed for India, not the New World.

    ANSWER: True. En route to India, Cabral's fleet of 13 ships was curving around the continent of Africa when they hit the Brazilian coast. However, some records suggest that the Portuguese already knew of Brazil's existence. Either way, Cabral stayed just nine days before leaving for India.

2. Pedro Cabral claimed this new land for Portugal and named it *Terra de Vera Cruz (Land of the True Cross)*. That name didn't stick. Where did the name Brazil come from?

    a. The name of a coastal tribe of Amerindians

    b. The name of the first Portuguese to found a successful colony in Brazil

    c. Brazil wood

    d. The Brazil nut

ANSWER: c. Brazil wood (*pau brasil*) was the first thing of value the Portuguese found in Brazil. It is used to make a red dye for textiles. The first permanent settlement in Brazil was founded by Martim Alfonso de Sousa in 1531.

3. TRUE or FALSE? Brazil is the only South American country to have had a resident European Emperor.

    ANSWER: True. When Napoleon chased the royal house of Portugal out of Europe, they took up residence in Rio. The King, Dom João VI, liked Brazil so much that he stayed in Brazil even after Napoleon was defeated. Brazil became the only nation in the Americas from which a European Empire was ruled.

4. Brazil has had several capitals since the first one was established in 1549. Which of the following cities has NOT been a capital of Brazil?

    a. Salvador da Bahia

    b. São Paulo

    c. Rio de Janeiro

    d. Brasilia

    ANSWER: b. São Paulo may be Brazil's industrial center, but, unlike the other three cities, it has never been a national capital.

5. TRUE or FALSE? The reign of Dom Pedro I, King of Brazil, is remembered as a Golden Age of Brazil.

    ANSWER: False. Dom Pedro I was a less-than-competent ruler, and was forced to abdicate in favor of his five-year-old son. It was the reign of his son,

Dom Pedro II, that is fondly remembered. During his 48 years in office, Brazil abolished slavery, became the most powerful nation in South America, and built its first railroad and telegraph lines.

6. The military has seized power in Brazil several times. In what year did Brazil finally return to democracy after a military regime?

   a. 1889

   b. 1930

   c. 1951

   d. 1985

   ANSWER: d. The military allowed a presidential election to take place in 1985. Opposition leader Tancredo Neves won the election, but died of a heart attack the day before he was to be inaugurated. His running mate, José Sarney, was inaugurated in his place, and Brazil has had democratic elections ever since.

7. Brazil has suffered several bouts of high inflation. TRUE or FALSE? President Itamar Franco and his Finance Minister, Fernando Henrique Cardoso, stabilized the economy in 1994.

   ANSWER: True. They introduced a new currency, the *Plano Real.* The effort was so successful that Brazilians elected Fernando Henrique Cardoso to the Presidency by a landslide in the 1994 elections.

8. Brazil is big, and so are many of its businesses. These can have big profits . . . or big losses. US shipping magnate Daniel K. Ludwig bought a huge tract of the Amazon in 1967 for a massive agribusiness project.

When he sold it in 1981, what was the result?

a. A loss of $8 million US

b. A loss of $800 million US

c. A profit of $8 million US

d. A profit of $800 million US

ANSWER: b. Ludwig's controversial Jari project was huge, both in size and cost. It was not a success, in part because of conflict with the Brazilians. The Brazilian press inflamed public opinion against Ludwig's "imperialist exploitation," and the Brazilian government pressured him to sell. Ludwig sold his project to a Brazilian consortium, at a loss of at least $800 million. *The New York Times* called it "perhaps the largest and most costly entrepreneurial effort ever made by one man."

9. TRUE or FALSE? There are more Japanese in Brazil than in any country except Japan.

   ANSWER: True. The Japanese have found Brazil to be a land of boundless opportunity.

10. In Brazil, a *jeito* is:

a. The national dish

b. An Afro-Brazilian religion

c. A way to side-step a rule

ANSWER: c. When an obstacle presents itself, Brazilians prefer to go around the rules. Such a maneuver is called a *jeito* or (if the maneuver is small) *jeitinho*. In business, it often consists of calling in a favor to have someone bend a regulation.

QUOTATIONS ABOUT BRAZIL

"Anyone who does not get along with (Brazilians) had better examine himself; the fault is his."

—From *I Like Brazil* by Jack Harding.

"This is a world between First and Third Worlds, comfortable only within its own relativity. Forty-seven percent of the landmass of South America that hardly considers itself part of South America at all! Yet it's South America taken to extremes: the best and worst in cordiality and cruelty, penchant for the absurd! The largest Catholic country, oh yes! Which means it's got the greatest number of illegal abortions, too. Five million in one recent year! The most saints, the most cults! The largest numbers who worship the Virgin Mary, Oxum and Oxalá, too! The most slaves came here, some three million forcibly removed from Africa, which at some points in Brazil is less than two thousand miles from the Americas, another record in proximity."

—From *Why Is This Country Dancing?* by John Krich.

"We say to these Brazilians we can supply you with cotton goods cheaper than you can buy them elsewhere. Will you buy them? By all means, say the Brazilians, and we will pay you with our sugar and coffee. No, say we, your sugar and coffee are produced by slave labour; we are men of principle and our consciences will not allow us to consume the product of slave labour. Well, anyone would imagine that the matter ended there, and we left the Brazilians to consume their own sugar and coffee. No such thing. We are men of principle, but we are also men of business, and we try to help the Brazilians out of their difficulty. We say

to them: Close to us and near at hand live some 40,000,000 industrious and thriving Germans, who are not as conscientious as we are; take your sugar to them; they will buy it from you, and you can pay us for our cottons with the money you thus receive. But the Brazilians represent that there will be some difficulty with this. The Germans live on the other side of the Atlantic; we must send them our sugar in ships; now our ocean. Our reply is ready. We have plenty of ships and they are at your service. It is true that slave-labor sugar would contaminate our warehouses, but ships are different things. But the Brazilians have another difficulty. They say the Germans are particular and have a fancy for refined sugar. It is not easy to refine sugar in Brazil, and these Germans do not like the trouble of refining it themselves. Again we step in with an expedient. We will not only carry your sugar but we will refine it for you too. It is sinful to consume slave-grown sugar, but there can be no harm in refining it, which in fact is to cleanse it from part of its original impurity. The Brazilians are at us again. Say they, we produce a great deal of sugar more than the Germans will buy. Our goodness is infinite; we ourselves will buy your surplus. It cannot be consumed at home, because the people of this country are men of conscience, but we will send it to the West Indies and Australia. The people who live there are only negroes and colonists, and what right have they to consciences? And now that you may plague us no more about these matters, we tell you at once, that, if the price of our own sugar should rise above a certain value, we will buy more of your slave-grown sugar and we will eat it ourselves."

—From an ironic 1841 speech by Lord Palmerston to the British Parliament. Brazil did not abolish slavery until 1888.

"Newly freed from slavery, lacking industrial skills, savings, literacy, property or any form of reparation on the part of the lackadaisical Brazilian government, the blacks must have wanted first of all refuge from the rigors of freedom. If during slavery runaways protected their liberty in palisaded villages in the wild, they now fled to the numerous steep hills that ring Rio's downtown district and divide the city roughly in half: the prosperous (white) south, and the darker, poorer north. Joined by discharged soldiers back from extinguishing a religious revolt in Canudos, and by members of the poorer fringe of white tradespeople and artisans, Rio's poorest blacks rummaged crates from the docks and zinc sheeting from the warehouses and began life uphill. They descended to the city to scrabble a living out of occasional odd jobs, backbreaking labor at the docks, domestic employment, street vending and, increasingly, petty crime and prostitution. For a sense of order and dignity they turned again to the two things slavery had not confiscated and used against them: samba and candomblé—music and religion, the end products of centuries of clandestine worship of the African gods. During the slavery period the Portuguese had banned African religions among the blacks they imported to their colony in Brazil, but for the most part they tolerated the all-night sessions of drumming, singing and dancing that often took place in the slave barracks. They never really understood that the dancing and the worship were indivisible...."

— Mexican journalist Alma Guillermoprieto, explaining the origins of the *favelas* (mountainside slums) of Rio de Janeiro in her book *Samba*.

"Twenty years ago I first visited Amazonia. On its landing approach to Manaus, 1,600 kilometers westward from the

mouth of the river, the twin-jet Caravelle passed over the Encontro das Águas (Meeting of the Waters), that point where the black Rio Negro and the pale, muddy Solimões converge to form a single massive stream. For maybe a kilometer the two colors of fast-flowing water boil along separately beside each other, forming curling and twining patterns at the border, where fish frolic and terns flutter and swoop, before finally merging into uniform café au lait. *The incongruous opera house in Manaus, built at the height of the* belle époque *rubber boom in the region, was then painted rosy pink and not its current battleship gray. Slums consisting of nests of floating boats* (cidades flutuantes) *cluttered the edge of town. Ashore, little was stirring. I saw a white-elephant steel mill and at midday strolled on uncrowded streets where women walked with umbrellas unfurled against the hot sun."*

— A description of Manaus in the 1960s from *Dreams of Amazonia* by Roger Stone.

"There we were when a violent storm struck Vicencia. The terrified mayor left for the hut that had been the seat of government to examine the damage and destruction wrought by the rain. We stayed inside watching through the window as the townspeople fled the storm, shielding themselves under palm trees and hats—running from side to side like shipwrecked rats. It was raining as hard inside the bar as out because the zinc roof was riddled with holes, and the door frame was the only spot that offered protection from the inclement weather. The one thing left standing after the waterfall was the banana vendor at the entrance to the bar. His bunches of bananas were arranged on the edge of the street, while water ran over his body, drenching his shirt sleeves and making him shiver with cold. But he didn't abandon his post at the fruit

stand. When the storm ended, Miguel bought a banana, and the poor guy thanked him by bowing reverently, because he wasn't used to anybody buying bananas that you could pick from your own tree merely by raising your arm."

—An Amazon scene from *The Impostors,* a comic novel by Uruguayan-born author Pablo Vierci (now a resident of São Paulo, Brazil).

"If it hadn't been for my arthritis I would never have met Helena again . . . the truth is that without this malady, our meeting in São Pedro thirty years later would never have occurred. She in Pacaembu and I in Alto dos Pinheiros, each moving in our different circles, neither of us frequenting nightclubs or parties and neither in the limelight, the chances of our paths crossing were negligible . . . Nevertheless, if one stops to think about it, a man and a woman who are both over fifty, arthritic, affluent, and living in São Paulo, would sooner or later be bound to turn up at the same time in Águas de São Pedro, the spa village where bourgeois and middle-class rheumatics reserve rooms in two or three principal hotels."

—A reunion of two adulterous lovers, from the short story "Twice with Helena" by Paulo Emílio Salles Gomes (later made into the film *Memorias de Helena*).

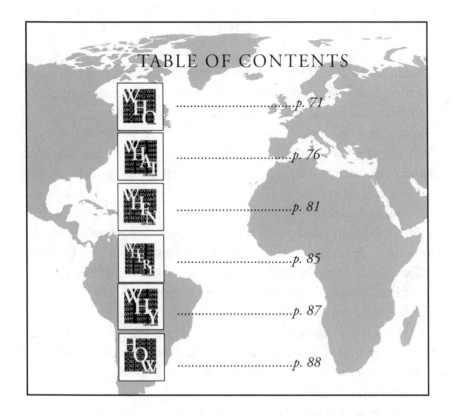

TABLE OF CONTENTS

THE BRAZILIANS

The majority of Brazilians (54.0%) consider themselves to be of European descent. The mixed-race groups form the next largest population: 39.9% are mestizos (white-Amerindian) or mulattos (white-black). Black and black-Amerindian Brazilians make up 5.9%. Asians now account for 0.9%. And although there is a large population of Amerindians in the Amazon, Amerindians make up only 0.2% of Brazil's population.

LITERATURE

Brazil is blessed with numerous writers, many of whom have achieved an international reputation. In the 20th century, Brazilian authors have dominated Portuguese literature, publishing far more books than authors native to Portugal. This list does not even include the many foreign-born writers who came to Brazil to live and write, such as Manuel Puig (born in Argentina) or Pablo Vierci (born in Uruguay).

Jorge Amado (1912–) is one of Brazil's most famous authors. A former journalist and politician, he was elected to Brazil's Congress on the Communist Party ticket. (He resigned from the Brazilian Communist Party in 1965.) He has been imprisoned several times and lived in exile from Brazil. Writing of the poor in his native state of Bahia, he wrote of the plight of black sugar cane workers in the 1935 book *Jubiabá,* which was translated into English in 1984. His 1966 novel *Dona Flor e seus dois maridos* (1969 English translation: *Dona Flor and Her Two Husbands*) was made into a highly successful Brazilian film in 1976.

Rubem Fonseca (1925–) is the mystery man of Brazilian letters; various reports list his background as a journalist, a lawyer, a policeman, and a worker for a Brazilian power and light company. He published his first collection of short stories in 1963. Fonseca's work soon gained a reputation for depictions of urban violence and explicit sexuality. His 1975 collection, *Feliz ano nova* (published in English in 1991 as *Happy New Year*) was banned by censors under the military dictatorship. His 1988 work, *Vast Emotions and Imperfect Thoughts*, was one of the best-selling books of recent years in Brazil.

João Guimarañes Rosa (1908–67) was raised on a farm in the rural highlands of Minas Gerais, which provided the backdrop for many of his stories. He went from a career in medicine to one in diplomacy, which led to extended stays in Germany, France, and Colombia. He mastered at least eight languages (including Japanese and Russian), and his linguistic talent is clearly evident in his writing. As James Joyce did in English, Guimarañes Rosa reconfigured Portuguese into his own literary language. This also makes his work difficult to translate. His masterpiece is the long novel *Grande Sertão: Veredas* (1956; translated into English as *The Devil to Pay in the Backlands*).

Clarice Lispector (1925–77) was born to Russian parents in the Ukraine, but her family emigrated to Brazil when she was two months old. Trained as a lawyer, she published her first novel at the age of 18. Later novels include *A paixão segundo G.H.* (1964, *The Passion According to G.H.*) and *A hora da estrela* (1977, translated into English in 1986 as *The Time of the Star*). Her short stories are even more distinguished than her novels; she is considered to be one of the finest writers of short fiction in the 20th century.

Joaquim Maria Machado de Assis (1839–1908) fought his way up to become one of Brazil's best-known writers of the 19th century. A mulatto, he was orphaned at an early age. Largely self-taught, Machado de Assis began as a printer and journalist, then became a Brazilian civil servant. His early fiction was sentimental; his masterworks all belong to his later, more satiric period. His *Memórias póstumas de Brás Cubas* (published in English as *Epitaph of a Small Winner* in 1952) and its sequel, *Quincas Borba* (1954 English translation as *Philosopher or Dog?*) remain his best known novels. Machado de Assis also published over 200 short stories and wrote in virtually every literary form; his *Collected Works* take up 31 volumes.

Paulo Emílio Salles Gomes (1916–77) made a career of film criticism, a specialty he began in 1941. Imprisoned in 1936 for protesting the dictatorial Vargas regime, he left Brazil for Europe. His single novel, *Tres mulheres de tres Pppes* was published in 1977 (translated into English in 1982 as *P.'s Three Women*). The novel consists of stories about three remarkable women, narrated by a man who signs his name only with the initial "P." The first of the three stories, "Twice with Helena," was later made into a film, *Memorias* *de Helena,* directed by David Neves. This novel brought Salles Gomes great renown as a comic stylist, but he did not live to profit from it; he died shortly after its publication.

Moacyr Scliar (1937–) is a prolific journalist, novelist, and writer of short stories. A descendant of Russian Jews, Scliar studied medicine and served for many years as Director of Public Health in the state of Rio Grande do Sul.

His 1968 prize-winning collection *The Carnival of the Animals* gained him critical acclaim. *The Centaur in the Garden* extended his reputation internationally; the protagonist of this tragicomic 1980 novel tries to lead a normal, middle-class existence, despite the fact that he is a Jewish centaur!

LIGHTS! CAMERA! ACTION!

 To adequately describe Brazilian cinema would take an entire book. Brazil has the largest and most vital film industry in South America. Dozens of fine Brazilian films are now available in the USA, subtitled in English. In addition to the film versions of literary works noted above, some notable Brazilian films (and foreign films about Brazil) include:

1. **O Boto (The Dolphin)** is not just any sea mammal; he's a sort of were-dolphin, capable of assuming human form. In a small Brazilian fishing village, he seduces a fisherman's daughter. But when she gives birth to the dolphin's child, a curse takes its toll on the town (1987, directed by Walter Lima Jr.).

2. **Black Orpheus** is a retelling of the Orpheus and Eurydice myth, set amid the poverty-stricken *favellas* (hillside slums) of Rio de Janeiro. This film won the Academy Award for Best Foreign Film (1958, directed by Marcel Camus).

3. **Bye Bye Brazil** could be described as the first "magical realist" road movie. Although the main characters are fictional, much of the film consists of an actual documentary of the film crew's journey across the Trans-Amazonian Highway (1979, directed by Carlos Diegues).

4. **The Emerald Forest** is a Hollywood film featuring Powers Boothe as an American engineer, who is working in the Amazon when his son is stolen by a native tribe. Over the years, in between construction projects, he searches for his lost child. But when they are finally reunited, the son becomes the teacher as he shows his father a different way to view the Amazon jungle (1985, directed by John Boorman).

5. **Quilombo** is a historical drama about the Republic of Palmares—a 17th century democratic community of runaway slaves, outcasts, and Brazilian Jews in the interior of Brazil. This idealized but fascinating film depicts life in this unique community, and its eventual destruction at the hands of a Portuguese army (1984, directed by Carlos Diegues).

LANGUAGE

The official language of Brazil is Portuguese, but the Portuguese of Brazil is not identical to the Portuguese spoken in Portugal. The most obvious difference is the many words that come from the languages of Brazilian Indians. In fact, until its use was prohibited by law in 1757, a majority of Brazilians spoke a version of Tupi-Guaraní, an Amerindian lingua franca that had first been written down by Jesuit missionaries.

Language

Linguists have categorized 209 different languages spoken in modern Brazil—*Ethnologue: Languages of the World,* 12th Edition from their Web site at (http://www.sil.org/ethnologue/ethnologue. html).

BUSINESS IN BRAZIL

Remember that Brazilians almost always make an effort to be charming. This in no way obstructs their desire to get what they want.

> *"The gentleness factor is ubiquitous. Even the Brazilian political leader who brought the country to the verge of fascism, President Getúlio Vargas, radiated this quality. A plump-faced, benevolent, "father-of-the-poor" figure, he could not have been more different in style than his contemporaries (some would say soulmates) Adolf Hitler and Benito Mussolini."*

—From *The Brazilians* by Joseph A. Page.

BRAZILIAN BUSINESS PERSONALITIES

Roberto Marinho is perhaps the most powerful media magnate in Latin America. He is the owner of *O Globo,* Brazil's leading daily newspaper. He is also the founder of *TV Globo,* the largest and most successful television network. With 94 affiliates, *TV Globo* is a third larger than its closest competitor; its evening news broadcast is watched by half of all television viewers. The network also self-produces about three-quarters of its shows. Marinho's success has been helped by his comfortable relationship with the military dictators who ruled Brazil from 1964 to 1985.

President Fernando Henrique Cardoso (often referred to in the press by his initials, FHC) came to prominence during the administration of his predecessor, President Itamar Franco. As Itamar Franco's Finance Minister, FHC was responsible for stabilizing Brazil's economy and reigning in inflation. On 1 July 1994, Brazil introduced a new currency, the *Plano Real.* FHC's program, the *Real Plan,* was a success, and propelled him to the Presidency in the 1994 elections. He continues to cautiously guide the Brazilian economy, allowing private investment to compete with the Brazilian oil monopoly (*Petrobrás*) and the telecommunications monopoly (*Telebras*).

Maximum Risk: Daniel K. Ludwig's Jari Project

The late Daniel K. Ludwig was a US shipping magnate and entrepreneur who, in 1967, purchased a tract in the Amazon jungle nearly the size of the state of Connecticut. The forest was cleared and sown with rice and pulp trees. This massive agribusiness venture, called the Jari Project, soon encountered obstacles. Conservationists protested the massive deforestation. The Brazilian media inflamed the people over the Jari Project's neocolonial overtones. Brazilian politicians became obstructive. Ludwig's autocratic personality aggravated the situation; nick-named "the Invisible Billionaire," he lacked the social skills that Brazilians value. Fourteen years later, Ludwig had to "sell" his project to a consortium of 23 private Brazilian companies. (He received no money for his shares, but the Brazilians assumed his losses and promised him a share of future profits.) Ludwig had lost over $800 million US (some estimates reach $1 billion) on the project—one of the largest business losses by a single entrepreneur in history.

BUSINESS SUCCESS IN BRAZIL

Caveat: Brazil levies income tax on foreign exporters if the exporter is determined to be present in Brazil. Presence is established by two factors:

1. The closing of sales contracts in Brazil

2. The existence of a Brazilian agent or representative with power of attorney (whether implied or expressly granted)

Foreigners are often surprised to discover that Brazilian income taxes are paid every month. Brazilians file their income taxes twelve times a year!

In addition to standard arrangements with local agents and representatives, foreign businesses can market goods in Brazil through a trading company. Brazilian trading companies, modeled after such organizations in Japan and Germany, were designed to assist the export of Brazilian goods. However, they can also act as intermediaries in the import process. Brazilian trading companies are known under such designations as *empresas comerciais exportadoras, companhias comerciais,* or *companhias de comercio exterior.*

Franchises were introduced into Brazil in the 1970s. They are now one of the fastest growing sectors in Brazil. There are no regulations in Brazil specifically addressing franchises. Joint ventures and licensing agreements are also used.

Brazilian law makes it difficult to form branch offices. However, Brazil's legal code favors the formation of corporations and limited liability companies.

Consumers list price as the major factor in deciding which product to buy. Second to this in importance is quality, followed by delivery and after-sales support.

Brazil is a major advertising market, with world-class advertising agencies. Television is the most important venue, followed by radio and print advertising. There are also numerous trade publications.

LEGAL AFFAIRS IN BRAZIL

Copyright violations remain a problem in Brazil. To cut down on video piracy, all videotapes now carry a stamp from Cocine, the Brazilian film agency.

Vigilance is necessary to protect one's copyright. When a trademark is not used in Brazil for more than two years, Brazilian law allows anyone to file for cancellation of that registered trademark. Many internationally known trademarks have been taken over through this policy.

The spiraling crime rate in cities like Rio de Janeiro has brought back the use of police death squads. Real and suspected criminals have been tortured and killed. The large numbers of homeless children are especially vulnerable to these extralegal squads, who view the children as potential criminals.

LEADING BUSINESSES IN BRAZIL

The following businesses are some of the largest employers in Brazil:

Autolatina Brasil SA
São Paulo.
Motor vehicles. 48,000 employees.

Banco Bradesco SA
Osasco.
National Commercial bank. 74,580 employees.

Battistella Industria e Comercio Ltda
Lages.
Farm machinery and equipment. 21,500 employees.

Caixa Economica Federal
Brasilia.
National commercial bank. 65,000 employees.

Companhia de Saneamento Basico do Estado de São Paulo SABESP
São Paulo.
Water supply. 22,000 employees.

Empresa Brasileira de Correios e Telegrafos
Brasilia.
Postal service. 70,000 employees.

Encol SA Engenharia Comercio e Industria
Brasilia.
Single-family housing construction. 21,063 employees.

Luguide Industria e Comercio de Confeccoes Ltda
São Paulo.
Men's and boys' clothing. 50,000 employees.

Petroleo Brasileiro SA Petrobras
Rio de Janeiro.
Petroleum refining. 51,399 employees.

Rede Ferroviaria Federal SA
Rio de Janeiro.
Railroads. 45,074 employees.

Telecomunicacoes de São Paulo SA Telesp
Rio de Janeiro.
Telephone communications. 23,000 employees.

Varig SA (Viacao Aerea Rio Grandense)
São Paulo.
Air transportation. 21,495 employees.

The following are some of the largest newspaper publishers in Brazil:

D C I Editora Jornalistica Ltda
São Paulo.
1,035 employees.

Empresa Folha da manha SA
São Paulo.
3,000 employees.

Gazeta Mercantil SA
São Paulo.
2,228 employees.

S/A O Estado de São Paulo
São Paulo.
1,035 employees.
Jornal do Brasil SA
Rio de Janeiro.
1,950 employees.
O Globo Empresa Jornalistica Brasileira Ltda
Rio de Janeiro.
2,300 employees.
S/A Correio Brasiliense
Brasilia.
1,200 employees.
S/A Estado de Minas
Belo Horizonte
1,761 employees.

BRAZILIAN HISTORY

Until 1500: Unlike the Mayans or Incas, the Amerindians of Brazil do not form centralized civilizations or build great cities. Brazil's Amerindians leave few artifacts behind for archaeologists to study. Brazil is home to numerous Amerindian tribes who live diverse lifestyles. The coastal Tupi tribe are among the first to meet Europeans, and many Brazilian names for flora, fauna, and places are of Tupi origin.

1500: Portuguese explorer Pedro Cabral, leading a fleet of 13 ships ostensibly bound for India, becomes the first known European to reach Brazil. Landing near present-day Porto Seguro on 22 April 1500, Cabral claims Brazil for the Portuguese crown. Some records suggest that the Portuguese already knew of Brazil's existence. Cabral stays just nine days, enough time to build a cross and name the country Terra de Vera Cruz (Land of the True Cross). Cabral then continues on to India via the African route. He takes with him samples of pau brasil, a wood that produces a red dye. It is this wood that eventually gives the country its name.

Early 1500s: The Portuguese are uninterested in colonization, and the only item of value they find is Brazil wood for dying textiles. They trade metal tools to the Amerindians for providing the wood, but the trade is never highly profitable.

1531: To preempt occupation by other European powers, King João III of Portugal sends out the first colonizing expedition. The settlement of São Vicente is established by Martim Alfonso de Sousa. This settlement eventually becomes a profitable sugar-producing center, after African slaves are imported to work the plantations.

1534: King João III divides the Brazilian coast into 12 captaincies. Only four manage to build permanent settlements. Four are destroyed by Amerindians, and the other four never build settlements at all.

1549: Tomé de Sousa is appointed as the first governor of Brazil. Salvador da Bahia becomes the capital, a position it will hold until 1763.

1554: São Paulo is established. The settlement specializes in expeditions into the interior to capture Amerindians for slaves.

1555–1654: French and Dutch settlers establish colonies in remote areas of the Brazilian coast. Not until 1654 are they driven out by the Portuguese.

1690s: After nearly two centuries of searching, Portuguese explorers find gold in Brazil. Thousands of people pour into the Minas Gerais gold fields. In the next hundred years, 400,000 Portuguese emigrants come to Brazil, most of them lured by gold. Two million African slaves are imported during the same period. By 1750, gold production in Minas Gerais declines.

1807: Napoleon invades Portugal, capturing Lisbon. The Portuguese prince regent (the future Dom João VI) and his entire court flee to Brazil. The Brazilians welcome him, and he rules Brazil as viceroy. An avid naturalist, Dom João enjoys Brazil so much that he declines to return to Portugal after Napoleon is defeated in 1815.

1816: After the death of his mother, Dom João VI becomes King of Portugal. He still refuses to return to Europe, and declares Rio to be the new capital of the Portuguese empire. This makes Brazil the only country in the Americas to be the ruling seat of a European king.

1820s: Unable to compete with West Indian sugar production, Brazil's sugar exports fall. Coffee soon replaces sugar as Brazil's main export.

1821: Finally convinced that Portugal cannot be ruled from Brazil, Dom João VI reluctantly returns to Europe. He leaves his son, the prince regent, in Brazil.

1822: The prince regent declares Brazil independent from Portugal, and rules the Kingdom of Portugal as Dom Pedro I. An incompetent ruler, in 1831 he is forced to abdicate in favor of his five-year-old son.

1825–28: Brazil fights a war with Argentina over control of Uruguay. Neither side wins a decisive victory. After British intervention, Uruguay becomes an independent buffer state between Brazil and Argentina.

1834: With Dom Pedro II still a minor, Brazil lacks a strong ruler. Some factions demand a republic, others a monarchy. After a period of civil war, some democratic concessions are made via the constitutional amendment of 1834, which sets up provincial legislators.

1841: Finally of age, Dom Pedro II is enthroned as the second Emperor of Brazil. An enlightened, progressive monarch, his 48-year reign is remembered as Brazil's Golden Age. The Emperor encourages parliamentary democracy, European immigration, and infrastructure development (including Brazil's first railroad and telegraph). He also presides over the abolition of slavery, which costs him the support of the rich coffee planters.

1851–52: Brazil fights a war with Argentina. Brazil wins.

1864–70: The War of the Triple Alliance pits Paraguay against not only Brazil but Argentina and Uruguay as well. Paraguay loses; Brazil annexes some Paraguayan territory.

1889: A military coup, supported by coffee planters and republicans, ousts the Emperor. Dom Pedro II is exiled to Europe. The

Republic of Brazil is born, but the military remains in control until 1894.

1890: Providing material for automobile tires, Brazil's rubber exports boom. But Brazil's monopoly on natural rubber is broken when plantations in Southeast Asia (using stolen Brazilian rubber tree seeds) start rubber production in 1910.

1903: Bolivia is persuaded to cede territory to Brazil.

1917: Following German attacks on Brazilian shipping, Brazil enters the First World War on the Allied side.

1930: With Brazil suffering from the Great Depression, Getúlio Vargas is brought to power via a coup. Although he rules autocratically, he guides Brazil through the Depression and World War II (again on the Allied side). He rules Brazil until 1945, when he is ousted by a coup. He regains the presidency in the 1950 elections. He then rules until 1954, when he commits suicide rather than be ousted by another military coup.

1960: Brazil caps a massive industrialization era by inaugurating the new city of Brasilia as the capital. Fueled by government spending, inflation soars.

1964: After several unpopular presidents in a row, the military seizes power. Many Brazilians support the coup at first. The regime's human rights abuses soon change their minds. But the economy grows steadily, so the military manages to stay in power until 1985.

1985: Faced with increased protests from the Brazilian people, the military allows a presidential election to take place in 1985. Although the military's candidate is expected to win, opposition leader Tancredo Neves wins the election. Brazilians celebrate . . . until Neves dies of a heart attack the day before he is to be inaugurated. His running mate, José Sarney, becomes president. Sarney's term is marked by a return to high rates of inflation.

1989: Fernando Collor de Mello, a former karate champion, is elected president. He resigns amid corruption charges in 1992, and Vice President Itamar Franco ascends to the presidency. Franco stabilizes the economy with the introduction of a new currency, the Plano Real, in 1994.

1994: Itamar Franco's Finance Minister, Fernando Henrique Cardoso, is credited with the success of Brazil's economic plan. (He becomes known as "the Father of the Real.") He is elected to the presidency in the 1994 elections and takes office on 1 January 1995.

BRAZILIAN GEOGRAPHY

BRAZIL

FLAG AND MAP OF BRAZIL

The yellow and green of Brazil's flag are considered Brazil's national colors. Wearing both of these colors may offend some Brazilians.

In the center of the Brazilian flag is a depiction of the night sky as it was over Rio on 15 November 1889, when the Republic of Brazil was declared. The sky-field is bisected by the motto *"Ordem e Progresso"* (*"Order and Progress"*).

Size: 3,300,171 square miles

Population: 160,737,489

Brazil is the largest and most populous member of the Mercosur Customs Trade Union (along with Argentina, Chile, Paraguay, and Uruguay). Collectively, Mercosur represents a population of 213,611,000.

HOW TO TELL BRAZIL AND BRAZILIANS FROM THEIR NEIGHBORS

It is impossible to describe Brazil without using extremes.

1. Brazil is the largest nation in South America. It is slightly larger than the lower 48 states of the USA. Taking up almost half of South America's landmass, Brazil shares borders with all but two South American nations (Ecuador and Chile).

2. São Paulo is the most populous metropolis in South America, with a population of some 17 million (or about one in every nine Brazilians). São Paulo accounts for half of Brazil's industrial production.

3. Despite massive deforestation and pollution, Brazil still contains more plant and animal species than anywhere else on earth. The Amazon—the world's largest river—is centered in Brazil, and remains the world's largest tropical rain forest. Brazil is also home to the world's largest wetlands, known as the Pantanal.

4. Brazilians watch mostly Brazilian-made television, as opposed to virtually every other Latin American nation, where much of the broadcasts consist of American-made shows dubbed into Spanish.

5. While Brazil has known successive boom times—
producing first sugar, then gold, rubber, and coffee—
most Brazilians are wretchedly poor. Nutrition and
health care are so lacking that, in 1983, almost half of
Brazil's 18-year-old men could not pass their military
induction physicals. Some Brazilians have nicknamed
their country "Belindia"—implying that Brazil combines the production capacity of Belgium with the per-
capita income of India.

BRAZILIAN BEHAVIOR

Why are Brazilians the way they are?

Brazil is so huge and multicultural that generalizations are difficult. The predominant culture is Portuguese, which yields such
characteristics as the love of family, the importance of honor, and an
outward show of emotion. The expression "jealous as a Portuguese"
is centuries old, and is illustrative of the traditional Portuguese relationship between the sexes. To this day, juries often acquit a
Brazilian man who kills his adulterous wife on the grounds that he
was only "defending his honor." A strain of violence coexists in
Brazilian culture with great hospitality and courtesy.

*What has replaced sports, the samba, and politics as Brazil's #1 form of
entertainment?*

The most popular form of entertainment in Brazil is the television soap opera, known as the *telenova*. For three hours each
evening, Monday through Saturday, Brazilian-produced telenovas
entertain the public with melodramatic tales of sex, crime, and
redemption. So popular are these telenovas that the real-life murder
of a telenova actress by her on- and off-screen lover grabbed public
attention away from the 1992 impeachment of Brazilian President
Fernando Collor de Mello.

Conflict resolution in Brazil

On top of a rigid class system and an unforgiving natural environment, Brazilians have been burdened with draconian laws and an inert bureaucracy. Rather than struggle against impossible odds, Brazilians find ways to cheat the system. The term *jeito* (and its diminutive form *jeitinho*) refers to a characteristically Brazilian way to get around the rules. Many business obstacles can be overcome by a judiciously applied *jeito*. But be aware that such favors must always be repaid, one way or another.

How do Brazilians dress?

Dress in Brazil is more casual than anywhere else in the Americas. There are, however, regional variations.

HOW CAN I FIND MORE INFORMATION ABOUT BRAZIL?

Here are a few resources to start with:

Getting Through Customs' Web site at **http://www. getcustoms.com** tracks current holidays in Brazil. They also post Cultural I.Q. Quizzes, gift-giving guidelines, a demo of the PASSPORT database, and further international information. Telephone: (610) 353-9894; fax (610) 353-6994.

Embassy of Brazil
3006 Massachusetts Avenue, NW
Washington, DC 20008
Telephone: (202) 745-2700; fax: (202) 745-2827
The Embassy of Brazil has a Web site (official):
http://www.brasil.emb.nw.dc.us.

The **United States Information Service (USIS) office in Brasilia** is accessible via WWW (official): **http://www.usia.gov/posts/brasilia.html**.

Brazilian Tourism Office
551 Fifth Avenue #590
New York, NY 10176
Telephone: (212) 286-9600; fax: (212) 490-9294

EMBRATUR—Brazilian Tourism Agency.
http://www.embratur.gov.br/

Brasil Web—This site serves as a window to Brasil, with information about culture, history, daily news events, and web servers in the country.
http://www.escape.com/~jvgkny/Brasil.Web.html

The International Academy at Santa Barbara at **http://www.iasb.org/cwl** publishes Current World Leaders, an excellent resource for data on political leaders and parties in Brazil. Telephone: (800) 530-2682 or (805) 965-5010 for subscription information.

The Bureau of Consular Affairs at **http://travel.state.gov** can give you detailed information on obtaining passports, visa requirements, and consular affairs bulletins.

The Center for Disease Control at **http://www.cdc.gov/** provides valuable medical information, as well as information on any outbreaks of virulent infections in Brazil.

Like all Web sites, the preceding Internet addresses are subject to change, and there is no guarantee that they will continue to provide the data we list here.

Chile

WHAT'S YOUR CULTURAL I.Q.?

1. How long is it? TRUE or FALSE? Chile is so long that, if placed in the USA, it would stretch from New York City to Los Angeles.

   ANSWER: True. Additionally, Chile has over 6,000km of coastline.

2. Which of the following is one of the fathers of Chilean independence?

   a. Diego de Almagro

   b. Pedro de Valdivia

   c. Bernardo O'Higgins

   d. Salvador Allende

   ANSWER: c. Chilean-born hero Bernardo O'Higgins helped drive out the Spanish, but was forced into exile by Chile's new leaders.

3. TRUE or FALSE? Chile is one of the most seismically active nations on earth.

   ANSWER: True. Set squarely in the Pacific's "Ring of Fire," Chile has 55 active volcanos and is subject to frequent earthquakes.

4. In the War of the Pacific, which of the following countries did Chile not acquire land from?

   a. Argentina

   b. Bolivia

   c. Peru

   ANSWER: a. Argentina was the only neighbor that Chile did not fight (and take land from) in this war.

5. The popular 1995 film *Il Postino (The Postman)* depicted the relationship between the exiled Chilean poet Pablo Neruda and an Italian postman. TRUE or FALSE? That film was based on a book by another Chilean author, Antonió Skarmeta.

   ANSWER: True. The film was inspired by Skarmeta's novel *Ardiente paciencia (Burning Patience)*.

6. Which one of the following Chilean authors has not yet won the Nobel Prize for Literature?

   a. Isabel Allende

   b. Gabriela Mistral

   c. Pablo Neruda

   ANSWER: a. Isabel Allende has never received a Nobel.

7. TRUE or FALSE? The Galápagos Islands are under Chilean control.

   ANSWER: False. The Galápagos belong to Ecuador. Chile controls Easter Island.

8. Chile's abundant mineral wealth includes which of the following?

   a. Copper

   b. Nitrate

   c. Iron

   d. All of the above

   ANSWER: d. Chile mines and exports copper, nitrates, and iron.

9. TRUE or FALSE? The Chilean snack break known as *once* is taken at 11 a.m.

   ANSWER: False. Although *once* means "eleven" in Spanish, an *once* is enjoyed in late afternoon.

10. What was unusual about the government of Dr. Salvador Allende, who became President of Chile in 1970?

    a. He was the first Marxist to be freely elected as leader in Latin America

    b. He instituted major land reforms and expropriated the copper industry

    c. He was overthrown in a coup in 1973

    d. All of the above

    e. None of the above

    ANSWER: d. The only Marxist head of state elected (to date) in Latin America, he was deposed by a military junta in September 1973 and died during the takeover.

QUOTATIONS ABOUT CHILE

"It's not true that Chile is bordered by the Andes, by the Saltpeter Desert, by the Pacific Ocean, by the meeting of two oceans: it's just the opposite. It's the Andes that are bordered by Chile . . . "

—Chilean poet Nicanor Parra, from his prose-poem, *The Borders of Chile*.

"I'm sorry, but I'm afraid I just can't take Chile seriously. For me, it's torture, There's something about it that makes me, well, nervous.

"It's a funny shape. It's long: it has over 5,000 miles of coast stretching all the way from deserts in the north to the frozen waste of Tierra del Fuego in the south. It's thin. Some people say it looks as if Brazil and Argentina are trying to push it into the Pacific. Other people, I don't know why, say it's like a long, thin, highly polished jackboot. Most important, it's too long to fit on Chilean television. For weather reports, they have to cut it up into three chunks. Which, when we live in an age dominated by the media, could be dangerous."

—From Peter Biddlecombe's *Around the World—On Expenses*, a seriocomic memoir of international business travel.

"Temuco is a pioneer town, one of those towns that have no past, though it does have hardware stores. Since the Indians can't read, the stores hang their eye-catching signs out on the streets: an enormous saw, a giant cooking pot, a Cyclopean padlock, a mammoth spoon. Farther along the street, shoe stores—a colossal boot.

"Temuco was the farthest outpost of Chilean life in the southern territories, and therefore it had a long bloody history behind it.

"When the Spanish conquistadors pushed them back, after three hundred years of fighting, the Araucanian Indians retreated to those cold regions. But the Chileans continued what they called 'the pacification of Araucania,' their war of blood and fire to turn our countrymen out of their own lands. Every kind of weapon was used against the Indians, unsparingly: carbine blasts, the burning of villages, and later, a more fatherly method, alcohol and the law. The lawyer became a specialist at stripping them of their fields, the judge sentenced them when they protested, the priest threatened them with eternal fire."

—From the memoirs of poet Pablo Neruda, in which he recalls his Chilean hometown.

"The pilot flying towards the Straits of Magellan sees below him, a little to the south of the Gallego River, an ancient lava flow, an erupted waste of a thickness of sixty feet that crushes down the plain on which it has congealed. Farther south he meets a second flow, then a third; and thereafter every hump on the glove, every mound a few hundred feet high, carries a crater in its flank."

—French pilot Antoine de Saint-Expuréry from his book about his days as a South American mail pilot, *Wind, Sand and Stars.*

"Years of dictatorship by the last Prussian army in the world have not separated Chileans from Chile. The military rulers have prevented them from living like human beings, but they have not been able to prevent them from surviving like Chileans."

—Argentine journalist Jacobo Timmerman, from his book, *Chile: Death in the South.*

TABLE OF CONTENTS

THE CHILEANS

The majority (89.7%) of Chileans are of European or mestizo descent. Amerindians make up most of the remainder, primarily Araucanian (also known as Mapuche), but with some Aymara as well. There are also a few thousand Polynesians (Rapa Nui) on Easter Island.

The original immigrants to Chile during the colonial period were Spanish. Later immigrants came from Italy and Germany. Of course, Chile's mineral wealth has attracted miners and prospectors from all over the world.

LITERATURE

Chileans pride themselves on their literary tradition. Since the 1920s, Chile has challenged Argentina's place as South America's biggest producer of books in the Spanish language.

Chile's most noted authors include:

Isabel Allende (1942–) is distantly related to Salvador Allende, Chile's Marxist president who died during the coup in 1973. Educated in English boarding schools, she worked as a multilingual journalist for many years. Her first novel, *La casa de los espíritus* (*The House of the Spirits*), published in 1982, depicted the violence of the Pinochet regime. She currently lives in San Francisco.

José Donoso (1924–) has written some strange novels. His 1966 novel *El lugar sin límites* (*Hell Has No Limits*) is set in a brothel, and the narrator of his 1970 novel *El obsceno pájaro de la noche* (*The Obscene Bird of Night*) is a schizophrenic.

Gabriela Mistral (1889–1957), a teacher and poet, became the first Latin American to win the Nobel Prize for Literature (in 1945). Her poetry concentrates on children, love, and death. Her most famous collection is *Los sonetos de la muerte* (*Sonnets of Death*). After being awarded the Nobel, she was appointed a Chilean consul to the USA.

Nicanor Parra (1914–) bills himself as the anti-Neruda. Reflecting his training as a scientist, his poems are objective and unlyrical—the direct opposite of Pablo Neruda. He studied engineering at Brown University in Rhode Island and later taught at the University of Chile. His collection *Poemas y antipeomas* (*Poems and Antipoems*) was published in 1954.

Pablo Neruda (1904–73) was the pen name of Ricardo Neftalí Reyes, who took the name Neruda from a 19th-century Czech writer. Chile's most famous poet, he became Chile's second Nobel Laureate in Literature (awarded in 1971). He was elected to the Chilean Senate as a Communist in 1945, but just a few years later he was forced into exile. Neruda was only 20 years old when he produced one of his most popular collections: *Veinte poemas de amor y una cancion desperada* (*Twenty Love Poems and One Song of Despair*). This volume has sold over a million copies worldwide.

Antonió Skarmeta (1940–) is the author of the novel *Ardiente paciencia* (*Burning Patience*), which was the inspiration for the 1995 Italian film *Il Postino* (*The Postman*). The film focuses on a year in exile for Pablo Neruda and his friendship with an Italian postman. Skarmeta now lives in Berlin.

INVITATION TO THE DANCE

While some Chileans dance to the Argentine tango, Chile has its own indigenous form of popular dance. It is called the *cueca,* and, like the tango, it is both erotic and powerful.

LIGHTS! CAMERA! ACTION!

The Chilean film industry has produced a variety of movies over the years, although few of them have been released outside Latin America. The 1973 overthrow of the Allende government inspired over a dozen films and documentaries. Most of these films were made outside of Chile, and generally depicted the US Central Intelligence Agency as the villain. The following films are particularly enlightening about Chile and the Chileans:

1. **Enough Praying** dramatizes the moral dilemmas of a young priest, portrayed by Marcello Romo. His congregation contains wealthy, upper-class members, as well a some of the poorest Chileans. The disparity in their lives leads him to question the ethics of the status quo (1973, directed by Aldo Francia).

2. **The Jackal of Nahueltoro** is a documentary-style re-creation of a horrific event in Chilean history: A farm laborer murders his common-law wife and her four children while in a drunken stupor. Director Littin provides a moving portrayal of the lives of Chile's poorest citizens.

   Released during a time of intense debate over the poor, it became the most widely seen film in the history of Chilean cinema—the director even prepared inexpensive 16mm prints for distribution to Chilean jails (1970, directed by Michael Littin).

3. **The Knight of the Sword** is a lush historical drama. It follows the career of Argentine-born Jose de San Martin, the general who fought for the liberation of Chile, Peru and Argentina (1970, directed by Leopoldo Torre Nilsson).

4. **Missing** is a Hollywood film, inspired by a true story, centered on a young American writer who disappears in Chile during the 1973 coup. When the writer's bohemian wife (portrayed by Sissy Spacek) cannot find him, his estranged father comes down from the US to search. Jack Lemmon is marvelous as the patriotic, middle-class father, and the film is largely about the father's painful education in international politics.

   Unforgettable moments: This film offers many haunting images. In one scene, Beth is outside after curfew, running from one sheltered, concealed doorway to another. While hiding, she sees a white horse inexplicably running down the street, pursued by a car full of soldiers.

   In another scene, soldiers are harassing women for wearing trousers—under the junta, women were ordered to wear skirts! (1982, directed by Constantin Costa-Gavras).

5. **What Is To Be Done** takes place just before the election of Salvador Allende as president of Chile. This co-production of Chile and the USA depicts a woman in the Peace Corps, torn between her love for a Maoist revolutionary and a mysterious American—who may or may not be an agent of the CIA (1972, directed by Saul Landau, Nina Serrano, and Raul Ruiz).

Other foreign films inspired by the 1973 overthrow of the government of Salvador Allende include:

6. **The Battle of Chile** A three-part documentary; co-produced by Cuba and Chile. Part III, entitled *Power of the People,* depicts Allende's fall (1980, directed by Patricio Guzman).

7. **Born of Fire** An East German documentary on the coup (1979, directed by Walter Heynowski and Gerhard Scheumann).

8. **It's Raining on Santiago** An international production, co-released by Film Marquise and Bulgarofilm, outlining the collusion between the CIA and General Pinochet (1975, directed by Helvio Soto).

9. **A Night Over Chile** A co-production of the USSR and Chile, focusing on the doomed resistance of Marxists loyal to Allende on the night of the coup (1977, directed by Sebastian Alarcon and Alexander Kosarev).

10. **The Spiral** A French collaboration credited to six directors. This film blames US business interests for ordering the coup (1976, directed by Silvio Tendler, et al.).

LANGUAGE

The official language of Chile is Spanish. In fact, the Chileans speak a very conservative form of Spanish. Unlike most of Latin America, where the second-person plural is replaced by the third-person plural, the Chileans continue to use the second-person plural. Chile is actually a good place to study classical Spanish in its pure form.

Linguists have categorized eight different languages spoken in modern Chile—*Ethnologue: Languages of the World,* 12th Edition from their Web site at (http://www.sil.org/ethnologue/ethnologue. html).

BUSINESS IN CHILE

BUSINESS SUCCESS IN CHILE

There are approximately 3,000 importers in Chile, many of whom act as local distributors for foreign products. Finding the right local distributor or agent can be a challenge. The selection can be narrowed down by eliminating importers who are unfamiliar with your type of product or who currently carry your competitor's products. But there are other factors to consider. A good local agent will have an aggressive sales force which reaches a wide area (including Chile's free trade zones). Most importers have their main office in or near Santiago.

Franchises have experienced tremendous growth in Chile in the 1990s. Some 65 different foreign firms have franchises in Chile. Fast-food franchises have been especially successful. There are no laws in Chile specifically aimed at franchises.

Shopping malls have also experienced rapid expansion. Chilean shoppers have a tradition of window-shopping and comparing products before buying. Shopping through catalogs has not been popular. Direct marketing of products to consumers is rare, although such marketing of services to businesses has been successful. The resistance of consumers to catalog shopping and direct marketing is attributed to widespread distrust of warranty and service guarantees.

Buying decisions are usually made on the basis of price. Products from North America and Europe face strong competition from inexpensive goods from Asia. Where after-sale service is important, local customer support becomes a factor, but price remains the most important determinant.

Chile's unusual geography has led to the development of a traveling sales force. Businesses have become accustomed to having salesmen demonstrate products in their offices, rather than going to a showroom.

Except for direct marketing, advertising runs the full spectrum in Chile. Television, radio, newspapers, magazines, and billboards are all used.

English is commonly understood in the business sector, but all materials should be translated into Spanish.

What is the "Chilean Model"?

Unlike many military dictatorships, the regime of General Augusto Pinochet (which ruled Chile from 1973 to 1989) actually did bring a degree of prosperity to Chile. Installing harsh free-market guidelines, the Chileans lowered trade barriers, reduced their expenditures, and privatized inefficient industries. This "Chilean Model" was touted as a guideline for several ex-Communist governments in Eastern Europe and the former USSR.

They liked the way Pinochet created prosperity while restricting human rights. However, none of these countries managed to implement the "Chilean Model."

Chile has asked to join NAFTA, the North American Free Trade Agreement. The addition of Chile would require a name change, and it was thought that the word "North" could simply be deleted, leaving the American Free Trade Agreement. However, it was discovered that *afta* was Brazilian slang for mouth sore! If and when Chile is ever admitted, the name of the agreement will undergo major alterations.

LEGAL AFFAIRS IN CHILE

Divorce—as it is understood in most countries—is not a legal option in Chile. Due to the influence of the Catholic Church (which proscribes divorce), divorce is not legal in Chile. Legal separations (either temporary or permanent) are obtainable, but even these remedies can be difficult to obtain. Such separations are sometimes referred to as "divorce," but Chileans who are separated may not remarry.

When a bill was proposed to legalize divorce in 1995, Santiago Archbishop Carlos Oviedo articulated the Church's opposition, opining that divorce would be "contrary to the common good of the country." The Catholic Church maintains considerable influence, even though only 10% of Chile's Catholics attend Mass on Sundays.

LEADING BUSINESSES IN CHILE

The following businesses are some of the largest employers in Chile:

Amencenes Paris Ltda
Santiago.
Department stores. 4,200 employees.

Astilleros y Maestranza de la Armada
Valparaiso.
Shipbuilding and repairing. 3,500 employees.

Banco del Estado de Chile
Santiago.
State commercial bank. 7,000 employees.
Calderon Confecciones S A C
Santiago.
Wines and spirits. 3,000 employees.
Cia de Petroleos de Chile SA
Santiago.
Petroleum products. 5,000 employees.
Cia de Telefonos de Chile SA
Santiago.
Chemicals and allied products. 7,700 employees.
Constructora Copeva Ltda
Santiago.
Single-family housing construction. 3,479 employees.
Contreras Morales Lucia
Talca.
Grocery stores. 160,018 employees.
Corporacion Nacional del Cobre de Chile
Santiago.
Copper ores. 27,260 employees.
Empresa Constructora Predericksen y Cia Ltda
Santiago.
Single-family housing construction. 3,500 employees.
Empresa Constructora Tecsa SA
Santiago.
Industrial buildings and warehouses. 3,800 employees.
Empresa de Obras y Montajes
Santiago.
Engineering services. 5,280 employees.
Empresa Nacional de Minera
Santiago.
Single-family housing construction. 3,350 employees.
Gordo y Cia Eulogio
Santiago.
Excavation work. 4,000 employees.

Universidad de Santiago de Chile
Santiago.
University. 3,400 employees.
Witt Alimentos SA
Santiago.
Ice cream and frozen desserts. 3,605 employees.

The following are some of the largest newspaper publishers in Chile:

Empresa El Mercurio SA Periodistica
Santiago.
1,600 employees.
Publisher of *El Mercurio,* the largest daily newspaper in Chile. This paper alone takes in some 58% of all Chilean newspaper advertising revenues.
Editorial Lord Cochrane SA
Santiago.
800 employees.
Empresa Periodistica la Nacion SA
Santiago.
400 employees.
Publisher of *La Nacion,* the state-owned daily newspaper.

CHILEAN HISTORY

Until 1533: Much of Chile is part of the powerful Inca Empire.

1533: After the Spanish conquer the center of the Inca Empire in Peru, an expedition led by Diego de Almagro tries to conquer Chile. It fails.

1541: The second Spanish expedition, led by Pedro de Valdivia, is successful. The outpost of Santiago is founded.

1810: Chilean patriots Bernardo O'Higgins and José Miguel de Carrera lead an army against their Spanish overlords and win.

1818: Chile finally declares its independence from Spain.

1837–39: Chile fights the Peru-Bolivia confederation and wins, resulting in the breakup of the confederation. Chile secures valuable nitrate deposits in the north.

1879–83: Chile fights the War of the Pacific against Peru and Bolivia. Chile wins again, and annexes Bolivia's seacoast.

1880: Chile's eastern boundary is settled by treaty with Argentina.

1945: Neutral in World War I, Chile finally joins the Allies by declaring war against Japan.

1970: Dr. Salvador Allende is elected president, the first freely elected Marxist head of any Latin American country. He institutes land reform and expropriations of copper mines.

1973: A military coup overthrows the government; Allende is killed.

1973–89: The military government of General Augusto Pinochet rules Chile. Civil rights are repressed, but economic stability is restored.

1990: Democratic government is restored to Chile with the election of Patricio Aylwin. Pinochet remains influential as commander-in-chief of the army.

1994: Eduardo Frei is elected president of Chile. He presses for investigation of the human rights abuses of Pinochet's military regime. Many of his efforts are blocked by friends of the military.

1995: Chile requests membership in the North American Free Trade Agreement (NAFTA). However, the US Congress fails to approve Chile's "fast track" application. Action on Chile's application is not expected until 1997 at the earliest.

CHILEAN GEOGRAPHY

FLAG AND MAP OF CHILE

Size: 292,135 square miles

Population: 14,161,216

Chile is one of the major countries of the Southern Cone of South America. Chile is a new associate member of the Mercosur Customs Trade Union. The other Mercosur members are Argentina, Brazil, Paraguay, and Uruguay. Collectively, Mercosur represents a population of 213,611,000.

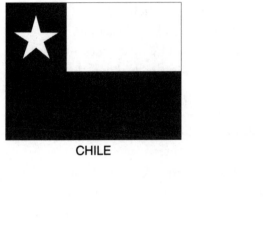

CHILE

Arica

Antofagasta

Valparaiso

Concepcion

CHILE

Puerto Montt

Punta
Arenas

HOW TO TELL CHILE AND THE CHILEANS FROM THEIR NEIGHBORS

No one likes being mistaken for someone else. Here are a few facts that differentiate Chile from its neighboring countries:

1. The Andes Mountains run down the western side of South America. Chile runs from the Andes to the Pacific Ocean. Chile's constant rival, Argentina, lies on the other side of the Andes, and has four times as much land area as Chile.

2. In the north, Chile borders two smaller countries: Peru and Bolivia. In the 19th century, Chile fought two wars with these countries. Chile was victorious both times, which yielded its current northern borders. Bolivia has never forgiven Chile, because Chile annexed Bolivia's only seacoast. (Landlocked Bolivia still maintains a small navy on Lake Titicaca, just in case it ever gets its coastline back from Chile!)

3. If it's Argentine, the Chileans have a different version of it. For example: Argentine cowboys are called *gauchos*. Chilean cowboys are called *huasos*. Argentina's urban slums are called *villas miserias*. Chile's slums are called *callampas*. Argentina's national dance is the *tango*. Chile's national dance is the *cueca*. (Both are described as displays of dominance and submission in the form of a dance.)

CHILEAN BEHAVIOR

Why are Chileans the way they are?

Chileans always explain their uniqueness in terms of geography. Their country was isolated and ignored by Spain. Their long, narrow nation is divided into distinct regions, all of which have different climates and conditions. And the ever-present danger of earthquakes reminds Chileans how powerless they are.

Why do you want to avoid pouring the wine in Chile?

Because the wine-growing Chileans have developed several nonverbal idiosyncrasies about wine pouring; pour the wine in the wrong way and you've managed to insult them. "The wrong way" includes holding the bottle backwards (with your palm up instead of down) or pouring so the wine splashes against the opposite side of the glass.

What is an once *and how did it get its name?*

An *once* refers to an afternoon drink, which is taken around the time the British have their tea. While an *once* can be any alcoholic drink (with or without an accompanying snack), it was traditionally an alcoholic drink called *aguardiente*. *Once* means "eleven," and it is the eleven letters in the word aguardiente that allegedly gives the *once* its name.

How do Chileans dress?

Chileans are not as formal as the Argentines, but they do dress conservatively.

What concerns does a traveler have in Chile?

Sunburn is a risk in Chile for two reasons: the altitude and the Antarctic ozone hole. Wear sunglasses and sunblock. Remember that the higher you go into the Andes, the less atmosphere protects you from the sun.

In the Andes, altitude sickness presents a problem in areas over 6,000 feet above sea level. There is no effective predictor of who will succumb and who won't. People of different ages, sexes, and health are struck down. The best way to avoid altitude sickness is to acclimate yourself to the altitude. Once you get to 6,000 feet, schedule a rest period at each increase of 3,000 feet.

Finally, Chile is one of the most tectonically active nations on the planet. Earthquakes can occur at any place, at any time, throughout most of Chile.

HOW CAN I FIND MORE INFORMATION ABOUT CHILE?

Here are a few resources to start with:

> **Getting Through Customs'** Web site at **http://www. getcustoms.com** tracks current holidays in Chile. They also

post Cultural I.Q. Quizzes, gift-giving guidelines, a demo of the PASSPORT database, and further international information. Telephone: (610) 353-9894; fax (610) 353-6994.

Embassy of Chile
1732 Massachusetts Avenue, NW
Washington, DC 20036
Telephone: (202) 785-1746; fax: (202) 887-5579

Servicio Nacional de Turismo
Av. Providencia 1550, P.O. Box 14082
Santiago, Chile
Telephone: (56-2) 236 14 16; fax: (56-2) 236 14 17; telex: 240137 Serna Cl
http://www.segegob.cl/sernatur/inicio.html

Chile Online
http://www.ChileOnline.com

Bienvenido a Chile
3014 Massachusetts Avenue, NW
Washington, DC 20008
Telephone: (202) 483-4410; fax: (202) 328-3712; telex: 440049
(clickable map) **http://www.dcc.uchile.cl/chile/chile.html**

The International Academy at Santa Barbara at **http://www.iasb.org/cwl** publishes Current World Leaders, an excellent resource for data on political leaders and parties in Chile. Telephone: (800) 530-2682 or (805) 965-5010 for subscription information.

The Bureau of Consular Affairs at **http://travel.state.gov** can give you detailed information on obtaining passports, visa requirements, and consular affairs bulletins.

The Center for Disease Control at **http://www.cdc.gov/** provides valuable medical information, as well as information on any outbreaks of virulent infections in Chile.

Like all Web sites, the preceding Internet addresses are subject to change, and there is no guarantee that they will continue to provide the data we list here.

Colombia

WHAT'S YOUR CULTURAL I.Q.?

1. TRUE or FALSE? Christopher Columbus landed in Colombia on his fourth and final voyage to the New World.

   ANSWER: False. Although Colombia is named after Christopher Columbus, he never set foot on Colombian soil. The first Europeans to reach Colombia were led by Alonso de Ojeda in 1499.

2. Believing Colombia to be the site of El Dorado (the lost city of gold), the Spanish quickly explored and conquered the country. They found few mineral resources. However, thanks to the Chibcha Indians, they did find one amazingly productive mine. What was the product of this mine?

   a. Gold

   b. Silver

   c. Salt

   d. Emeralds

   ANSWER: c. During the Colonial era, Colombia's one truly astonishing mine was the salt mine at Zipaquirá. Once worked by the Chibcha, this hugely productive mine is so large that it now contains an underground cathedral!

3. TRUE or FALSE? Colombia is the only nation in South America to have coastlines on both the Pacific and the Caribbean.

   ANSWER: True. Several Central American nations have both Pacific and Caribbean coasts, but Colombia is the only such country in South America.

4. After defeating the Spanish in the northern part of South America in 1819, Venezuelan freedom fighter Simón Bolívar, attempted to combine which of the following countries into his Confederation of Gran Colombia?

   > a. Colombia and Panama
   >
   > b. Ecuador and Venezuela
   >
   > c. Peru and Bolivia
   >
   > d. All of the above

   ANSWER: d. He failed. Only Colombia and Panama remained together within a few years of the death of *El Libertador* in 1830.

5. TRUE or FALSE? Over the years, Colombia has been known by such diverse names as the *República de Nueva Granada* and the *Estados Unidos de Colombia* (the United States of Colombia).

   ANSWER: True. And more besides.

6. Once Colombian politics divided into two rival groups (the Liberals and the Conservatives) in 1948, political

violence was assured. How many civil wars did Colombia suffer?

a. Eight

b. Five

c. Three

d. One

ANSWER: a. Their rivalry resulted in eight civil wars in Colombia, cumulating in the 1948 War, which cost the lives of 300,000 Colombians.

7. TRUE or FALSE? Only due to the assistance of the USA did Panama successfully declare its independence from Colombia in 1903.

ANSWER: True. This event, unique in Latin American history, occurred so that US President Teddy Roosevelt could build (and then control) the Panama Canal.

8. Colombian entrepreneur Lorenzo Jaramillo has added recognition to his Colombian automobile manufacturing business by "pirating" the name of an old US automobile. That car is:

a. Nash Rambler

b. Willys

c. Metropolitan

d. DuPont

ANSWER: b. Jaramillo is producing four-wheel drive vehicles under the name Willys, which Chrysler never locally trademarked.

9. TRUE or FALSE? Gabriel García Márquez is the only Colombian to win the Nobel Prize for Literature.

ANSWER: True. The author of the such classic novels as *One Hundred Years of Solitude, Love in the Time of Cholera,* and *The General in his Labyrinth,* he won the Nobel in 1982.

10. Colombia's long literary tradition includes masters of multiple literary styles. Which of these literary styles is associated with Colombia's Gabriel García Márquez?

   a. *Nueva sensibilidad* (new sensibility)

   b. *Modernism* (modernism)

   c. *Nudists* (beat poetry)

   d. *Realism mágic* (magic realism)

ANSWER: d. This style, favored by García Márquez and others, intertwines dreams and mythic archetypes with reality.

QUOTATIONS ABOUT COLOMBIA

" . . . *the acoustics in Bogotá are almost painfully good. Perhaps this is because of the altitude. Nothing escapes you—no sound in the next room, no voice in the court-yard, no footstep on the stairs. As for the traffic outside, it seems even noisier than Third Avenue; the taxi-horns job at your nerves like pins.*"

—British novelist Christopher Sherwood, in his travelogue *The Condor and the Cows.*

"*One morning, after almost two years of crossing, they became the first mortals to see the western slopes of the mountain range. From the cloudy summit they saw the immense aquatic expanse of the great swamp as it spread out toward the other side of the world. But they never found the sea."*

—Part of the history of the fictional town of Macon, by Gabriel García Márquez in his novel *One Hundred Years of Solitude.*

"Better a grave in Colombia than a jail in the United States!"

—The motto of *Los Extraditables,* an association of Colombian *narcotraficantes* (narcotics traffickers) who resisted extradition to the USA.

TABLE OF CONTENTS

THE COLOMBIANS

Although Colombia's rugged geography has kept its people in isolated groups, the length of the Spanish occupation (Colombia was one of the first colonies) has led to considerable interbreeding. The mestizos form the largest bloc at 58%. Whites, who hold much of the wealth and power in Colombia, make up 20%—a larger percentage than in some neighboring countries. Mulattos (persons of mixed black-white parentage) account for 14%, blacks account for 4%, and zambos (persons of mixed black and Indian descent) for 3%. Only 1% of Colombians are of pure Amerindian blood.

HOW TO TELL COLOMBIA AND THE COLOMBIANS FROM THEIR NEIGHBORS

Named after Christopher Columbus (who never actually set foot there), Colombia has a long and compelling history. From colonial Spaniards searching for the mythical El Dorado to today's *narcotraficantes,* Colombia has been a place where dreams of fabulous wealth meet with harsh reality.

1. Colombia borders Venezuela, Brazil, Peru, Ecuador, and Panama. It is the only South American country to have coasts on both the Caribbean and the Pacific.

2. After the Spanish were thrown out of South America, Colombia was united with three neighboring nations (Ecuador, Venezuela, and Panama) as the *Confederation of Gran Colombia.* Ecuador and Venezuela left the Confederation in 1830, and Colombia went through several name changes (see the section called "Identity Crisis?" later in this chapter).

3. The USA has a history of intervention in Latin America. However, the removal of Panama from Colombia in 1903 at the instigation of the USA is unique in Latin American history.

4. Colombia has a reputation (which may or may not be deserved) as the most dangerous nation for foreigners to visit in Latin America. Although the violence from narcoterrorists and guerrillas has died down, Colombia is currently the world's leader in kidnappings.

5. Colombia also has a reputation as a haven for smugglers. The illegal export of cocaine and marijuana from Colombia is well known, but long before that Colombian emeralds and exotic birds were being smuggled out. Smuggling occurs in the other direction as well. The hefty 36% taxes on imported goods has made it profitable to smuggle consumer goods into Columbia.

6. Colombia seem to have the longest greeting rituals in Latin America. Every conversation begins with long inquiries as to the health, welfare, location, and status of both the speakers and all relatives known to them. Attempting to move into the purpose of a conversation after a brief, simple *Hola!* will brand you as impolite.

One theory for the extensive greeting patterns of Colombians attributes them to Amerindian influence. Linguists have a maxim which states that "Indians are never in a hurry." Another theory maintains that long greetings result from geographic isolation. When travel is difficult, a visitor from another town is drained of all gossip upon arrival.

LITERATURE

Colombia has a long and glorious literary tradition. The country has produced numerous authors of note, including one winner of the Nobel Prize for Literature. They include:

Gabriel García Márquez (1928–) is Colombia's most famous author and celebrity, even though he has lived much of his life in exile (mostly in Mexico City). His first novel, *La hojarasca,* came out in 1955 (translated in 1972 as *Leaf Storm and Other Stories*). In 1967, his masterpiece *Cien años de soledad* gained him worldwide attention (published in English in 1970 as *One Hundred Years of Solitude*). Affectionately known as *Gabo,* García Márquez is a master of the literary style known as *realism mágic* (magic realism). In 1982 he became the first Colombian to date to win the Nobel Prize for Literature.

Jorge Isaacs (1837–95) studied for a medical career before becoming a journalist and writer. From Colombia's small Jewish community, Amerindians became the focus of much of his writings. His 1987 novel *María* (published in English in 1890 as *María: A South American Romance*) is still popular.

Porfirio Barba Jacob (1883–1942) became known as The Poet of Death for his avant-garde poetry (his work was considered reminiscent of Baudelaire). He became the most famous Colombian master of the style known as *nueva sensibilidad* (new sensibility—an odd title for irrationalism!).

José Asunción Silva (1865–96) is a Colombian poet known as an early practitioner of the literary trend known as modernism. In his short life he managed to produce a lasting collection of poetry called *Los Nocturnos.*

LIGHTS! CAMERA! ACTION!

Colombia's film industry has produced several movies. They include:

1. **El Immigrante Latino (The Latin Immigrant)** is a comedy about a Colombian musician who seeks fame and fortune in the US. He takes his life savings and moves to New York City. A classic comedy of cross-cultural errors (1972, directed by Gustavo Nieto Roa).

2. **Miracle in Rome** is a sentimental story of faith and undying love. Margarito, an ordinary man from a small Colombian town, must deal with the sudden death of his 7-year-old daughter. Twelve years later, when the town's cemetery is being moved, the girl's body is found to be in perfect condition. Over the objections of the local bishop, the townspeople declare that a miracle has taken place. Margarito must go to Rome to present his case. Based on a short story by Gabriel García Márquez (1989, directed by Lisandro Duque Naranjo).

3. **Rodrigo D: No Future** focuses on the aimless lives of a group of directionless teenage boys in Medellín. Rodrigo and his gang drift aimlessly from petty crime into carjacking, to the accompaniment of bad heavy-metal music. This was the first Colombian film to be chosen for competition at the Cannes Film Festival (1990, directed by Victor Gaviria).

LANGUAGE

The official language of Colombia is Spanish (which they call *castellano,* not español). Colombians have many regional terms, which are collectively known as *colombianismos.*

English is not widely spoken, although some international executives speak it.

Many Amerindians are bilingual in Spanish and their native language. Colombia's diverse Amerindian population speaks some 200 languages and dialects.

Linguists have categorized 79 different languages spoken in modern Colombia—*Ethnologue: Languages of the World,* 12th Edition from their Web site at (http://www.sil.org/ethnologue/ethnologue.html).

BUSINESS IN COLOMBIA

BUSINESS SUCCESS IN COLUMBIA

Caveat: Although most foreign consumer products are available in Colombia, foreign goods are heavily taxed—currently, there is a 20% import duty plus a 16% value-added tax. As a result, many goods are contraband, smuggled in without paying duties. To compete with contraband goods, warranties and quality after-sale support are vital.

The Colombian economy has experienced solid economic growth in recent decades. The country now has a large middle class and many affluent citizens. This market has attracted many foreign businesses to Colombia, despite high taxes and legal obstacles.

The Colombian Commercial Code requires registration of agreements between foreign companies and Colombian citizens. Although most foreign firms do set up a local agent, branch, subsidiary, or joint venture to distribute goods in Colombia, this is not required by law. Companies providing consumer goods to the private sector may sell directly to Colombian customers. Foreign companies may not bid for contracts with the Colombian government unless they have a Colombian representative.

Care should be taken when hiring a Colombian agent, since the cost of firing an agent is high. Upon termination, the standard agreement grants a Colombian agent an amount equal to one-twelfth of the agent's annual remuneration (whether that is in the form of royalties, profits, or commissions), multiplied by the number of years the agent has represented the company. In addition, the agent may seek further remuneration if the termination was determined to lack "just cause."

Franchise agreements are growing. In addition to fast-food outlets, franchises ranging from Holiday Inns to Sir Speedy Printers are present in Colombia. All franchise agreements must be registered with the *Instituto Colombiano de Comercio Exterior* (the Colombian Institute of Foreign Trade).

Joint ventures have been established in Colombia for many years. They are considered to be an important venue for transferring technology to Colombia.

Current legislation in Colombia makes international direct marketing difficult. Some Colombians now purchase items via catalogs, but they can legally make such purchases only from Colombian companies.

Brands from the USA have an advantage in Colombia. Many Colombians travel to or study in the United States, and are very familiar with US products. Also, the USA is much closer to Colombia than competing manufacturers in Europe or Asia. The United States is currently Colombia's largest trading partner.

Years of extensive advertising have left Colombians jaded. A massive advertising campaign is required to introduce a new product. Television is the primary venue; even low-income Colombian households usually possess a television. Radio and print are also used. A recent successful trend involves contests, for which a purchase is required to enter.

Colombian Entrepreneurship

Lorenzo Jaramillo learned the automobile business as a foreman at the Chrysler plant in Bogotá. Now he's producing his own cars, designed to run on Colombia's rough Andean roads. Not only has he found a niche, but he found an excellent way to market his cars: He's named them after a classic American brand. He discovered that, while Chrysler had trademarked the name "Jeep," it had failed to trademark the name "Willys."

continues

> *Willys Jeeps still had a fine reputation in Colombia, so Jaramillo formed Willys de Colombia S.A. Combining the good points of the original 1954 Willys Jeep and the contemporary US Army Hummer, he produced a vehicle that can haul 1.5 tons up mountain roads and can seat 13 people. "The multinational car manufacturers have forgotten that for many people in the Third World, a vehicle represents an income," he notes. Now producing 200 vehicles per month (in a converted tanning factory!), his company is swamped with orders.*

LEGAL AFFAIRS IN COLOMBIA

 There are more specially designated narcotics traffickers in Colombia than in any other country. US citizens are prohibited by law from doing business with any of the designated parties.

In the wake of narcoterrorism and violence from leftist guerrilla groups, paramilitary death squads have been active in Colombia. Involvement in these death squads reaches high into the military and government. In 1996, General Faruk Yanine was charged with forming a death squad. The chief of the armed forces, General Harold Bedoya, may not allow Yanine to be tried, despite the existence of videotapes showing Yanine's involvement.

LEADING BUSINESSES IN COLOMBIA

The following businesses are some of the largest employers in Colombia:

Almacenes Exito SA
Envigado.
5,000 employees.
Banco Cafetero SA
Bogotá.
Commercial bank. 7,258 employees.

Caja de Compensacion Familiar
Bogotá.
5,200 employees.
Carvajal SA
Cali.
4,492 employees.
Compania Colombiana de Tejidos SA
Medellin.
6,754 employees.
Empresa Colombiana de Petroleos
Bogotá.
Petroleum. 10,879 employees.
Empresa de Energia de Bogota
Bogotá.
Electricity. 4,200 employees.
Empresa de Telecomunicaciones de Sange Fe de Bogota
Bogotá.
Telephone communications. 4,000 employees.
Empresa Nacional de Telecommunicaciones
Bogotá.
Telephone communications. 6,000 employees.
Fabrica de Hilados y Tejidos del Hato SA
Medellin.
6,000 employees.
Gran Cadena de Almacenes Colombianos SA
Medellin.
7,425 employees.
Preparaciones de Belleza SA
Medellin.
4,800 employees.

The following are some of the largest newspapers in Colombia:

El Espectador
Bogotá.
One of the two daily newspapers with the largest nation-wide circulation.

El Tiempo
Bogotá.
One of the two daily newspapers with the largest nation-wide circulation.
El Colombiano
Medellín.
El Mundo
Medellín.
El Occidente
Cali.
El País
Cali.

COLOMBIAN GEOGRAPHY

FLAG AND MAP OF COLOMBIA

Francisco de Miranda, the Venezuelan-born military leader who liberated this part of South America, selected the Colombian flag's colors—yellow, blue, and red. The blue represents the sea, which separates South America from Spain. The red stands for the blood of freedom fighters. And the yellow was chosen to represent the new nations (perhaps in the hope that they would find gold). Only the width of the top yellow stripe separates the Colombian and Ecuadorian flags; the Venezuelan flag adds an arc of seven white stars to the same basic design.

Size: 440,762 square miles

Population: 36,20,251

About 90% of the population lives in the western half of Colombia. Colombia is divided into 32 *departamentos* (departments, or provinces). The white descendants of the Spanish settlers are concentrated in the Antioquia department (which includes Medellín), plus the coffee-growing regions. The black population is concentrated in coastal areas, especially the Chocó department and the nearby city of Cali. The Amerindian population lives in widely scattered groups throughout Colombia, many of them in the interior jungle areas along tributaries of the Amazon River.

COLOMBIAN HISTORY

Until 1499: Numerous Amerindian tribes are spread out over Colombia's rugged terrain. They include the Calima, Muiscas, Quimbaya, Sinú, and Tayrona peoples. Little is known about these tribes. Although they make finely crafted artifacts, most of them are not city builders like the Incas. When the Spaniards arrive, their gold and silver ornaments are melted down and their settlements are destroyed.

1499: Although Colombia is named after Christopher Columbus, he never actually set foot in the country. The first Europeans to reach Colombia were led by Alonso de Ojeda. On his second voyage to the New World, his party ventures into the Sierra Nevada de Santa Marta region. The local Amerindians possess gold ornaments, leading the Spaniards to believe that the golden city of El Dorado is located in Colombia. Ojeda then explores along the coast, where he is fatally wounded by the natives. The Indians also destroy Ojeda's settlement, San Sebastián de Urabá.

1525: Rodrigo de Bastidas founds Santa Marta, the first European settlement in Colombia to withstand the Amerindian opposition. The settlement declined after 1532 when the local Indians refused to supply it with food.

1533: Perdo de Heredia founds Cartagena, which soon becomes Colombia's main trading center and port.

1536: The conquest of the interior begins, when three Spanish expeditions work their way inland, linking up in Muisca territory. By playing one faction against another, the Spanish soon come to rule the Muisca peoples. These expeditions also established some of Colombia's most important towns, including Bogotá and Cali. Relatively little gold is found.

1717: The *Viceroyalty of Peru* is split up. Colombia is now administered as part of the *Viceroyalty of New Granada* (Virreynato de la Nueva Granada).

1781: A tax rebellion by the *Comuneros* in Socorro becomes the first Colombian revolt against Spain.

1808: Napoleon Bonaparte replaces the King of Spain with his brother, Joseph Bonaparte. Several Spanish colonial outposts, including several Colombian cities, refuse to recognize the new king's authority.

1815–17: Napoleon sends troops to Colombia, which reestablishes his authority.

1819: Venezuelan freedom fighter Simón Bolívar, known as *El Libertador,* succeeds in driving the Spanish out of *Gran Colombia* (Colombia, Ecuador, Venezuela, and Panama). He attempts to add Peru and Bolivia to Gran Colombia, but fails.

1828: With separatist movements threatening to pull *Gran Colombia* apart, Simón Bolívar appoints himself dictator. This also fails, and he resigns in 1830. He dies the same year. Ecuador and Venezuela leave *Gran Colombia*. Colombia itself becomes the *República de Nueva Granada*.

1849: Colombian politics divides into two groups, the Liberals and the Conservatives. Their rivalry will result in eight civil wars in Colombia.

1857: Colombia undergoes the first of several changes in name and constitution. (See the list of name changes on page 128.)

1948: After the assassination of a Liberal leader, the most violent of Colombia's civil wars breaks out. Known as *La Violencia,* 300,000 Colombians die in the fighting.

1953: As *La Violencia* threatens to tear Columbia apart, members of both the Liberal and Conservative parties support a military coup by General Gustavo Rojas Pinilla. This is Colombia's only military junta of the 20th century. He remains in power until 1957.

1957: Elections begin again, although choice is limited to approved Liberal and Conservative candidates. For the first time, women are allowed to vote in Colombia. The two major parties agreed to share political power (the presidency itself alternated between the Liberals and the Conservatives) for the next 16 years. All other political parties are suppressed, contributing to the eventual growth of guerrilla movements. This sharing of power is known as the National Front.

1974: The National Front extends its power-sharing agreement for another 17 years.

1980s: The rise of the *narcotraficantes,* with their enormous wealth and power, threatens to undermine the authority of the Colombian government. Guerrillas, such as the M-19 group, also fight the government.

1984: The *narcotraficantes* assassinate Justice Minister Rodrigo Lara Bonilla. In response, the Colombian government finally begins to extradite Colombian *narcotraficantes* wanted for trial by the USA. These drug lords, who become known as *Los Extraditables,* alternate violence with bribes to avoid being extradited to the US. They even offer to pay off Colombia's entire US $13 billion foreign debt! (The offer was declined.)

1985: In November, the M-19 guerrillas occupy the Colombian Palace of Justice in Bogotá. Government troops attack. Over 100 people, including 11 justices of the Colombian Supreme Court, are slain. Following this event, paramilitary death squads are formed to execute government opponents.

1990: Open elections are finally held, with candidates from outside the National Front. Some former guerrillas are elected, and violence by many guerrilla organizations ceases. M-19 lays down its arms, and becomes the legal political party ADM-19 (Allianza Democrática M-19).

1993: The last of the well-known *narcotraficantes,* Medellín cartel leader Pablo Escobar is killed. The new cartel leaders are less public, and less likely to assassinate government officials.

1996: President Ernesto Samper is charged with accepting US $6 million from *narcotraficantes* during his election campaign.

COLOMBIAN BEHAVIOR

Identity crisis?

The nation of Colombia has gone through numerous name changes. This may (or may not) have had an effect on the Colombian psyche.

- Spanish Colombia was first administered from the *Viceroyalty of Peru.*

- When this proved to be too cumbersome, the northern portion was split off and became the *Viceroyalty of New Granada (Virreynato de la Nueva Granada).*

- After declaring independence from Spain, it was part of *Gran Colombia,* which also included Ecuador, Venezuela, and Panama.

- When Ecuador and Venezuela left in 1830, the country became the *República de Nueva Granada.*

- When a new federalist constitution was created in 1857, it was renamed the *Confederació Granadina.*

- The constitution of 1863 yielded most powers to the *departamentos,* and the nation became *Estados Unidos de Colombia* (the United States of Colombia).

- This lasted only until 1866, when a centrist constitution was imposed and the country had a final name change to the *República de Colombia.*

And Colombians sometimes refer to their nation as *Locombia.* An anagram of Colombia, Locombia means "the mad country." Of course, Colombia is named after Christopher Columbus.

Why are Colombians the way they are?

Geography has molded the Colombian national character. Colombia's rugged topography has divided its people into isolated, self-sufficient groups. This is also the reason given for the traditional friendliness of Colombians; since few outsiders were seen, they were treated with great hospitality.

How do you handle time in Colombia?

First off, in important business settings, Colombians are often relatively punctual. But social rules are very lax. People may show up several hours late, or not show up at all. Some recommend making appointments with several different people during an evening, in the hope that at least one will show up at a reasonable time. Remember that Colombians are concerned with *aquí y ahora* (the here and now). The future is nebulous to most Colombians.

How do Colombians dress?

Dress is considered an important indicator of a person's status. Conservative but stylish business attire is expected. The high-altitude interior cities allow for heavier clothing than the hot coastal lowlands.

HOW CAN I FIND MORE INFORMATION ABOUT COLOMBIA?

 Here are a few resources to start with:

Getting Through Customs' Web site at **http://www. getcustoms.com** tracks current holidays in Colombia. They also post Cultural I.Q. Quizzes, gift-giving guidelines, a demo of the PASSPORT database, and further international information. Telephone: (610) 353-9894; fax (610) 353-6994.

Embassy of Colombia
Suite 218
1825 Connecticut Avenue, NW,
Washington, DC 20009
Telephone: (202) 332-7573; fax: (202) 232-8643

Colombia Government Tourist Office
140 E. 57th Street
New York, NY 10022
Telephone: (212) 688-0151

Colombia on the Internet—Internet Resources about Colombia and its culture, businesses, government, and economy. (English/Spanish)
http://www.latinworld.com/countries/colombia/

The International Academy at Santa Barbara at **http://www.iasb.org/cwl** publishes Current World Leaders, an excellent resource for data on political leaders and parties in Colombia. Telephone: (800) 530-2682 or (805) 965-5010 for subscription information.

The Bureau of Consular Affairs at **http://travel.state.gov** can give you detailed information on obtaining passports, visa requirements, and consular affairs bulletins.

The Center for Disease Control at **http://www.cdc.gov/** provides valuable medical information, as well as information on any outbreaks of virulent infections in Colombia.

The US Office of Foreign Assets Control (OFAC) at **http://www.fedbbs.access.gpo.gov** maintains a list of Colombian parties with whom citizens of the USA are prohibited from doing business with.

Like all Web sites, the preceding Internet addresses are subject to change, and there is no guarantee that they will continue to provide the data we list here.

Costa Rica

WHAT'S YOUR CULTURAL I.Q.?

1. TRUE or FALSE? In 1502, Christopher Columbus sailed right past Costa Rica, never knowing of its existence.

   ANSWER: False. On his fourth and final voyage to the New World, Christopher Columbus discovered Costa Rica on 18 September 1502. He spent 17 days there, near the present city of Puerto Limón.

2. The name Costa Rica refers to which of the following beliefs about the region?

   a. It offered agricultural riches

   b. It was rich in gold

   c. It was a lucky place, where everyone achieved success

   ANSWER: b. Columbus found that the local Amerindians possessed artifacts made of gold, which they traded to the Spaniards. The gold had been acquired from Amerindian tribes to the north or south, but the Spanish assumed that it was native to the region. So they named the area Costa Rica (Rich Coast). Far from being a prosperous place, the Spanish who settled there found no gold at all and a coast so pestilent that they settled in the central highlands . . . where agricultural riches finally came their way, centuries later.

3. TRUE or FALSE? The advanced, highly organized Amerindians of Costa Rica fought fiercely against the Spanish conquistadors.

   ANSWER: False. The sparse tribes of Costa Rica fought briefly, then virtually melted away from disease. So easily did the Spanish take Costa Rica that some historians call it a "settlement" rather than a "conquest." (The surviving Amerindians see it differently, of course.) There were too few Amerindians left to enslave or interbreed with, so Costa Rica today has no large mestizo (mixed European-Amerindian ancestry) population.

4. The Spanish settlers found themselves in possession of a country with highly varied geography. Which of the following are NOT found in Costa Rica?

   a. Rainy, swampy, malaria-ridden coasts

   b. Tropical rainforests

   c. Semiarid grasslands

   d. Fertile valleys with volcanic soil

   e. Mountain glaciers

   ANSWER: e. Costa Rica has mountains, but they're too warm for glaciers. The Caribbean coast is swampy (while the Pacific coast has a dry season, which makes it the preferred tourist destination). Costa Rica's rich volcanic soil has yielded agricultural riches, its arid grasslands are suitable for cattle ranching, and its rich rain forests—once heavily logged—now offer ecotourism.

5. TRUE or FALSE? For many years, Costa Rica was considered a useless backwater by the Spanish.

   ANSWER: True. When the Spaniards abandoned Costa Rica's malarial coastland for Panama's interior highlands, the Costa Ricans were cut off from the sea traffic which bound the Spanish Empire together. Export agriculture did not become very profitable until after Costa Rica achieved independence from Spain.

6. Costa Rica has a well-deserved reputation as the most peaceful and stable nation in Central America. However, Costa Rican history is not totally free of coups, dictators and violence. In what year was the last Costa Rican civil war?

   a. 1821

   b. 1857

   c. 1860

   d. 1948

   ANSWER: d. In 1948, a disputed election between Reformist and Conservative candidates for president spawned Costa Rica's last civil war, which took 2,000 lives. 1857 and 1860 were also violent years. In 1857, President Juan Rafael Mora raised a Costa Rican army to defeat the invading troops of US mercenary leader William Walker (the conqueror of Nicaragua). After losing the presidency, Mora tried to stage a coup in 1860, but he failed and was executed. Ironically, Costa Rica experienced no bloodshed in 1821, when it achieved independence from Spain—all the fighting occurred far from Costa Rican soil.

7. TRUE or FALSE? Today, Costa Rica has no army.

ANSWER: True. The Costa Rican army was abolished after the Civil War of 1948. Costa Rica gets by with a large police force.

8. In which of the following categories has a Costa Rican won a Nobel Prize?

> a. Literature
>
> b. Chemistry
>
> c. Peace
>
> d. Economics
>
> e. All of the above

ANSWER: c. Costa Rican President Oscar Arias received the 1987 Nobel Peace Prize for his work in negotiating a peace plan in neighboring Central American nations.

9. TRUE or FALSE? Today, Costa Rica is the wealthiest country in Central America.

ANSWER: False. Costa Rica is at the top of many lists (most peaceful, best educated), but it takes second place in wealth to Panama (in large part due to revenues from the Panama Canal). However, the wealth in Costa Rica is much more evenly distributed than in Panama.

10. Ticos (as Costa Ricans are called) worry about losing their sovereignty to foreign influences. What is the so-called "parallel government" of Costa Rica?

> a. The US Agency for International Development (USAID)
>
> b. The International Monetary Fund (IMF)

c. The anticommunist paramilitary troops trained by
the US Central Intelligence Agency (CIA)

d. A conspiracy of US senior citizens who have retired
to Costa Rica (AARP)

ANSWER: a. The US Agency for International Development is so omnipresent in Costa Rica that it has been accused of being a "parallel government." But the IMF and the CIA have been deeply involved in Costa Rican affairs as well. No one has accused the many American retirees of being a secret sinister force—yet.

QUOTATIONS ABOUT COSTA RICA

"Behind the rider a dazzling panorama slowly opened. To the north, the Barba Mountains and to the south the Aserri Mountains stretched out like the jaws of a pair of pliers whose axis was the Irazú Volcano. In the center of the expansive valley lay San José, the capital, like an urban island in a verdant agrarian sea. Along the mountainside small villages of whitewashed houses resembled piles of seashells thrown against the rocks. To the west where the enormous jaws of the pliers had not quite closed, the blue hills of the coast hid the Gulf of Nicoya."

—From the novel *Redemptions* by Carlos Gagini.

"If San Salvador and Guatemala City were hosed down, all the shacks cleared and the people rehoused in tidy bungalows, the buildings painted, the stray dogs collared and fed, the children given shoes, the trash picked up in the parks, the soldiers pensioned off—there is no army in

Costa Rica—and all the political prisoners released, those cities would, I think, begin to look a little like San José . . . Costa Ricans were proud of their decent government, their high literacy rate, their courtly manners. The only characteristic Costa Rica shares with her Central American neighbors is a common antipathy. You don't hear a good word about Guatemala or El Salvador; and Nicaragua and Panama—the countries Costa Rica is wedged between—are frankly loathed. Costa Rica is as smug as any of them, but has more reason to be so."

—From Paul Theroux's *The Old Patagonian Express.*

TABLE OF CONTENTS

THE COSTA RICANS

The majority (87.0%) of Costa Ricans are of direct European descent. Mestizos make up 7.0%, while blacks and mulattos account for 3.0%. The most recent immigrants are the Asians (most of them Chinese), who now constitute 2.0% of the population. The original Amerindian inhabitants of Costa Rica make up only 1.0%.

The Costa Ricans call themselves *ticos* (or *ticas* if you are speaking of women). Tradition says that this nickname came from the Costa Rican tendency to add tico as a diminutive or affectionate suffix, as in *momentico* (a short moment) or *chiqitico* (very small).

Costa Rica did import small numbers of black slaves from Jamaica, mostly to work on plantations. A small black population still lives in the Caribbean-coast province of Limón. Some of them still speak a Jamaican dialect of English rather than Spanish.

Note that most Costa Rican Amerindians dislike the term *indio* (Spanish for Indian), preferring to be called *indígena* (which means indigenous person). Although they number only some four or five thousand, the indígenas have 22 reservations in Costa Rica.

Costa Rica has the most egalitarian citizenry in Central America. Although 10% of Coast Ricans still live in poverty, the country also has the largest middle class in the region. Costa Rica's political leaders have made serious attempts to break down class and economic barriers. Costa Rica also boasts the region's highest literacy rate at 93%. Despite the culture of egalitarianism, there is a wealthy upper class, and three-quarters of the presidents before 1970 descended from just three of the original colonizers of Costa Rica.

LITERATURE

Prosperity in the 20th century has brought widespread literacy. Costa Rica has produced writers of note. A series of National Prizes for Literature has encouraged authors and increased their visibility.

Fabián Dobles (1918–) has published more than 20 books in his long career. He published his first novel, *Ese que llaman pueblo,* in 1942. He was the 1968 recipient of Costa Rica's National Prize for Literature. His work has been translated into German and Russian as well as English. Many of his stories and novels examine rural life in Costa Rica.

Carlos Gagini (1865–1925) was Costa Rica's first important author. His 1918 novel *El árbol enfermo* (translated into English in 1985 as *Redemptions*) depicts a love triangle between the daughter of a Costa Rican plantation owner and her two suitors: a Costa Rican poet and a US businessman. The characters represent the conflict between the Costa Ricans and the rich Americans who exploit their resources. (The beautiful daughter is eventually redeemed by the love of the Costa Rican poet.)

Carmen Naranjo (1930–) has served her country in several capacities, including as Ambassador to India (1972–74) and as Costa Rica's Minister of Culture (1974–76). Twice awarded Costa Rica's National Prize for Literature, her body of work includes six novels and seven books of poetry. Her short story "And We Sold the Rain" became the title story for a collection subtitled *Contemporary Fiction from Central America* (published in English in 1988). She now heads the Editorial Universitaria Centroamericana (EDUCA), the most influential publishing house in Central America.

Samuel Rovinski (1932–) writes in many genres, including prose, essays, film and theater. He has twice won Costa Rica's National Prize: in 1975 for his play *Un modelo para Rosaura* and in 1976 for his novel *Ceremonia de casta*. Themes in his work include urban strife and the lives of Jews in Central America.

LANGUAGE

The official language of Costa Rica is Spanish. The influence of the United States of America (including a large US expatriate community) has made English a virtual second language. Most upper-class

Costa Ricans have some familiarity with English. Menus in many restaurants are printed in both Spanish and English.

Linguists have categorized 10 different languages spoken in modern Costa Rica—*Ethnologue: Languages of the World,* 12th Edition from their Web site at (http://www.sil.org/ethnologue/ethnologue.html).

BUSINESS IN COSTA RICA

The government of Costa Rica supports business, both foreign and domestic. *Exportar es Bueno* (Export is good) is an offical policy slogan.

BUSINESS SUCCESS IN COSTA RICA

Caveat: Commercial Law in Costa Rica has undergone some recent alterations. Commercial licenses are no longer required for all businesses. While this reduces paperwork, it also eliminates the background check which had been part of the process of acquiring a license. To avoid the risk that your Costa Rican trading partners have misrepresented themselves, foreign companies are strongly recommended to have a check done on potential partners. Such a report can be commissioned through a firm like Dun & Bradstreet. Or, for US companies, the local US Department of Commerce District Office can provide a confidential financial report on Costa Rican companies.

Costa Rica is unusual in that foreign companies do not need to be represented by (or partnered with) a citizen of Costa Rica in order to do business. However, a local representative can be so useful that foregoing one is not recommended. At the very least, foreign companies should hire local legal representation.

The extensive presence of US citizens has had some influence on business practices in Costa Rica. However, true to the Latin norm, business in Costa Rica is based on personal relationships. Costa Ricans prefer doing business with people they know and like, so a relationship must first be built up. Furthermore, Costa Ricans insist upon time-consuming rituals of courtesy and politeness; these are considered national traits. Do not expect to do business as quickly as in the United States—or even in neighboring Panama.

Costa Rica has many fast-food franchises, including Pizza Hut–Costa Rica (which boasts the largest Pizza Hut in Latin America). However, the market is underserved in other types of franchises.

Registered licensing agreements are not common in Costa Rica, in part because foreigners are allowed to own businesses in Costa Rica. Many foreign firms simply set up a local factory, without sharing ownership with Costa Rican citizens. Joint ventures can be arranged. However, one should note that the prevailing sentiment of many Costa Ricans is against large foreign-owned businesses. The small farmer or family business is part of the Costa Rican mythos. Large-scale expansion is not necessarily viewed as a good thing.

The hard sell rarely works in Costa Rica. US products are considered prestigious and desirable, but they must be priced competitively. The potential for business expansion in Costa Rica is great. Be aware that US products must compete with products from Mexico; Costa Rica and Mexico have a Free Trade Agreement.

Newspaper advertisements have traditionally been the most successful marketing technique. Direct mail is in its infancy, and is rendered difficult because most residential houses do not have street addresses, making the compilation of mailing lists impossible.

Despite the prevalence of English in the business sectors, all materials should be translated into Spanish.

LEGAL AFFAIRS IN COSTA RICA

While Costa Rica has the best record of respecting human rights in Central America, Costa Rican women are often sentenced to more severe penalties than men for the same crimes. This tendency has been studied by Costa Rican researcher Alda Facio, for which she was awarded a 1996 Women's Human Rights Award (which is awarded by Woman, Law and Development International, a UN consultative group based in Washington, DC).

Costa Rica is a popular destination for North American retirees. Legal residence is granted for several reasons, including the investment of US $200,000 in certain industries. Projects which are considered in Costa Rica's national interest (such as reforestation or tourism) require only a US $50,000 investment.

LEADING BUSINESSES IN COSTA RICA

The following businesses are some of the largest employers in Costa Rica:

> **Banco Nacional de Costa Rica**
> *San José.*
> *National commercial bank. 3,612 employees.*
> **Caja Costarricense de Seguro Social**
> *San José.*
> *24,000 employees.*
> **Compania Bananera Atlantica Ltda**
> *San José.*
> *1,500 employees.*
> **Compania Nacional de Fuerza y Luz SA**
> *San José.*
> *1,552 employees.*
> **Cooperativa de Productores de Leche RL**
> *San José.*
> *2,110 employees.*

Corporacion Pipasa SA
Heredia.
1,800 employees.
Embotelladora Tica SA
Heredia.
1,300 employees.
Florida Ice & Farm Co. SA
San José.
1,500 employees.
Instituto Costarricense de Acueductos y Alcantarillados
San José.
2,800 employees.
Instituto Costarricense de Electricidad
San José.
9,000 employees.
Kativo Chemical Industries SA
San José.
1,850 employees.
Refinadora Costarricense de Petroleo SA
San José.
1,500 employees.
Scott Paper Company de Costa Rica
Heredia.
1,200 employees.

The following are the largest print and broadcast media concerns in Costa Rica:

La Nación
San José.
Newspapers and magazines. Daily circulation: 75,000.
La Prensa Libre
San José.
Newspapers. Daily circulation: 45,000.

La República
San José.
Newspapers. Daily circulation: 55,000.
The Tico Times
San José.
Costa Rica's largest English-language newspaper.

COSTA RICAN GEOGRAPHY

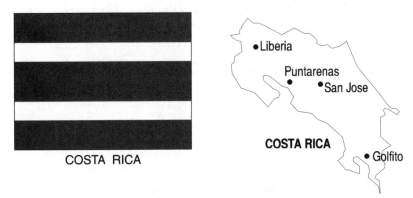

FLAG AND MAP OF COSTA RICA

Costa Rica's flag originated as the flag of the short-lived Central American Federation (blue, white, and blue stripes). The single red stripe in the center was added in 1848. Also added were the arms of Costa Rica, a busy symbol which includes seven stars (one for each province), two sailing ships (one for the Atlantic Ocean, one for the Pacific), three volcanoes, and a rising sun which symbolizes freedom.

Size: 12,730 square miles

Population: 3,419,174

One of the smaller nations in Central America, Costa Rica lies between Panama and Nicaragua. It has coasts on both the Caribbean and the Pacific.

COSTA RICAN HISTORY

Until 1502: Costa Rica is home to several small groups of Amerindians, including the Bribri and the Talamanca. Little is known of them, as they did not build cities like the Aztecs and Maya to the north or the Inca to the south.

1502: Christopher Columbus leads the first European expedition to visit Costa Rica, on his fourth and final voyage to the New World. He collects several gold decorations from the friendly Amerindians. Believing that the gold was mined locally (it wasn't), the Spanish name the region Costa Rica (Rich Coast).

1522: A Spanish expedition led by Gil Gonzá Dávila establishes an outpost in Costa Rica. It is temporarily successful, but the settlers eventually die of disease and malnutrition. Several other expeditions also fail, and the Amerindians become hostile.

1562: The new governor, Juan Vásquede Coronado establishes the first successful outpost. To avoid the disease-ridden coastal regions, he selects the central highlands for the site of his new city, which is named Cartago. The local Amerindians, already sparse, die off from disease. The Spanish find few Indians to enslave or marry, and Costa Rica never develops a significant mestizo population. Further cities are established in the highlands, and their remoteness from the coast keeps them out of the mainstream of the Spanish Empire.

1737: San José is founded. Agriculture spreads in the fertile valleys of the highlands, but Costa Rica is still considered a backwater.

1821: All of Central America declares its independence from Spain. The news does not even reach Costa Rica for a month.

1822: All of Central America is claimed by the Mexican Empire. Mexican troops never reach Costa Rica.

1823: Central America breaks away from Mexico. Costa Rica becomes the southernmost part of the new Central American Federation.

1838: The Central American Federation dissolves. Costa Rica is one of the five independent successor states. Export of Costa Rican coffee begins around this time.

1849: Coffee grower Juan Rafael Mora is elected president. During his 10 years in office, he raises Costa Rica's first army which defeats the US adventurer William Walker, who had conquered Nicaragua. His victorious army is blamed by Costa Ricans for bringing cholera into the country, and Mora is deposed in 1859. Mora tries to seize power in 1860, fails, and is executed.

1889: The vote is extended from the wealthy landowners to include poor farmers. Unlike its neighbors, Costa Rica manages to keep democratically elected leaders in charge.

1917: The minister of war, Frederico Tinoco, seizes power in a rare coup. He is ousted in 1919.

1934: The Costa Rican Communist Party incites a nationwide strike of banana workers.

1940: Rafael Angel Calderón Guardia is elected president. His reformist administration is supported by the Communists and opposed by the Conservative landowners.

1948: Running for reelection, Calderón is declared the loser in a disputed election. The Conservative candidate, Otilio Ulate is proclaimed the winner. The dispute escalates into civil war. Some 2,000 Costa Ricans are killed.

1949: Peace is restored, and Otilio Ulate becomes president. A new constitution extends the vote to all citizens over 18 (women and blacks had been excluded from voting). The Costa Rican army is dissolved.

1986: Oscar Arias is elected president of Costa Rica. He receives the Nobel Prize for Peace in 1987 for his work in negotiating a peace plan in neighboring Central American nations.

COSTA RICAN BEHAVIOR

 Costa Rica has a reputation as a Central America's most stable, peaceful, and hospitable nation. This reputation is true—up to a point. The facts are a little more complicated.

1. Costa Rica is Central America's most stable nation.

   True, Costa Rica has celebrated years of peaceful transitions from one elected government to another. But Costa Rica did suffer some periods of instability and dictatorship. The last civil war is still within living memory—it occurred back in 1948.

   Economic stability is another matter. In 1981, Costa Rica had the dubious distinction of becoming the first underdeveloped nation to suspend its international debt payments. Costa Rica survived this economic crisis only through further loans from the World Bank and the International Monetary Fund, plus assistance from the US Agency for International Development.

2. Costa Rica has no army.

   Costa Rica abolished its army after the 1948 Civil War. But this doesn't mean that the country lacks troops to enforce the government's will. Costa Rica has a fair-sized police force, under the direction of various governmental branches. These forces include the Civil Guard, the Rural Assistance Guard, the Metropolitan Police, the Special Investigation Police, and the commandos of the Immediate Action Unit.

   Costa Rica also has a surprising number of right-wing paramilitary groups, most of which are anticommunist. Some of these groups are linked to the government. Fortunately, Costa Rica does not yet seem to have any right-wing death squads.

3. Costa Ricans love Americans.

   Costa Ricans like most foreigners, especially US citizens. But there is a lot of prejudice against other Central Americans. *Ticos* see their neighbors as living lives of chaos and poverty, and don't want such things in peaceful Costa Rica. Most *ticos* like *norteamericanos;* some don't. Many are uneasy about the massive US presence in their nation. The US Agency for International Development is so omnipresent in Costa Rica that some accuse it of being a "parallel government." In 1988, half of the 170 Peace Corps volunteers in Costa Rica petitioned the US Embassy not to increase the number of volunteers; they claimed that US advisers were so numerous that they were putting Costa Ricans out of business! But Costa Rica has a tradition of hospitality, so visitors are usually treated with courtesy—whatever the private opinions of the hosts. Most *ticos* certainly have an affinity for the United States, its products, and its culture. But they want to be thought of as equals.

HOW CAN I FIND MORE INFORMATION ABOUT COSTA RICA?

Here are a few resources to start with:

Getting Through Customs' Web site at **http://www. getcustoms.com** tracks current holidays in Costa Rica. They also post Cultural I.Q. Quizzes, gift-giving guidelines, a demo of the PASSPORT database, and further international information. Telephone: (610) 353-9894; fax (610) 353-6994.

Embassy of Costa Rica
2114 S Street NW
Washington, DC 20008
Telephone: (202) 234-2945

Costa Rica Tourist Board ICT's US public relations
office is:
JGR and Associates
Ste. 5000
2600 Douglas Rd.
Coral Gables, FL 33134
Telephone: 305-446-9234; fax: 305-446-8215

Costa Rica Information Center—official online information center of Costa Rica, maintained by the Costa Rican
Tourist Board ICT, with information, pictures, animations,
videos, and so on.
http://www.tourism-costarica.com

Costa Rica's TravelWEB—for tourists, investors, and students, including general and political news and information
about language schools.
http://www.crica.com/

The International Academy at Santa Barbara at
http://www.iasb.org/cwl publishes Current World
Leaders, an excellent resource for data on political leaders
and parties in Costa Rica. Telephone: (800) 530-2682 or
(805) 965-5010 for subscription information.

The Bureau of Consular Affairs at **http://travel.state.gov**
can give you detailed information on obtaining passports,
visa requirements, and consular affairs bulletins.

The Center for Disease Control at **http://www.cdc.gov/**
provides valuable medical information, as well as information on any outbreaks of virulent infections in Costa Rica.

Like all Web sites, the preceding Internet addresses are subject to
change, and there is no guarantee that they will continue to provide
the data we list here.

Ecuador

WHAT'S YOUR CULTURAL I.Q.?

1. TRUE or FALSE? Ecuador takes it name from its inhabitants, the Ecuador Indians.

   ANSWER: False. The name Ecuador is derived from the word equator, on which this country lies. Ecuador had many Amerindian tribes, but none called the Ecuador.

2. If Atahualpa could have gotten along with Huascar, history might have been different. Atahualpa and Huascar were:

   a. Two tribes of Amerindians

   b. Two rulers of the Inca Empire

   c. Two Ecuadorian cities

   ANSWER: b. Just before the arrival of the conquistadores, the emperor of the mighty Inca Empire split everything between two sons, Atahualpa and Huascar. The half-brothers were soon at war for control of the whole empire. Atahualpa, emperor of the northern Inca Empire (based in Quito), eventually defeated his half-brother Huascar, leader of the southern Inca Empire (based in Cuzco, Peru). But Atahualpa's victory was short-lived. The battle-weary Incas could not stand up to the invading Spaniards. Atahualpa was captured, held for ransom, and then killed by the Spanish.

3. TRUE or FALSE? After taking control of Ecuador, the Spanish conquistadores amiably divided up the territory.

ANSWER: False. The conquistadores were as violent towards each other as they were to the Indians. Most of the leaders of the original Spanish expeditions had killed each other off within a few years.

4. After defeating the Spanish in the northern part of South America in 1819, Venezuelan freedom fighter Simón Bolívar kept the old Viceroyalty of New Granada together as his Confederation of Gran Colombia. Which of the following was NOT part of Gran Colombia?

> a. Ecuador
>
> b. Colombia
>
> c. Venezuela
>
> d. Costa Rica
>
> e. Panama

ANSWER: d. Costa Rica was not part of Gran Colombia—it was governed out of Guatemala at that time.

5. TRUE or FALSE? During the mid-19th-century reign of Dictator Gabriel García Moreno, only Catholics were permitted Ecuadorian citizenship.

ANSWER: True. García Moreno, who seized power in 1859, is still considered a model ruler by Conservative

Ecuadorians. His reign ended with his assassination in 1875.

6. How many times did perennial President José María Velasco Ibarra take office?

   a. Three

   b. Four

   c. Five

   d. Seven

   ANSWER: c. Velasco Ibarra was elected president in 1934, 1944, 1952, 1960, and 1968, but only got to complete one full term in office. The other four were cut short by coups or revolts.

7. TRUE or FALSE? Ecuador lost half its territory to Peru in 1941.

   ANSWER: True. Peru invaded Ecuador in 1941, demanding possession of the Oriente (the Ecuadorian part of the Amazon). The United States was unwilling to allow a South American military crisis to continue during the Second World War, so it prevailed on Ecuador to surrender its territory. Ecuador did so, but has resented the loss of its land ever since.

8. After the Second World War, which of the following became Ecuador's primary legal cash crop?

   a. Bananas

   b. Cacao

   c. Coffee

   d. Roses

ANSWER: a. After insect pests damaged cacao production in the 1920s, bananas became Ecuador's most
important legal crop. (Ecuador is not a primary producer of illegal crops like cocaine or marijuana, but the
actual amount grown is difficult to estimate.)

9. TRUE or FALSE? Ecuador administers Easter Island,
an important source of tourism.

   ANSWER: False. Ecuador administers the Galápagos
   Islands. (Chile administers Easter Island.)

10. Ecuador and its inhabitants are subject to many forces
beyond their control. Which of these is NOT usually
one of them:

   a. Earthquakes

   b. Volcanos

   c. Fluctuations in the El Niño Current

   d. Tornados

   ANSWER: d. Ecuador's highlands tend to inhibit the
   formation of tornados.

QUOTATIONS ABOUT ECUADOR

*"Guayaquil is built along a river, a city with many parks
and squares and statues. The parks are full of tropical trees
and shrubs and vines. A tree that fans out like an umbrel-
la, as wide as it is tall, shades the stone benches. The people do a great deal of sitting . . . A hunchback with
withered legs was playing crude bamboo pan-pipes, a
mournful Oriental music with the sadness of the high*

mountains. In deep sadness there is no place for sentimentality. It is as final as the mountains: a fact. There it is."

—From William S. Burrough's novel, *Queer.*

"In the past, that (Guayaquil's) waterfront had teemed with commerce, and ships from all over the planet delivered meat and grain and vegetables and fruit and vehicles and clothing and machinery and household appliances, and so on, and carried away in fair exchange, Ecuadorian coffee and cocoa and sugar and petroleum and gold, and Indian arts and crafts, including 'Panama' hats, which had always come from Ecuador and not from Panama."

—From *Galápagos* by Kurt Vonnegut.

"Now and then a young Huao would come into some cash, by selling a blowgun or spear, or a harpy eagle, or a jaguar cub, or by earning slave wages as a boatman for a tour guide or as a laborer for the (Petrochemical) Company, and he would bring an entourage of other Huaorani with him to Rosita's and spend everything he had buying his friends fried chicken and soft drinks. This was not profligacy: the Huaorani ideal is to be independent and self-reliant, and every effort is made to give the appearance, at least, of being so clearly in tune with the abundance of the forest that one is without fear of need . . . There is no higher manifestation of this ideal state than unqualified generosity, and no act more generous than to give away food."

—From *Savages,* Joe Kane's account of the stone-age Huaorani Amerindians and their contact with oil companies.

"If you manage to make it to San Lorenzo during the first days of the new year—and this is no easy stunt—you'll be

blessed by a happening so unlikely that you'd be excused for wondering whether you've stumbled onto the wrong continent, or into the wrong century. San Lorenzo lies among the mangrove swamps of South America's Pacific coast, but the imagination races to pre-colonial Africa. Muddy streets are filled with black children in small groups, dancing and beating on makeshift drums. Their faces and bodies are painted in red and yellow, and their singing refers to Macumba (voodoo) spirits such as el Rivel, who steals corpses, or la Tunda, who frightens bad children to death."

—From *Wild Planet: 1001 Extraordinary Events for the Inspired Traveler,* by Tom Clynes.

TABLE OF CONTENTS

THE ECUADORIANS

As in neighboring Peru, most of the population of Ecuador has Amerindian blood.

Amerindians and mestizos each account for about 40% of Ecuador's population. The remaining 20% breaks down into 15% white and 5% black. These figures are rounded off, which suggests probable inaccuracies. The count of Amerindians still living in jungle areas is little more than a guess.

HOW TO TELL ECUADOR AND THE ECUADORIANS FROM THEIR NEIGHBORS

1. First of all, if the country doesn't touch the equator, it can't be Ecuador. The name Ecuador is derived from the word equator.

2. Ecuador borders only two neighbors: Colombia and Chile. It is one of only two South American nations not to share a border with Brazil.

3. After the Spanish were defeated, Ecuador spent the next eight years as part of the Confederation of Gran Colombia, along with Venezuela, Colombia, and Panama. The Confederation broke up in 1830, and Ecuador became an independent state.

4. Until oil exportation began in 1972, Ecuador was the quintessential "banana republic"—small, poor, and agricultural. Ecuador's major export is still bananas, but the oil revenues have dwarfed its agricultural output. (Whether or not oil has helped Ecuador's poor is open to debate.)

5. Ecuador's border dispute with Peru broke out into fighting in early 1995.

LITERATURE

Tiny Ecuador has produced several important authors. They include:

Demetrio Aguilar Malta (1909–81) was a multi-talented Ecuadorian writer, painter, and film director. The mestizo title character in his first novel, *Don Goyo* (translated into English in 1980) hates the whites who try to exploit his coastal island—an unusual attitude for the protagonist of a book published in 1933. He set some of his later novels in a fictional South American nation called Santorontón. Aguilar Malta also served as Ecuador's Ambassador to Mexico.

Jorge Carrera Andrade (1903–78) was another writer/diplomat. He served in several capacities, including as Ecuador's ambassador to Venezuela, the UK, and France. Ecuador's Indians were a frequent topic in his work. His collections include *Selected Poems*, published in 1972. He was born in Quito, and died there as well.

Jorge Icaza (1906–78) was born, worked, and died in Quito. A poet, playwright, and novelist, he was also a teacher and civil servant. Only one of his novels has been translated into English: his 1934 work *Huasipungo* (English edition published in 1964 as *Huasipungo: The Villagers*). Detailing the lives of Amerindians forced to work for an oil company, it ends with a Quechua rallying cry of *Nucanchic huasipungo! (Our plot of land!)*.

Adalberto Ortiz (1914–) has been a poet, novelist, educator, and diplomat. His 1943 award-winning novel *Juyungo* (translated into English in 1982) focuses on the travails of a coastal lowlands zambo (person of mixed black and Amerindian descent) named Juyungo, who kills two whites to protect his family.

LANGUAGE

The official language of Ecuador is Spanish. Many Amerindians are bilingual in Spanish and their native language.

There are 22 different languages spoken in modern Ecuador— *Ethnologue: Languages of the World,* 12th Edition from their Web site at (http://www.sil.org/ethnologue/ethnologue.html).

BUSINESS IN ECUADOR

ECUADORIANS WHO INFLUENCE BUSINESS

Abdala Bucaram, a former mayor of Guayaquil, took office as president of Ecuador in 1996. He was ousted from the presidency on 6 February 1997. From his exile in Panama, he plans his triumphant return.

A populist outsider—he is of Lebanese ancestry, unlike most members of Ecuador's Spanish-descended ruling class—his unconventional antics earned him the nickname El Loco (The Madman). These very eccentricities gave Ecuador's congress the excuse to oust him on the grounds of "mental incapacity."

While president, Bucaram first won the hearts of Ecuador's poor by handing out his monthly salary in the streets. Although his erratic handling of the Ecuadorian economy lost him much of his popular support, some poor Ecuadorians still adore him.

The international business community, however, viewed his presidency with trepidation. The US ambassador to Ecuador, Leslie Alexander, admitted that corruption was reaching record levels under the Bucaram administration. Bucaram appointed an energy minister named Alfredo Adum who boasted that the only thing he knows about the oil industry is what he puts in his car. Ten days after taking office, Adum tried to stop oil drilling in the Oriente by the Maxus Energy Corporation due to a contract dispute. Bucaram stood by Adum, even when the energy minister punched and kicked two union leaders and publicly insulted the Ecuadorian press.

Despite his ouster, Bucaram seems confident that he is not through with Ecuadorian politics. Twice before he has fled to Panama, and both times he returned to take even bigger government jobs. Nor is he apologetic for his idiosyncratic style. "Tradition is what destroyed Ecuador," he asserts. "Formality and lies are what destroyed the homeland during the past 170 years of bad government."

Valerio Grefa may be the most powerful Amerindian politician in South America. The discovery of oil in the Ecuadorian Amazon put international oil companies in daily contact with the indigenous peoples, some of whom were living a stone-age existence. This resulted in violent changes in the lives of the Indians. On top of occasional violent clashes, there was bad publicity for the oil companies and threats of boycotts by environmental groups.

A former schoolteacher, Valerio Grefa came to the forefront as an intermediary between the oil companies and the Amerindians. He now can demand revenues from virtually any exploitation of land inhabited by Amerindians. As the head of the Coordinating Council of the Indigenous Nations of the Amazon Basin, his influence extends beyond Ecuador into Colombia, Venezuela, Brazil, Bolivia, and Peru.

BUSINESS SUCCESS IN ECUADOR

> *Caveat: Ecuador has a complex legal code. The use of a local attorney is considered vital for foreign businesses.*

It is difficult to sell products or services in Ecuador without a local agent. Such a local representative is required by law to sell to the government. These local agents have considerable protection under Ecuadorian law, making it difficult and expensive for foreign businesses to change agents. Especially nettlesome is Ecuador's Decree 1038-A, which prohibits foreign businesses from unilaterally modifying, terminating, or failing to renew a contractual agreement with its local agent without just cause. The determination of what constitutes "just cause" is up to the Ecuadorian courts.

The number of franchises in Ecuador continues to grow. As with the aforementioned local agents, Ecuador's Commercial Code tends to favor the local franchisee.

Direct marketing is in its infancy in Ecuador. Its growth is coming primarily from television (both broadcast and cable). Such marketing has proven effective in selling consumer goods and physical fitness items.

Joint ventures can be set up in Ecuador. Most foreign investors find that setting up a corporation or branch is preferable to such options as partnerships, limited liability companies, or mixed economy (using both public and private capital) endeavors.

As of 1 June 1996, Ecuador instituted a new invoicing system to facilitate the collection of taxes. Under the new law, a sales receipt must be issued for any transaction over 10,000 sucres (about $3 US).

Newspapers have been the primary venue for advertising, although television is increasingly used in the larger cities. Radio advertising runs a distant third. Cinemas should also be considered, since movie theaters in Ecuador traditionally run about 15 minutes of advertisements before each feature.

While English is spoken by many business executives, all promotional materials should be translated into Spanish.

LEGAL AFFAIRS IN ECUADOR

Ecuador continues to have great difficulties with its legal system, which is complex, politicized, unevenly applied, and slow-moving. In addition, it has in the past been susceptible to bribery, both to bring a case to a speedy trial and to assure a favorable outcome. Human rights monitors report continued violations, including arbitrary arrests and "disappearances." Whether or not a detention is legal, a court order must be issued for a prisoner to be released, which requires legal funds that many poor Ecuadorians do not have. It remains to be seen if reforms instituted in 1996 will improve matters.

LEADING BUSINESSES IN ECUADOR

The following businesses are some of the largest employers in Ecuador:

Autoridad Portuaria de Guayaquil
Guayaquil.
1,267 employees.
Compania Azucarera Valdez SA
Guayaquil.
3,000 employees.
Cuerpo de Ingenieros del Ejercito
Quito.
3,000 employees.
Empresa Estatal de Telecomunicaciones
Quito.
6,000 employees.
Estar CA
Machala.
2,000 employees.
Hildago e Hildago SA
Quito.
8,000 employees.
Importadora el Rosado Cia Ltda
Guayaquil.
2,500 employees.
Omnibus BB de Transportes SA
Quito.
3,000 employees.
Petroindustrial
Quito.
5,000 employees.
Sociedad Agricola e Industrial San Carlos SA
Guayaquil.
2,000 employees.

The following are the newspapers with the largest circulation in Ecuador:

> ### El Universo
> *Guayaquil.*
> *Circulation: 160,000.*
> ### Extra
> *Guayaquil.*
> *Circulation: 150,000.*
> ### El Comercio
> *Quito.*
> *Circulation: 90,000.*
> ### Ultimas Noticias
> *Quito.*
> *Circulation: 60,000.*
> ### El Mercurio
> *Cuenca.*
> *Circulation: 12,000.*

ECUADORIAN HISTORY

Before 1438: Several Amerindian cultures rise and fall. Around the 11th century A.D., the dominant tribes are the Caras on the coast and the Quitus in the interior highlands. Later, the Duchicela take control of Ecuador's north and the Cañari occupy the south. The Inca have not yet entered Ecuador.

1438–1532: The Inca, whose empire is based in nearby Peru, become the preeminent Amerindian people in Ecuador. They impose their language, Quechua, over their subject peoples, bringing linguistic unity to their multitribal empire.

1526: The first Europeans arrive in Ecuador, when a small force led by Bartolomé Ruiz de Andrade lands in northern Ecuador.

1532: The Inca Empire is rocked by a civil war. The Emperor Atahualpa, leader of the northern Inca Empire (based in Quito), battles his half-brother Huascar, leader of the southern Inca Empire (based in Cuzco, Peru). Atahualpa emerges as the winner and moves the capital of the reunited Inca Empire to Cuzco. The same year, an expedition led by Francisco Pizarro captures Atahualpa and executes him. The Spaniards begin their conquest of the now-leaderless Inca.

1534: The Inca stronghold of Quito is conquered by Sebastían de Benálcazar. The Spaniards must rebuild the town, which the retreating Inca burnt before fleeing.

1537: The Spanish victors fight among themselves, and Francisco Pizarro is slain. His brother, Gonzalo Pizarro, becomes governor.

1541: Gonzalo's lieutenant, Francisco de Orellana, journeys from Quito in search of gold. His expedition becomes the first to sail down the Amazon all the way to the Atlantic. This early journey establishes Ecuador's claim to the Upper Amazon, which the Ecuadorians call the Oriente.

1548: Representatives of the Spanish crown defeat the rebel conquistadores, and consolidate their hold on what is now the Viceroyalty of Peru, which initially includes Ecuador.

1780–83: The remaining Incas make their last stand, led by Tupac Amaru.

1739: As the colonial population grows, administration of the Viceroyalty from Lima becomes more difficult. The northwest, including Ecuador, is split off and becomes part of the Viceroyalty of New Granada.

1767: The Jesuit missionaries, who have been the only effective advocates for the Amerindians, are expelled from Ecuador (and the rest of the New World).

1809: The first revolt of Ecuadorian-born whites against Spanish rule occurs on 10 August. Ecuador continues to celebrate this day as *Primer Grito de la Independencia* (First Cry of Independence).

1822: The main Spanish army in Ecuador is defeated by a force led by Antonio José de Sucre, who is later venerated as Ecuador's national hero.

1822–30: Simón Bolívar rules as dictator. Bolívar combines Ecuador with Venezuela, Colombia, and Panama into the Confederation of Gran Colombia.

1830: Ecuador and Venezuela both leave Gran Colombia and become independent nations.

1852: Slavery is abolished in Ecuador.

1859–75: Dictator Gabriel García Moreno brings stability to Ecuador, until his assassination in 1875. His Conservative reign is marked by religious intolerance, and only Catholics are permitted citizenship. Chaos follows his death.

1895–1912: Dictator Flavio Eloy Alfaro rules as a Liberal dictator. He undoes García Moreno's pro-Catholic policies. He is slain by a mob in Quito in 1912, but his policies are continued by his successor, General Leonidas Plaza Gutiérrez.

Mid-1920s: Insects damage the cacao crop, one of Ecuador's main exports.

1934: José María Velasco Ibarra takes office as president for the first time. He is elected president five times (in 1934, 1944, 1952, 1960, and 1968), yet he only completes one full term (1952 to 1956) in office; the others are cut short by military coups and revolts. An expert orator, Velasco manages to be all things to all men, drawing support from Communists to Conservatives.

1941: Peru invades Ecuador, demanding possession of the Oriente. Unwilling to allow a South American military crisis to continue during the Second World War, the great powers in this Hemisphere (the USA, Argentina, and Brazil) force Ecuador to surrender half its territory to Peru. Ecuadorian resentment over this continues today, and Ecuadorian maps depict the pre-1941 Ecuador.

1948–60: Ecuador enters an era of unprecedented stability, with three consecutive democratically elected presidents and peaceful transfers of power. Banana exports soar.

1960s: Military juntas rule for most of the decade. José María Velasco Ibarra is reelected president for the fifth time in 1968, but in 1970 he suspends Congress and assumes dictatorial powers.

1972: A military coup overthrows Velasco.

1979: Ecuador returns to democratic rule with the election of Jaime Roldós Aguilera. He dies in an airplane crash in 1981 but power is transferred smoothly to his vice president, Osvaldo Hurtado Larrea.

1982: Fluctuations in the El Niño Current result in massive floods in Ecuador during the 1982–1983 season.

1987: A severe earthquake causes widespread damage, including the loss of 40 km of oil pipeline.

1995: In January, military forces from Ecuador and Peru fight inconclusively over the disputed border in the Cordillera del Cóndor region. Thanks to better positioning and superior weapons, the Ecuadorians have the advantange. However, the border remains undelineated, and the brief conflict costs Ecuador an estimated $340 million US (about 2% of Ecuador's gross domestic product). This further exacerbates Ecuador's critical budget deficit, requiring cuts in government subsidies and capital spending.

1996: Abdala Bucaram, nicknamed El Loco (The Madman), becomes president.

1997: The Ecuadorian congress ousts Bucaram from the presidency on the grounds of "mental incapacity." A caretaker government is appointed until the 1998 elections.

ECUADORIAN GEOGRAPHY

ECUADOR

FLAG AND MAP OF ECUADOR

The flag of Ecuador has an identical color scheme as the Colombian flag, which is not surprising, since they are derived from the same source. The Venezuelan-born military leader, Francisco de Miranda, who liberated this part of South America, selected the colors—

yellow, blue, and red. The blue represents the sea, which separates South America from Spain. The red stands for the blood of freedom fighters. And the yellow was chosen to represent the new nations (perhaps in the hope that they would find gold). Only the width of the top yellow stripe separates the Ecuadorian and Colombian flag; the Venezuelan flag adds an arc of seven white stars to the same basic design.

Size: 105,037 square miles

Population: 10,890,950

One of the smallest nations in South America, Ecuador lies directly on the equator.

Darwin Slept Here: The Galápagos

The Galápagos Islands were claimed by Ecuador in 1832. An archipelago of 13 major islands and many smaller ones, they were not inhabited by humans before their accidental discovery by the Bishop of Panama in 1535. The islands became a favorite resupply base for seafarers in the South Pacific. Aside from water and firewood, the islands offered a species of giant tortoise (the galápago, from which the islands take their name). The easily caught turtles could be kept alive on board a ship for as long as a year, providing fresh meat. The island's unique life-forms were first detailed by Charles Darwin in 1835. Today, the islands are an increasingly important source of ecotourism dollars for Ecuador.

ECUADORIAN BEHAVIOR

Why are Ecuadorians the way they are?

Ecuadorians have an attitude for a reason: They lost half their land to Peru in 1941, which made tiny Ecuador even tinier. Peru wanted the Oriente and invaded it. Since the Second World War was underway, the United States was unwilling to send troops to South America. So, backed up by Argentina and Brazil, the USA prevailed upon Ecuador to surrender half its territory. Ecuador and Peru have had bad relations ever since. Most Ecuadorian maps stubbornly refuse to recognize the country's diminished borders; they still show the old, twice-as-large Ecuador. And many Ecuadorians also harbor resentment against the nations who rewarded Peru's aggression: the USA, Argentina, and Brazil.

Are there differences between Ecuadorians?

Certainly. Aside from racial and class differences, there is the usual rivalry between the coast and the interior. The coastal people tend to be more relaxed and informal. For example, the inhabitants of Quito (who are known as Quiteños) tend to be formal, conservative, and very Catholic. Some of them deride the inhabitants of coastal Guayaquil. The Guayaquileños tend to be carefree and liberal.

Why are there such mixed feelings about Ecuador's oil resources?

Ignoring for a moment the protests of foreign environmentalists, why do many Ecuadorians rue the day oil was discovered? In any Ecuadorian city, you can see the graffito *Más petróleo* = *más pobreza* (More petroleum = more poverty).

The fact is, relatively few Ecuadorians have profited from the oil boom. The sudden influx of oil income caused rampant inflation, which is devastating to people already living a marginal existence. The oil money that went to wealthy Ecuadorians immediately went out of the country: no one keeps their money in rapidly devaluating Ecuadorian currency (the sucre has been falling against the dollar since 1987). Worse, Ecuador's foreign debt has exploded, to some $12 billion. Foreign lenders demand austerity programs from Ecuador's government, resulting in civil service layoffs and cuts in the food and fuel subsidies. Penniless Amerindians, displaced from their Amazon homes by oil companies, come to Ecuador's cities and swell the ranks of the poor. So Ecuador's poor are indeed getting poorer.

The foreign oil interests are now in a good position, since Ecuador is now so deeply in debt that it must continue to export oil.

Is literacy important in Ecuador?

It is if you want to vote; Ecuador makes literacy—in Spanish—a requirement for voting. This effectively disenfranchises many Amerindians living in their traditional environments.

How do Ecuadorians dress?

Conservative business attire is expected.

HOW CAN I FIND MORE INFORMATION ABOUT ECUADOR?

Here are a few resources to start with:

Getting Through Customs' Web site at **http://www.getcustoms.com** tracks current holidays in Ecuador. They also post Cultural I.Q. Quizzes, gift-giving guidelines, a demo of the PASSPORT database, and further international information. Telephone: (610) 353-9894; fax (610) 353-6994.

Embassy of Ecuador
2535 15th Street NW
Washington, DC 20009
Telephone: (202) 234-7200
Embassy of Ecuador Web site:
http://www.ecuador.org/ecuador/

Ministerio de Turismo de Ecuador
http://mia.lac.net/mintur/

Ecuador [upenn.edu]
http://www.seas.upenn.edu/~leer/ecuador/

FunkyFish Ecuador Guide—Web site with extensive
information on Ecuador.
http://www.qni.com/~mj/

The International Academy at Santa Barbara at
http://www.iasb.org/cwl publishes Current World
Leaders, an excellent resource for data on political leaders
and parties in Ecuador. Telephone: (800) 530-2682 or
(805) 965-5010 for subscription information.

The Bureau of Consular Affairs at http://travel.state.gov
can give you detailed information on obtaining passports,
visa requirements, and consular affairs bulletins.

The Center for Disease Control at http://www.cdc.gov/
provides valuable medical information, as well as information about any outbreaks of virulent infections in Ecuador.

Like all Web sites, the preceding Internet addresses are subject to
change, and there is no guarantee that they will continue to provide
the data we list here.

El Salvador

WHAT'S YOUR CULTURAL I.Q.?

1. Who is credited with leading the first European expedition into El Salvador?

   a. Hernán Cortés

   b. Pedro de Alvarado

   c. Augustín Farabundo Martí

   ANSWER: b. Sent from Mexico by Cortés, Pedro de Alvarado fought his way through Guatemala and reached El Salvador in 1524.

2. The Spanish ruled El Salvador out of Guatemala City. TRUE or FALSE? El Salvador's capital of San Salvador became the second-most important city in the Captaincy-General of Guatemala.

   ANSWER: True. However, San Salvador was not loyal to the Captaincy-General of Guatemala. Twice (in 1811 and 1814) it revolted against Spanish rule.

3. What is *La Mantanza?*

   a. The Salvadoran national dish

   b. The first type of coffee to thrive in El Salvador

c. A blight that kills Salvadoran fruit crops

d. The 1932 massacre of Salvadorans by the government

ANSWER: d. To suppress a popular uprising, Dictator Maximilano Hernández Martínez ordered the execution of some 30,000 peasants, an event referred to as *La Mantanza* (The Massacre).

4. El Salvador's agricultural wealth derives from the fertility of its volcanic soil. TRUE or FALSE? The country has so many volcanoes that at least one can be seen from almost anywhere in the country.

ANSWER: True. Fortunately, most of El Salvador's numerous volcanoes are dormant or extinct.

5. The founder of the Central American Socialist Party, Augustín Farabundo Martí, led the Salvadoran poor against the government in 1932. Martí was captured and executed. A hero to many Salvadorans, his name lives on in which of the following?

a. The FMLN guerrilla organization

b. El Salvador's national university

c. The country's largest volcano

ANSWER: a. The initials FMLN stand for *Frente Martí Liberacion Nacional,* usually translated into English as the Farabundo Martí National Liberation Front.

6. TRUE or FALSE? Catholic Archbishop Oscar Arnulfo Romero was awarded the Nobel Peace Prize for his attempts to mediate between the government and the guerrillas.

ANSWER: False. Archbishop Romero had been nominated for the Nobel Peace Prize, but had not won it at the time of his assassination in March 1980.

7. Which of these followed the 1989 presidential election, which put Alfredo Cristiani of the right-wing ARENA Party into power?

    a. Violence by the Communist FMLN guerrillas increased

    b. Violence by government death squads increased

    c. Six Jesuit priests at the University of Central America were slain

    d. The USA cut military aid to El Salvador by 50%

    e. All of the above

ANSWER: e. This all occurred after the first open national elections, in which people could vote for previously banned groups like the FMLN.

8. A Salvadoran peace treaty was signed on 16 January 1992. TRUE or FALSE? The 12-year civil war cost the lives of at least 70,000 Salvadorans.

ANSWER: True. In addition, more than 10 times that many fled into exile.

9. What is boj?

    a. A harvest festival

    b. A traditional Amerindian dance

    c. A sugarcane-based liquor

    d. Covert funding from the USA

ANSWER: c. The legend around boj says that a devil pricked his finger and let a drop of his blood drip into the liquor. This accounts for the drink's alleged personality-altering traits.

10. El Salvador has long been an oligarchy, run by fourteen wealthy families (known as *Los Catorce*). TRUE or FALSE? These fourteen have now consolidated and intermarried; El Salvador is now dominated by just six families.

ANSWER: False. Just the opposite: in the past century and a half or so, the original 14 families have expanded into about 250 families.

QUOTATIONS ABOUT EL SALVADOR

"Cacahautique is a village that palpably represents the transition from an indigenous camp to a Christian community. The thatched roofs are interspersed with Arabian tile roofs that were adopted into colonial architecture without reservation. Hunters use shotguns and arrows. The vocabulary is a picturesque mix of Castilian and lenca, and the creation myth mixes Catholicism with the terrifying pantheism of the local tribes. I still remember the dread I felt as a child when I passed by the hut where a woman lived, who, I was assured, turned herself by night into a pig."

—Salvadoran author Francisco Gavidia, from his short story "The She-Wolf."

"If they kill me, I shall arise in the hearts of the Salvadoran people."

—Catholic Archbishop Oscar Arnulfo Romero, shortly before his assassination on 24 March 1980.

"Terror is the given of the place. Black-and-white police cars cruise in pairs, each with the barrel of a rifle extruding from an open window. Roadblocks materialize at random, soldiers fanning out from trucks and taking positions, fingers always on triggers, safeties clicking on and off. Aim is taken as if to pass the time. Every morning El Diario de Hoy *and* La Prensa Gráfica *carry cautionary stories. 'Una madre y sus dos hijos fueron asesinados con arma cortante (corvo) por ocho sujetos desconocidos el lunes en la noche': A mother and her two sons hacked to death in their beds by sight desconocidos, unknown men . . .*

"It is largely from these reports in the newspapers that the United States embassy compiles its body counts, which are transmitted to Washington in a weekly dispatch referred to by embassy people as 'the grim-gram.' These counts are presented in a kind of tortured code that fails to obscure what is taken for granted in El Salvador, that government forces do most of the killing."

—From *Salvador* by Joan Didion.

"Everybody here was sick of the war. Billboards pictured a mutilated kid with the caption WHY ARE WE DOING THIS? The impression I had was of a people saying, 'Enough is enough. Let's get this damn thing over with.' The Communists didn't have more money to pour in here, and we Americans were fed up with the entire thing because every time we opened up a newspaper our allies had killed six nuns or blown up something or done something else that made us sick. Posters from both sides proclaimed, 'We don't want to do this anymore.'"

—From Jim Rogers' travelogue *Investment Biker: Around the World with Jim Rogers.*

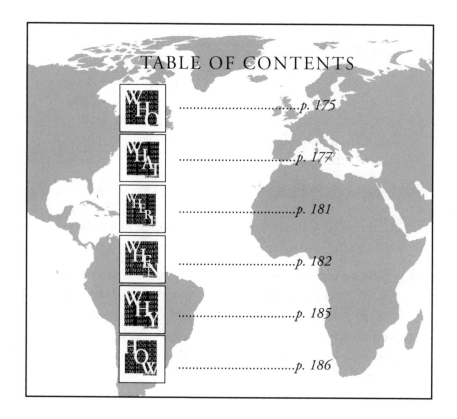

TABLE OF CONTENTS

THE SALVADORANS

The vast majority of Salvadorans have some Amerindian ancestry.
Most Salvadorans (89%) are mestizo, of mixed Amerindian and
European descent. About 10% are Amerindians. This leaves just
1%, most of whom are white. The nation's oligarchy comes from
this 1%.

HOW TO TELL EL SALVADOR AND THE SALVADORANS FROM THEIR NEIGHBORS

1. El Salvador is the only Central American nation without a coastline on the Caribbean. Salvador's only coast

is on the Pacific. It borders Guatemala to the northwest and Honduras to the northeast.

2. El Salvador is the smallest nation in Central America. It is also the most densely populated. Salvadorans have frequently left to seek work in neighboring countries—something that has caused friction with sparsely populated Honduras.

3. El Salvador is a land of volcanoes (most of which, fortunately, are extinct). The most recent major eruption occurred back in 1957. The volcanic soil of El Salvador is extraordinarily fertile.

4. Over a decade of civil war between the government and guerrillas came to an end in 1992 with the signing of peace accords. A United Nations Observer Mission monitored compliance with the accords through 1995. An estimated 70,000 Salvadorans lost their lives, and more than 750,000 fled the country.

LITERATURE

El Salvador's literary development has been hampered by the government, which has frequently forced authors into exile.

Manlio Argueta (1935–) became part of a literary group at Salvador's National University in the mid-1950s. Like other members of the group, Argueta was persecuted and exiled by the Salvadoran government. Primarily a poet, he has also written four novels. His 1980 novel *Un día en la vida* (published in English in 1984 as *One Day of Life*) was awarded the National Prize by Salvador's Catholic University. He now lives in Costa Rica.

Francisco Gavida (1875–1955) was a playwright, poet, and author of fiction. He also translated French poetry into Spanish.

Dalton Roque (1935–75) spent much of his life in prison or in exile from El Salvador. He studied to become a lawyer before joining the Communist Party in 1955. He wrote award-winning poetry and is best known for the novel *Miguel Mármol,* which was not published until 1982, long after his death. (It was translated into English in 1986.) Returning from exile, he joined the ERP guerrillas and was killed in a factional dispute within the group in 1972.

LANGUAGE

The official language of El Salvador is Spanish. Many members of the elite have some familiarity with English.

The use of indigenous languages has been in sharp decline, in part because government repression was often aimed at traditional Amerindians. Since the 1932 massacres, it became safer to speak Spanish than a native tongue. Only two Amerindian languages are still commonly used—Nahuatil (sometimes called Pipil) and Lenca. Despite recent cultural revival movements, fewer people now speak an Amerindian tongue as their first language.

Linguists have categorized five different languages spoken in modern El Salvador—*Ethnologue: Languages of the World,* 12th Edition from their Web site at (http://www.sil.org/ethnologue/ethnologue.html).

BUSINESS IN EL SALVADOR

"In El Salvador the government had set up a special project to establish a stock market, which might open in a year.

"Much to my own surprise, I decided to invest here, figuring the worst was over. The country's most important industry was textiles, but it also produced shoes, furniture,

chemicals, fertilizers, pharmaceuticals, cosmetics—the list went on and on. Exports of manufactured goods, mostly to other Central American countries, accounted for 24 percent of its foreign-exchange earnings. And all this even though a war had raged here over the past twelve years . . .

"Looking for a means to invest, I finally wound up with the guy whose job it was to develop the stock market . . . I was a year or so early, here before the market had officially opened, so I'd have to do something unorthodox if I wanted to buy right now, right at what I thought was the bottom.

"So, I did something I almost never do: I bought shares in a large private project, the newly developing free-trade industrial park. I saw the end of the war staring me in the face, and I figured coffee and sugar prices were certain to rise someday. I was certain El Salvador had to be a winner."

—From Jim Rogers' travelogue *Investment Biker: Around the World with Jim Rogers.* Rogers, a Wall Street investment banker who specializes in foreign investments, motorcycled through Guatemala in October of 1991.

BUSINESS SUCCESS IN EL SALVADOR

Caveat: At this writing, El Salvador's nascent intellectual property laws offer little protection. Computer software, data bases, and sound recordings are not protected by copyright in El Salvador. As a result, El Salvador has a higher rate of software piracy than any other Latin American country.

Many foreign firms market their products through the large Salvadoran retailers, which have distribution chains already in place. (The exceptions are the large Salvadoran department stores, which buy their products directly from foreign manufacturers.)

Some foreign firms appoint their own agent or distributor. As elsewhere, Salvadoran law regulates the type of contract that may be used for a distributor, and under what circumstances the contract may be altered or revoked.

Franchising is relatively new to El Salvador. Since the mid-1990s, some fast-food and video-rental franchises have been started. Joint ventures are also possible, and are regulated by the Salvadoran Commercial Code.

Advertising in El Salvador is done through newspapers and radio (both of which are currently inexpensive), and television. Billboards and leaflets are also used.

Marketing techniques are unsophisticated (thus far) in El Salvador. There is little telemarketing or direct sales. As competition increases, contests and raffles are sometimes used. Providing good after-sales service will give a product an edge.

Despite knowledge of English by many business executives, all materials should be translated into Spanish.

LEGAL AFFAIRS IN EL SALVADOR

Human rights issues remain the primary legal concern in El Salvador. Although the use of government death squads has fallen since the 1992 peace accords, such squads still exist.

The Salvadoran prison system remains corrupt and incompetent. Overcrowding is standard in every prison. Detainees can be held for extensive periods of time while crimes are investigated . . . as long as 120 days for serious offenses. Court backlogs can cause a prisoner to wait, in prison, for as long as three years before coming to trial.

LEADING BUSINESSES IN EL SALVADOR

The following businesses are some of the largest employers in El Salvador:

Administracion Nacional de Telecommunicaciones
San Salvador.
Telephone network. 7,097 employees.

Comision Ejecutiva Hidroelectrica de Rio Lempa
San Salvador.
Electric power. 2,950 employees.

Empresas Adoc SA
Soyapango.
4,000 employees.

Instituto de Seguro Social Salvadoreno
San Salvador.
4,684 employees.

Instituto Nacional de Azucar
San Salvador.
2,492 employees.

Sigma SA
San Salvador.
2,000 employees.

The following are the largest print media concerns in El Salvador:

La Prensa Gráfica
San Salvador.
Daily newspaper.
Founded in 1915, this is El Salvador's leading newspaper.

El Diario de Hoy
San Salvador.
Daily newspaper.
Founded in 1936, this ultraconservative newspaper is seen as the voice of the oligarchy—and, consequently, the business community.

Diario El Mundo
San Salvador.
Daily newspaper.
Founded in 1968, this is the least conservative major newspaper in El Salvador. It accepts advertising from people who are in opposition to the oligarchy.

SALVADORAN GEOGRAPHY

FLAG AND MAP OF EL SALVADOR

El Salvador's flag originated as the flag of the short-lived Central American Federation (blue, white, and blue stripes). In addition to the three horizontal stripes, the national seal and motto is often added in the center. El Salvador's motto is "God, Union, Liberty."

Size: 8,124 square miles
Population: 5,870,481

The smallest nation in Central America, El Salvador is bordered by Guatemala and Honduras. It is the sole Central American nation with a coastline only on the Pacific.

El Salvador has more than 25 extinct volcanoes. You are rarely out of sight of a volcano anywhere in the country. Since the volcanic soil is extremely fertile, towns frequently developed right at the base of volcanoes.

SALVADORAN HISTORY

Circa 800 B.C.: The first identifiable civilization in the region, the Olmecs, achieve supremacy in El Salvador, Guatemala, and southern Mexico.

Circa 200 B.C.: Pre-Columbian civilization reaches its "Golden Age" in Mesoamerica—an area stretching from the southern US to Nicaragua. The Mayans build large cities and temples. Mayan city-states (never unified) rule all of Mesoamerica until around A.D. 900, at which time the great Mayan cities are abandoned for reasons unknown.

Circa A.D. 1000: Nahuatil-speaking tribes entered El Salvador from Mexico. The Salvadoran Nahuatl groups (frequently called the Pipil) are related to both the Aztecs and the Toltecs. The Nahuatil people call their country *Cuzcatian,* a name which means "Land of Jewels and Precious Things." Another tribe, the Lenca, live in the east and south of El Salvador. Their origin is unknown.

1519: Hernán Cortés leads the first European expedition to subdue Mexico. After conquering central Mexico, he sends his men to conquer Yucatán and adjacent areas.

1524: After fighting its way through Guatemala, an expedition led by Pedro de Alvarado, a lieutenant of Cortés', becomes the first Spanish force to set foot on Salvadoran soil. He then conquers the Nahuatil over the course of several years.

1528: San Salvador is founded by the Spanish. By 1700, it becomes the second most important city in the region, and a center for anti-Spanish sentiment.

1530: San Miguel is founded.

1552: Sonsonate is founded. It soon becomes a center for exporting cacao and indigo dyes.

1570: The Captaincy-General of Guatemala is created, a domain that includes El Salvador (in fact, it runs as far south as Costa Rica). El Salvador's incredibly rich volcanic soil encourages the Spanish to establish plantations with Amerindian slaves.

1786: The political status of El Salvador is raised to an Indentancy. This makes El Salvador the equal of Honduras and Nicaragua.

1811: San Salvador leads Central America's first revolt against Spanish rule. It fails. The process is repeated in 1814 and fails again.

1821: Mexico declares itself independent from Spain, and also claims Central America (including El Salvador) as part of the Mexican Empire.

1823: Meeting in Guatemala City, the five Central American states (Guatemala, El Salvador, Honduras, Nicaragua, and Costa Rica) declare themselves to be the United Provinces of Central America, independent from Mexico.

1825: Salvadoran Manuel José Arce becomes the first president of the United Provinces of Central America.

1834: San Salvador becomes the capital city of the United Provinces.

1838: Following years of internecine fighting, the United Provinces of Central America dissolves. However, El Salvador hopes for a reconciliation, and does not officially call itself a republic until 1856. El Salvador suffers from internal conflict as well as interventions from Guatemala and Honduras.

1859–63: Gerardo Barrios serves as president and establishes the coffee industry.

1863–71: Francisco Dueñas serves as president. He rewrites the Constitution to ensure Conservative rule, setting the pattern for oligarchic rule by the Fourteen Families (*Los Catorce*).

1903–27: The presidency of El Salvador alternates between members of the Meléndez and the Quinóñez families.

1931: Coffee prices plummet due to the Great Depression. A disputed presidential election plunges the country into chaos. The minister of war, General Maximilano Hernández Martínez, seizes power. He rules as dictator until 1944.

1932: The founder of the Central American Socialist party, Augustín Farabundo Martí, leads an uprising against the government. He is captured and executed. The government executes some

30,000 peasants, an event referred to as *La Mantanza* (The Massacre).

1950: El Salvador promulgates a new constitution. Some improvements are made in human rights and the welfare of the poor.

1956: Lt. Colonel José María Lemus becomes president in a fraudulent election. Government oppression of the poor returns.

1960: Reformist officers stage a coup. The following year, conservative officers stage a counter-coup.

1962: Another new constitution is adopted.

1969: El Salvador and Honduras stage a brief conflict known as the "Soccer War."

1972: Reformist candidates are elected, but the electoral commission manipulates the votes so they are not seated. A coup attempt by reformist officers is put down.

1974: Conservatives win in fraudulent elections.

1976: Attempts at land reform are blocked by wealthy landowners.

1980s: Violence by both guerrillas and the government escalates. Some priests in the Catholic Church adopt "Liberation Theology," calling for aid to the poor and opposition to the government. Death squads execute many Salvadorans. Aid from the USA pours in to combat Communist guerrillas.

1980: Catholic Archbishop Oscar Arnulfo Romero, a nominee for the Nobel Peace Prize, is assassinated while celebrating Mass. That same year, four churchwomen from the USA are raped and killed. Both actions are traced to government death squads.

1987: Costa Rican President Oscar Arias coordinates regional peace negotiations. The violence continues.

1989: For the first time, the Communist FMLN is allowed to participate in national elections. But the presidency is won by Alfredo Cristiani of the Rightist ARENA Party. Violence resumes. Six Jesuit priests at the University of Central America are executed by government death squads.

1990: The USA mediates peace talks while cutting its aid to El Salvador's government.

1992: A peace treaty was signed by all parties on 16 January. The war cost the lives of at least 70,000 Salvadorans.

1994: The ARENA Party wins fewer seats in the legislative elections but still holds the largest block of seats. The ARENA candidate for president, Calderón Sol, wins in runoff elections.

SALVADORAN BEHAVIOR

Why are Salvadorans the way they are?

As the Irish discovered during the Potato Famine, basing your economy on a single crop is a dangerous thing. By the 1920s, 95% of El Salvador's export earnings came from coffee.

For many years, thousands of landless peasants worked the coffee plantations for sustenance wages. When the demand for coffee plummeted during the Great Depression, these poor Salvadorans lost what little they had. A charismatic leader, Augustín Farabundo Martí, led the destitute in an uprising against the government. The Salvadoran government responded by executing some 30,000 peasants, an event referred to as *La Mantanza* (The Massacre). Martí was captured and placed in front of a firing squad. His name lives on in the title of the FMLN guerrilla organization (*Frente Martí Liberacion Nacional*).

Since *La Mantanza,* the lines were clearly drawn. Elite in the government did whatever was necessary to stay in power, including the use of death squads. The poor's only hope was to depose the oligarchy.

The 1992 peace agreement brought an end to the formal conflict between the government and the guerrillas. But the animosities remained. The crime rate in El Salvador skyrocketed, as thousands of fighting men (on both sides) were discharged. And death squads continue to operate, although now their targets may be suspected criminals rather than suspected guerrillas.

Who runs El Salvador?

Since shortly after independence, El Salvador has been an oligarchy. The Fourteen Families (*Los Catorce*) were the largest landowners, and they ran the country for their benefit. In the past 160 years, the original 14 families have expanded into about 250 families. Their wealth has expanded beyond land and agriculture into banking and manufacturing. They remain exceedingly influential.

What is boj?

Boj is a sweet sugarcane liquor. Legend says that a devil pricked his finger and let a drop of his blood mix with the liquor—the better to seduce a pretty harp player. Today, when drunken Salvadorans fight, it is blamed on the "blood of the devil" which they consumed.

HOW CAN I FIND MORE INFORMATION ABOUT EL SALVADOR?

Here are a few resources to start with:

Getting Through Customs' Web site at **http://www.getcustoms.com** tracks current holidays in El Salvador. They also post Cultural I.Q. Quizzes, gift-giving guidelines, a demo of the PASSPORT database, and further international information. Telephone: (610) 353-9894; fax (610) 353-6994.

Embassy of El Salvador
2308 California Street NW
Washington, DC 20008
Telephone: (202) 265-9671

El Salvador Index— General information site on El Salvador.
http://lanic.utexas.edu/la/ca/salvador/

The International Academy at Santa Barbara at **http://www.iasb.org/cwl** publishes Current World Leaders, an excellent resource for data on political leaders and parties in El Salvador. Telephone: (800) 530-2682 or (805) 965-5010 for subscription information.

The Bureau of Consular Affairs at **http://travel.state.gov** can give you detailed information on obtaining passports, visa requirements, and consular affairs bulletins.

The Center for Disease Control at **http://www.cdc.gov/** provides valuable medical information, as well as information on any outbreaks of virulent infections in El Salvador.

Like all Web sites, the preceding Internet addresses are subject to change, and there is no guarantee that they will continue to provide the data we list here.

Guatemala

WHAT'S YOUR CULTURAL I.Q.?

1. The first capital of Guatemala was Santiago de los Caballeros de Guatemala. Founded in 1527, it was destroyed in 1543. What disaster overtook the capital?

    a. An earthquake

    b. A volcano

    c. Mudslides

    d. Locusts

    ANSWER: c. The capital was destroyed by mudslides. (It has since been rebuilt as Ciudad Vieja.) Nearby Antigua then became the capital. Antigua itself was leveled by an earthquake in 1773. Three years later, the current capital, Guatemala City, was founded.

2. TRUE or FALSE? Created in 1570, the Captaincy-General of Guatemala controlled Central America from Yucatán to Costa Rica.

    ANSWER: True. Virtually all of Central America south of Mexico was ruled out of Guatemala.

3. Along with Mexico, Guatemala declared independence from Spain in 1821. Soon Guatemala was part of

United Provinces of Central America. In what city was the first National Assembly convened?

a. Mexico City, Mexico

b. Managua, Nicaragua

c. Tegucigalpa, Honduras

d. Guatemala City, Guatemala

ANSWER: d. The United Provinces began as a continuation of the old Captaincy-General of Guatemala. The National Assembly of the United Provinces convened in Guatemala City. They wouldn't have met in Mexico City—Mexico was never a member of the United Provinces.

4. The United Provinces broke up in 1838, and Guatemala became an independent nation. TRUE or FALSE? A border dispute between Guatemala and British Honduras was finally settled once and for all in 1859.

ANSWER: False. Guatemala and the United Kingdom did sign a treaty in 1859, but the UK never fulfilled its part of the treaty: a promise to build a road from Belize City to Guatemala City. As a result, Guatemala continued to claim the disputed territory until 1992!

5. Justo Rufino Barrios ruled Guatemala from 1873 to 1885, and became known as "the Great Reformer." Which of the following actions did he take as president of Guatemala?

a. He encouraged the growth of the coffee-growing industry

b. He promoted European immigration into Guatemala

c. He built roads, schools, and a modern banking system

d. He limited the power of the Roman Catholic Church

e. All of the above

ANSWER: e. But his last attempt at reform caused his death: Rufino Barrios died in 1885 while trying to forcibly reunite the United Provinces.

6. In the latter half of the 20th century, Guatemala suffered from a long-running civil war. TRUE or FALSE? With the signing of a peace treaty in 1996, Guatemala's civil war ended after 36 years.

   ANSWER: True. The 36-year-long insurgency was the longest-running civil war in Central America.

7. Which of the following Nobel Prizes have been awarded to Guatemalans?

   a. The 1967 Nobel Prize for Literature to Miguel Ángel Asturias

   b. The 1993 Nobel Prize for Peace to Rigoberta Menchú Tum

   c. The 1989 Nobel Prize for Mathematics to Efraín Ríos Montt

   d. a. and b.

   ANSWER: d. Guatemalans have won the Literature and Peace Nobels. There is no Nobel Prize awarded in Mathematics—and the only numbers associated with dictator Efraín Ríos Montt are the uncounted numbers of Guatemalans killed in his counterinsurgency campaigns.

8. Guatemala has a higher proportion of Amerindians in its population than any other Central American nation. TRUE or FALSE? All of Guatemala's Amerindians are descended from the Mayans.

ANSWER: False. Guatemala's Amerindians come from many tribes, and speak dozens of different languages—not all of which are mutually intelligible.

9. The so-called "Guatemalan solution" has become well known throughout Central America. What is it?

a. Allowing foreign corporations (like United Fruit) to build a local infrastructure

b. Killing all suspect populations as a counterinsurgency technique

c. Declaring a public holiday and festival to distract the public from grievances

d. Uniting in a federation like the United Provinces of Central America

ANSWER: b. The Guatemalan government became known for depopulating hundreds of suspect villages during the course of the 36-year-old civil war.

10. TRUE or FALSE? The term *ladinización* refers to the process of granting property to landless peasants in Guatemala.

ANSWER: False. The Guatemalans use the term *Ladino* to designate populations following a "Latin" (mainstream) lifestyle—as opposed to traditional Amerindian cultural patterns. *Ladinización* refers to the acculturation process whereby traditional Amerindians drop their traditional ways and become part of the mainstream culture. Aspects of *ladinización* include wearing Western clothes instead of traditional, handwoven Amerindian garments, or speaking Spanish instead of an indigenous language.

QUOTATIONS ABOUT GUATEMALA

"(The United Provinces of Guatemala) was nominally a confederation . . . though for the next eighty years the foreign traveler continued to call them 'Guatemala' and to treat his adventuring in the jungles of Costa Rica and Nicaragua and his canoe trips across El Salvador's Lake Ilopango as travel in Guatemala . . . Civil war was almost immediate in the five countries: it was woodsman against townie, conservative against liberal, Indian against Spaniard, tenant farmer against landlord. The provinces battled, and unity disintegrated in saber charges and cannon fire. Within fifteen years, the area was political and social bedlam, or, as one historian has written, 'quintuple confusion.'"

—From Paul Theroux's *The Old Patagonian Express.*

"The arrival of the fruit companies often brought the host countries their first real infrastructure. In Guatemala . . . United Fruit built (and owned) the main highways, the railroads, and the only port on the Caribbean coast. It handled cable communications throughout the region, and traveling news reporters relied on the company's Tropical Radio to send their dispatches."

—From *The Good Neighbor: How the United States Wrote the History of Central America and the Caribbean* by George Black.

"The dilapidated blue and white taxi pulled off down Sixth Avenue. The two of us, separated by the colonel's bulk, did not even dare to look at each other, frightened we would give everything away with an indiscreet smile, as we left the Panamerican Hotel behind us, and the neon

*sign of the Jardín de Italia which had just come on with
the others in the dusk . . . "*

—From the novel *To Bury Our Fathers* by Sergio Ramírez. The narrator and his compatriot are Sandinista guerrillas, who are in the process of kidnapping a colonel in Guatemala City.

> *"In Guatemala, the Lord's Will was being invoked by the country's rulers against their own people. At 11 p.m. on February 15 (1982) . . . the Guatemalan army appeared at the Ixil village of Santo Tomás Ixcán and began firing automatic weapons into its homes. Families who were not killed outright were dragged outside and shot. The bodies were then carried into the village church. The killings continued for two more days. The church was set afire, and then the entire village.*
>
> *"To achieve this military victory, the army used linguistic differences, deploying Indian soldiers to areas where the tribal languages were alien to them. This strategy made it easier to dehumanize the enemy . . . Sometimes, however, the army needed to communicate with the Indians to carry out its 'civic action' and relief projects in occupied territory. For this more specialized task, it turned to American missionaries . . . "*

—From *Thy Will Be Done* by Gerard Colby with Charlotte Dennett. The authors have documented the complicity of US missionary translators with Latin American dictatorships. These dictatorships were supported by international business concerns, who in turn contributed to the missionary societies.

> *"The way things were done in Guatemala took a little getting used to. On the surface of things, the country paid a reasonable amount of respect to logic. Guatemala itself was divided into twenty-three regions, or states, called*

departamentos, *and its cities were divided into gerry-mandered sectors called* zonas. *The streets that had a roughly north/south orientation were called* avenidas, *and the cross streets were called streets, or* calles. *To locate an address you had to know the* zona *because the numbered* calles *and* avenidas *repeated themselves in each sector.*

"Beyond this point, nothing else in the entire country made sense. Reason was not a part of the national Weltanschauung. *Nothing was reliable or dependable because no one paid any attention to the formalities that were necessary for an organized society. That is, rules. Here the rules were uniformly disobeyed or ignored or made exception to. None of which mattered anyway, since the rules themselves constantly were being changed by people who seemed to have an understanding about something of which no one else had been informed. What was important here was convention, knowing 'the way things were done,' and learning how things were done was largely a process of trial and error. The big surprise was that, in Guatemala, the errors could cost you your life."*

—From the *Body of Truth* by David L. Lindsey. Lindsey's protagonist, Houston Police Detective Stuart Haydon, must track down a missing woman in Guatemala.

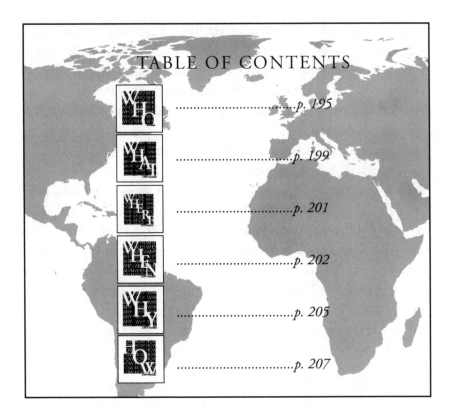

TABLE OF CONTENTS

THE GUATEMALANS

In a conflicted society, the division of population into ethnic groups becomes controversial. Here is perhaps the most useful way to break down Guatemalan society: the numbers of Amerindians and mestizos (persons of mixed Amerindian and Hispanic ancestry) are roughly equal; each constitutes 45% of Guatemala's population. Persons of direct European ancestry account for 5%. The oligarchy comes primarily from this group. Blacks make up 2%. The remaining 3% are mixed-race or Asian (mostly Chinese).

However, the term *Ladino* is sometimes used to define all non-Amerindian populations. This would include mestizos, whites, blacks, Asians, and even Amerindians who no longer follow an indigenous lifestyle (as in wearing traditional clothes or speaking an indigenous language). As societal upheavals bring more Amerindians into contact with the outside world, the process of *ladinización* has increased. Cheap, mass-produced Western clothes have also led many Amerindians to reject their traditional style of clothing.

Although exact figures are difficult to ascertain, Guatemala has the largest Amerindian population in Central America. The Amerindians themselves are not in agreement about what they prefer to be called. Some prefer the term Maya. However, Guatemala has many different Amerindian tribes, and not all are descended from the Mayans. Non-Mayan Amerindians generally prefer the term *indígena*. The old term *indio* is now a deliberate insult.

The citizens of Guatemala refer to themselves as *guatemaltecos*.

HOW TO TELL GUATEMALA AND THE GUATEMALANS FROM THEIR NEIGHBORS

Most of Latin America is overwhelmingly Roman Catholic, but at least one-quarter of Guatemalans are Protestants—most of them in the evangelical tradition. The leader of the evangelical Sahddai sect (to which former president Jorge Serrano belonged) believes that Guatemala is cursed because its Amerindians worshipped the devil in the form of a plumed, flying serpent. That image may be fanciful, but it seems appropriate as a political metaphor. To millions of poor Guatemalans who have suffered decades of violence and impoverishment, Guatemala has been a land accursed. It is too soon to tell if the new peace treaty will change that.

1. Guatemala borders Mexico to the north and west, Belize to the northeast, and Honduras and El Salvador to the east. It has a long coastline on the Pacific and a short coast in the Caribbean (specifically, on the Gulf of Honduras).

2. Superlatives—most of them undesirable—are needed to describe Guatemala. It has the largest population in

Central America (excluding Mexico, which is considered part of North America). Guatemala has the highest infant mortality rate in Central America, and the lowest life expectancy and lowest literacy rates.

3. The longest-running insurgency in Latin America officially ended with the signing of a peace treaty on 29 December 1996. This civil war lasted for 36 years, and cost thousands of lives.

4. The long civil war was accompanied by years of government crackdowns. To tourists, Guatemala is touted as "the Country of Eternal Spring." Some *guatemaltecos* wryly suggest that it should be "the Country of Eternal Repression." Although foreign business executives visiting Guatemala have relatively little to fear, the people have suffered decades of human rights violations, death-squad activity, and outright genocide.

LITERATURE

Although the development of literature has been hampered by poverty and a low literacy rate, Guatemala has nevertheless produced one author who has been awarded a Nobel Prize for Literature (as well as a Peace Prize-winner who has written an autobiography.)

Miguel Ángel Asturias (1899–1974) spent much of his life in exile for his political writing. His first major work, published in 1929, was a translation of *Popol Vuh,* the sacred Quiché book of the Mayans. While working as a journalist, he wrote a series of stories inspired by Guatemalan legends (published in 1930 as *Leyendas de Guatemala*). His next work, *El señor presidente,* was so explosive that it could not be published in Guatemala until 1946. Forced into exile, Asturias continued to attack the exploitation of Guatemala by both its leaders and foreign corporations. He took on the United Fruit Company in his so-called "banana republic trilogy" (*Strong*

Wind, The Green Pope, and *The Eyes of the Interred*), which he began in 1950. He was awarded the 1966 Lenin Peace Prize and the 1967 Nobel Prize for Literature. His fame (and a change in Guatemala's leadership) brought him acceptance at home, and he was appointed Guatemala's ambassador to France. He resigned that position in 1971 when yet another dictatorship took control of Guatemala.

Rigoberta Menchú Tum (1959–) is best known as an activist, working on behalf of her fellow Mayans. She was awarded the 1992 Nobel Peace Prize for these labors. She published an autobiography in 1984, entitled *I, Rigoberta Menchú: An Indian Woman in Guatemala.*

Rodrigo Rey Rosa (1958–) is a young Guatemalan writer whose work has been translated into English by the distinguished US author Paul Bowles (best known for his North African stories, such as *The Sheltering Sky*). Rey Rosa's short stories, collected in *The Beggar's Knife* (1985) and *Dust On Her Tongue* (1989) are written with a poetic sensibility—the words are minimal but they convey deeper meaning. His 1991 novel, *The Pelcari Project,* is an allegory about Central American political propaganda and parrots. Curiously, most of Rey Rosa's work has appeared in English, never in Spanish. He currently lives in Tangier, Morocco.

LANGUAGE

The official language of Guatemala is Spanish. Many upper-class Guatemalans have some familiarity with English. So do some Guatemalans who fled to the United States as refugees, then returned (voluntarily or otherwise).

There are many different indigenous languages, not all of which are mutually intelligible. In remote areas of Guatemala, there are Amerindians who speak only their native language.

Linguists have categorized 53 different languages spoken in modern Guatemala.—*Ethnologue: Languages of the World,* 12th Edition from their Web site at (http://www.sil.org/ethnologue/ethnologue.html).

BUSINESS IN GUATEMALA

> *Caveat: Guatemala does poorly in enforcing copyright law. Furthermore, Guatemalan law does not protect either trade secrets or sound recordings. Currently, Guatemala closely trails El Salvador and Paraguay for Latin America's highest rate of software piracy.*

As elsewhere in Latin America, successful business relationships hinge on friendly social relationships. Most Guatemalan decision-makers are free to base their decisions on gut instincts. If they dislike you—or even if you just made a poor first impression—they will not do business with you. Guatemalan decision-makers tend to be open and blunt-spoken. (It is as if many traditional Hispanic nicities and polite circumlocutions have been lost over the brutal years of the civil war.) Foreigners are frequently surprised at the accessibility of the decision-makers. Even high-ranking leaders in business and government tend to be willing to see foreign executives.

Product sales in Guatemala are almost evenly split between items sold directly by foreign firms and items sold through a Guatemalan agent or distributor.

Several franchises have been very successful in Guatemala. Current franchises are concentrated in the fast-food and hospitality sectors. Joint ventures are complex in Guatemala; they are not the preferred way to do business.

The price of consumer goods is the single most important factor in deciding to buy. After-sale service is an important factor. Products made in the USA have a positive image in the Guatemalan market, both for quality and for warranty. Guatemala is a small market, and a negative reputation (especially for such things as after-sale service) spreads quickly.

Telemarketing is uncommon in Guatemala, as are sales via mail order. Advertising is done in all the usual methods—radio, television, magazines, and newspapers. The number of highway billboards is growing throughout Guatemala.

Despite the use of English by many business executives, all materials should be translated into Spanish.

LEGAL AFFAIRS IN GUATEMALA

Joint venture legislation is unusual in that the joint venture is not regulated as a company or legal entity. Instead, Guatemalan law regulates the joint venture as a contract between two parties.

The women's movement is still in its infancy in Guatemala. Women only received the right to vote in 1945, and the country remains highly patriarchal. Under current law, only women may be charged with adultery.

The following businesses are some of the largest employers in Guatemala:

Almacenes Paiz SA
Guatemala City.
4,000 employees.
Compania Bananera Guatemalteca Independiente SA
Guatemala City.
3,960 employees.
Compania de Jarabes y Bebidas Gaseosas
la Mariposa SA
Guatemala City.
1,600 employees.
Compania Industrial Liztex SA
Guatemala City.
1,300 employees.
Instituto Nacional de Electrificacion
Guatemala City.
4,200 employees.

It has been both dangerous and unprofitable to be a journalist in Guatemala. Although official censorship has been relatively light, offending journalists were frequent victims of the death squads. Between 1978 and 1985, an astonishing 47 Guatemalan journalists were slain! Over a hundred others fled into exile. News outlets themselves could be subject to violence. In the 1988, the offices of the news magazine *La Epoca* were firebombed and destroyed. Radio journalists were frequent targets of violence.

The following are some of Guatemala's largest daily newspapers:

Prensa Libre
Guatemala City.
Diario El Grafico
Guatemala City.
Siglo Veintiuno
Guatemala City.
Diario La Republica
Guatemala City.
Diario La Hora
Guatemala City.

GUATEMALAN GEOGRAPHY

GUATEMALA

FLAG AND MAP OF GUATEMALA

Guatemala's flag originated as the flag of the short-lived Central American Federation (blue, white, and blue stripes). Additional yellow and red stripes were added in 1851, but these were removed in 1871.

Size: 42,042 square miles

Population: 10,998,602

One of the largest nations in Central America, Guatemala is flanked by Mexico, Belize, Honduras, and El Salvador. It has coasts on both the Caribbean and the Pacific.

GUATEMALAN HISTORY

Circa 800 B.C.: The first identifiable civilization in the region, the Olmecs, achieves supremacy in Guatemala and southern Mexico.

Circa 200 B.C.: Pre-Columbian civilization reaches its "Golden Age" in Mesoamerica—an area stretching from the southern USA to Nicaragua. The Mayans build large cities and temples. Mayan city-states (never unified) rule all of Mesoamerica until around A.D. 900—at which time the great Mayan cities are abandoned for reasons unknown.

Circa A.D. 1200: One of the successors to the Mayan hegemony, the warlike Toltecs, extend their rule as far south as Yucatán. Around A.D. 1200 they abandon their southern outposts and return north into Mexico. A tribe known as the Itzá occupy the former Toltec cities, and become the leading power in the region.

Circa A.D. 1450: A tribe known as the Xiú overthrow the hegemony of the Itzá Yucatán becomes a battleground as city-states war for supremacy.

1519: Hernán Cortés leads the first European expedition to subdue Mexico. After conquering central Mexico, he turns his attention south to Yucatán. Although the city-states of Yucatán are still warring with each other, they manage to repulse the Spanish.

1524: An expedition led by Pedro de Alvarado, a lieutenant of Cortés, makes the first Spanish inroads into Guatemala. He spends years conquering the resisting Amerindians.

1527: A capital of the Guatemala region is founded at what is now Ciudad Vieja, near Antigua. It is destroyed by a mudslide in 1543, whereupon Antigua becomes the capital.

1530: A Spanish expedition led by a father and son (both of whom were named Francisco de Montejo) begins the conquest of Yucatán. This pacification is not completed until 1546.

1570: The Captaincy-General of Guatemala is created. Its rule extends as far south as Costa Rica. Although the Spanish find few mineral resources in Guatemala, its rich soil encourages them to set up plantations with Amerindian slaves.

1773: Antigua is destroyed by an earthquake. The capital is moved nearby to the new outpost of Guatemala City in 1776.

1821: Following Mexico's lead, Guatemala declares independence from Spain. Mexico extends its control over Central America, including Guatemala.

1823: Meeting in Guatamala City, the five Central American states (Guatemala, Honduras, El Salvador, Nicaragua, and Costa Rica) unite as the United Provinces of Central America, and declare independence from Mexico.

1838: Following years of internecine fighting, the United Provinces of Central America are dissolved. Guatemala becomes a solitary independent state, led by Rafael Carrera. A semiliterate mestizo pig farmer, Carrera seizes power during an Amerindian uprising. He remains dictator until 1865, and undoes all the reforms enacted by the leaders of the United Provinces.

1859: During Rafael Carrera's reign, Guatemala and the United Kingdom sign a treaty that recognizes the existence and borders of the future British Honduras (later Belize). However, since the British never fulfill the treaty's provision to build a road from Belize City to Guatemala City, Guatemala continues to claim Belize's territory. Belize formally becomes a colony known as British Honduras in 1862, while the USA is embroiled with the US Civil War (and unable to enforce the Monroe Doctrine).

1871: A revolution returns the Liberals to power in Guatemala.

1873: Liberal Justo Rufino Barrios, hailed as "the Great Reformer," becomes president. He encourages European immigration, coffee-growing, and reduces the power of the Catholic Church. His improvements include roads, schools, and a modern banking system. He dies in 1885 while trying to forcibly reunite the United Provinces.

1898: Manuel Estrada Cabera comes to power in a rigged election for the presidency. He holds onto power until 1920. Cabera gives huge concessions to the foreign plantation owners, especially the United Fruit Company. He is ousted in a bloody coup in 1920.

1931: General Jorge Ubico y Castañeda seizes power. He rules until 1944, the last of the great caudillo dictators. Although Ubico admires Spain's Fascist leader Federico Franco, he keeps Guatemala neutral in World War II.

1944: Juan José Arévalo is elected president. Calling himself a "Spiritual Socialist," he enacts reforms and grants political liberties. He also survives 25 coup attempts by Conservative forces during his six-year term in office!

1951: Colonel Jacobo Arbenz Guzmán is elected president. He continues Arévalo's reforms. He expropriates some land from foreign owners, including the United Fruit Company. Angered, the United States supports a coup to overthrow him.

1954: The coup which ousted President Jacobo Arbenz returns power to the conservative oligarchy in Guatemala. There are no free and fair elections in Guatemala until the 1990s.

1966: The Guatemalan military and death squads begin to make thousands of Guatemalan citizens "disappear."

1970: The leader of the 1966 counterinsurgency campaign, Colonel Arana Osorio, becomes president. Osorio, nicknamed "the Jackal of Zacapa," rules for four years, during which over 15,000 citizens are slain.

1982: General Efraín Ríos Montt seizes power. His 16-month dictatorship is marked by a scorched-earth campaign against rebels. His ruthlessness restores a measure of order, and is popular with the oligarchy. In the same year, four separate rebel organizations unite under the title URNG (Guatemalan National Revolutionary Unit).

1989: General Efraín Ríos Montt once again seizes power. He rules as dictator until 1990.

1991: Jorge Serrano is elected president. His inauguration marks the first time in 51 years that one freely elected civilian government follows another in Guatemala. In 1993, faced with public unrest and official corruption, Serrano dissolves the Congress and Supreme Court. His attempt to seize dictatorial powers—referred to as an *autogolpe* (an auto-coup)—fails, and he is forced to flee into exile.

1992: Guatemala finally relinquishes its claim to Belize's territory. Also, Rigoberta Menchú Tum wins the 1992 Nobel Peace Prize for her work with Guatemala's Mayan Indians.

1996: After five years of negotiations, President Alvaro Arzu signs a peace treaty with URNG guerrilla front leader Rolando Moran and Amerindian peace activist Rigoberta Menchú. This brings Guatemala's 36-year civil war to an end.

1997: The URNG guerrilla army is demobilized.

GUATEMALAN BEHAVIOR

Why are Guatemalans the way they are?

Setting aside the Sahddai theory that Guatemala is cursed due to devil-worshipping Amerindians, is there any reason for Guatemala's misfortune?

Certainly the United States bears some responsibility. US players range from multinational corporations like United Fruit to anticommunist politicians. But Guatemala did much of its counterinsurgency on its own. Unlike El Salvador, where the counterinsurgency programs were financed by the USA, the Guatemalan government received relatively little US funding. Outsiders helped train the Guatemalan forces—not only from the USA, but Argentina, Taiwan, and Israel as well. But one suspects that the government would've cracked down on potential threats even without outside advice.

Guatemala may not be able to hold itself together except by force. Almost half of Guatemala's population are Amerindians living some approximation of their traditional ways. Western civilization has never, ever been good to Amerindians. Since the arrival of the Spanish in 1524, Europeans have brought misery and death to their lives. So why should they want to be part of Western civilization?

Of course, as with Amerindians elsewhere, Guatemala's *indígenas* do not necessarily get along with each other. The tribes were warring with each other when the Spanish arrived, and certain groups disagree to this day. The various Amerindian languages are not mutually intelligible.

In the 1996 peace treaty, the government promised to resettle some 100,000 displaced Amerindians. Even though the USA promised some $40 million in aid in 1997, it will be remarkable (and unprecedented) if the Guatemalan government can keep its promises.

What is the "Guatemalan solution"?

All of Latin America is now familiar with the "Guatemalan solution," which is "kill all your opponents." But this was not the only counterinsurgency technique used in Guatemala.

After displacing Amerindians from their ancestral homes, the government set up "model villages." These settlements not only kept the Amerindian populations under guard (and away from the rebels), they subjected them to pro-government propaganda. Whether the Guatemalan government won any hearts and minds is difficult to say.

HOW CAN I FIND MORE INFORMATION ABOUT GUATEMALA?

Here are a few resources to start with:

Getting Through Customs' Web site at **http://www. getcustoms.com** tracks current holidays in Guatemala. They also post Cultural I.Q. Quizzes, gift-giving guidelines, a demo of the PASSPORT database, and further international information. Telephone: (610) 353-9894; fax (610) 353-6994.

Embassy of Guatemala
2220 R Street NW
Washington, DC 20008
Telephone: (202) 745-4952

Guatemala Tourist Commission
299 Alhambra Circle, Suite 510
Coral Gables, FL 33134
Telephone: (800) 742-4529 or (305) 442-0651; fax: (305) 442-1013

Guatemala Online—a guide for Guatemalan business, investing, tourism, and general information. **http://www3.quetzalnet.com/quetzalnet/**

The International Academy at Santa Barbara at **http://www.iasb.org/cwl** publishes *Current World Leaders,* an excellent resource for data on political leaders and parties in Guatemala. Telephone: (800) 530-2682 or (805) 965-5010 for subscription information.

The Bureau of Consular Affairs at **http://travel.state.gov** can give you detailed information on obtaining passports, visa requirements, and consular affairs bulletins.

The Center for Disease Control at **http://www.cdc.gov/** provides valuable medical information, as well as information on any outbreaks of virulent infections in Guatemala.

Like all Web sites, the preceding Internet addresses are subject to change, and there is no guarantee that they will continue to provide the data we list here.

Honduras

WHAT'S YOUR CULTURAL I.Q.?

1. Christopher Columbus landed in Honduras in 1502. TRUE or FALSE? Honduras was the first landfall for Columbus on the American mainland.

    ANSWER: True. Columbus' first three voyages took him to the Caribbean islands. It was not until his fourth and final voyage to the New World that Columbus actually set foot on the mainland. He "discovered" Honduras on 14 August 1502 (of course, this was no discovery to the Amerindian inhabitants). The deep offshore waters inspired the name Honduras, which means "deep" in Spanish.

2. Which of the following people landed at Trujillo (which is on the Caribbean coast of Honduras)?

    a. Christopher Columbus

    b. American writer O. Henry

    c. The Dutch pirate van Horn and the British pirate Aury Morgan

    d. US mercenary leader William Walker

    e. All of the above

ANSWER: e. Columbus landed at (or near) present-day Trujillo, O. Henry spent time hiding out from the law there, Dutch and British pirates attacked it several times (and burned the town in 1643), and William Walker was executed there. Trujillo was also the first capital of Honduras.

3. Of the many Amerindian groups of Honduras, the Lenca were the only tribe to mount a serious offense against the Spanish. TRUE or FALSE? The Spanish turned the tide by inviting the Lenca chief to a meeting, then executing him.

ANSWER: True. The Lenca chief Lempira led 30,000 warriors against the Spanish in 1537. The next year, Lempira was taken and killed while under a flag of truce. By 1539, the Spanish had suppressed the Lenca revolt. Modern Honduras honors Lempira by naming the national currency after him.

4. In 1537, the capital of Honduras was moved from Trujillo to the cooler interior. This new capital of Honduras was:

    a. Comayagua

    b. Comayagüela

    c. Tegucigalpa

    d. San Pedro Sula

ANSWER: a. Honduras' capital was moved to Comayagua until 1880, when it was moved to its present location of Tegucigalpa.

5. Central America became independent from Spain in 1821, and soon united in a short-lived association

known as the Central American Federation, which was composed of Guatemala, Honduras, El Salvador, Nicaragua, and Costa Rica. TRUE or FALSE? The leader of this Federation was a Honduran.

ANSWER: True. The Honduran general, Francisco Morazán, became the first leader of the Central American Federation. The Federation collapsed in 1838.

6. Honduras has suffered a turbulent political history. All of the following presidents brought temporary peace to Honduras. Which one is also remembered as a brutal dictator? (The dates they took office appear in parentheses.)

   a. Marco Aurelio Soto (1876)

   b. Luis Brográn (1883)

   c. General Tiburcio Carías Andino (1933)

   d. Juan Manuel Gálvez (1949)

ANSWER: c. While the other presidents made some reforms to Honduras, General Tiburcio Carías Andino ruled with an iron hand and made no improvements to Honduras. His 16-year dictatorship was marked by political repression and a lack of progress.

7. US citizen Sam (the Banana Man) Zemurray is considered the man responsible for turning Honduras into the prototypical banana republic. Zemurray did far more than simply buy land to grow bananas; he deposed Honduran governments at will. TRUE or FALSE? Zemurray's US mercenary ally, General Lee Christmas, eventually became president of Honduras.

ANSWER: False—but just barely. Lee Christmas didn't become president, but he did become commander-in-chief of the entire Honduran army.

8. Competition for control of the banana market was fierce. Which company eventually won out to become Honduras' top producer (as well as the most influential business in Honduras)?

    a. Sam Zemurray's Cuyamel Fruit Company

b. The United Fruit Company (which eventually became United Brands)

    c. The Vaccaro Brothers (which became Standard Fruit)

    ANSWER: b. United Fruit became the leader after buying out Zemurray's company in 1929. This made United Fruit the primary target during the 1954 general strike.

9. After decades of dominating the Honduran economy, United Fruit was the target of a strike in 1954. TRUE or FALSE? The strike was broken without United Fruit making any concessions.

    ANSWER: False. United Fruit did have to make some concessions to the workers. But the lasting significance of the 1954 strike was the unified opposition of Central Americans to the foreign corporations that controlled their destinies.

10. In the 1980s, revolutions in neighboring Nicaragua and El Salvador had wide-ranging effects on Honduras. Which of the following was NOT one of these effects?

    a. The USA trained Nicaraguan Contras on Honduran soil

    b. The USA trained Salvadoran troops on Honduran soil

c. Thousands of refugees fled to Honduras from
El Salvador and Nicaragua

d. In 1988, Hondurans demonstrated their support for
US policy in mass rallies

e. The Honduran economy went into a tailspin after peace was declared
in 1990 and the millions of dollars in US aid ceased

ANSWER: d. There were mass rallies in Honduras in 1988, but they were anti-USA, not pro-USA. Even though the training of foreign troops on Honduran soil was bringing in millions of US dollars, the Honduran people wanted the United States and the foreign troops off their soil. The sentiment was so strong that Honduran president José Simeón Azcona del Hoyo was forced to ask the US military to leave.

QUOTATIONS ABOUT HONDURAS

"Most of Honduras is a nation of empty forests, swampy coasts, and sieve-like borders. It is a land made for smugglers and conspirators."

—From the book *With the Contras* by Christopher Dickey.

"General Fernández was standing in front of the large window in his office watching the light fall on a garden thick with gardenias and banana trees in bloom and contemplating in the distance the city orphaned by the sea. December was sewing needlework of cold onto the glass, and the north wind coming out of the mouth of the dormant volcano was beating against the windowpanes . . .

"'The people love me,' the general murmured as if to
himself, standing before the window once again. 'The
barefoot love me because I've given them everything,' he
repeated in a monologue of conviction. 'It's the educated
and cultured people who are against me, the ones who are
already up in the world, the ones who can read and learn
liberal slogans. The real people love me.'"

—From the short story *April in the Forenoon* by Julio Escoto.

"If any one man gave birth to the banana-republic stereotype, it was Sam (the Banana Man) Zemurray, a
Bessarabian immigrant to the United States who started
his career by buying overripe bananas from United Fruit
and peddling them in New Orleans. In 1910, he bought
up fifteen thousand acres of Honduras's Caribbean Coast.
The following year he joined forces with former President
Manuel Bonilla and an American mercenary named Lee
Christmas to overthrow a Liberal regime that had offend-
ed the State Department by getting up to its neck in debt
to Britain and becoming too friendly with the
Nicaraguan leader Zelaya. Zemurray, Bonilla, and
Christmas landed their troops at Trujillo, O. Henry's old
stomping ground, and the US consul named a new president of Honduras.

"In their north-coast enclave, the banana companies
received five hundred hectares of free land for every kilometer of railroad they built. The result was a serpentine
maze of tracks that crisscrossed the flatlands of the coast,
but no railway was ever laid to serve the capital
city, Tegucigalpa. In this splendid isolation, the companies

ran Honduras much more effectively than the central government."

—From *The Good Neighbor: How the United States Wrote the History of Central America and the Caribbean* by George Black.

> *"On the arrival of the first Europeans, the Miskito Indians were as purebred as the other tribes but with one important cultural difference. The women were ready and willing to take the Europeans (English buccaneers, mostly) as husbands, if only for an hour or two. There was no stigma on the child, who was considered Miskito. So while other tribes were cut down by disease and bullets, the Miskitos flourished and looked less and less like Indians.*
>
> *"Europeans or Africans: It didn't really matter. When a Portuguese slave ship (commanded by the slaves, who had killed the captain and crew) was wrecked south of Cabo Gracias a Dios, the slaves quickly became part of the tribe. The Spanish named the resulting subgroup Zambos (probably from ambos, meaning both) which became Sambo in English . . .*
>
> *"The Miskitos, being the seedy, fun-loving folk that they were, traditionally allied themselves with the British buccaneers against the straightlaced Catholic Spaniards. In 1687, the British formalized the arrangement by shipping the Sambo chief to Jamaica, dressing him up in a 'cocked hat,' red coat, shirt, and broadsword, presenting him with a certificate, and crowning him King of Mosquitia with a typical British feeling for pomp. The Miskitos loved it and the system continued almost without a break well into the nineteenth century, when Britain agreed to withdraw from the Shore."*

—From *The Fever Coast Log* by Gordon Chaplin.

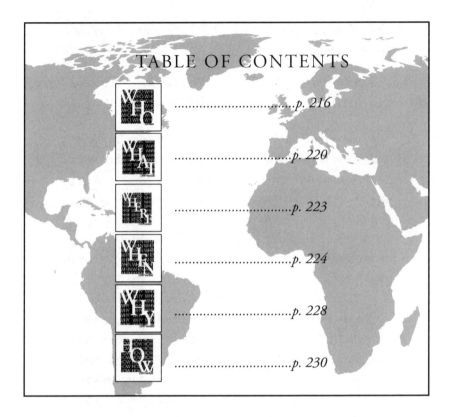

TABLE OF CONTENTS

THE HONDURANS

Honduras has one of the highest populations of mestizos—89.9%—in Central America. Amerindians form the next largest group at 6.7%, followed by black and black-Amerindian Hondurans at 2.1%. Honduras also has one of the lowest percentages—1.3%—of persons of direct European descent.

Unlike its neighbors, Honduras was not historically dominated by a landholding elite. After independence from Spain, northern Honduras was controlled by foreign-owned banana companies. These companies were often more influential than the government at Tegucigalpa.

The Hondurans refer to themselves as *hondureños*.

HOW TO TELL HONDURAS AND THE HONDURANS FROM
THEIR NEIGHBORS

Honduras is the second-largest nation in Central America. Only
Nicaragua is larger.

1. If there was ever a country which fit the stereotype of a
    banana republic, it's Honduras. The US-owned banana
    companies owned much of the land and exerted a
    tremendous influence on the development of
    Honduras. Coffee has replaced bananas as the biggest
    Honduran agricultural export, but the foreign interests
    are still influential.

2. Honduras borders Guatemala to the west, El Salvador
    to the southwest, and Nicaragua to the southeast.
    Belize (the former British Honduras) lies across the
    Gulf of Honduras, but the two countries do not share a
    border. Honduras has a long coastline on the
    Caribbean and a short coastline on the Pacific Ocean.

3. Honduras did fight a short war with neighboring El
    Salvador in 1969. It became known as the Soccer War,
    since the precipitating incident was an attack on
    Honduran soccer fans at a World Cup qualifying game
    in San Salvador. However, the actual cause was the
    Salvadoran immigrants living and working in
    Honduras. Tiny El Salvador is overpopulated; large
    Honduras has a much lower population density. But
    both countries are poor, so Hondurans see illegal
    Salvadoran immigrants as taking work and resources
    from Hondurans.

4. Honduras went from being the wealthiest country in
    Central America (during colonial times) to one of the
    poorest (by the middle of the 20th century). In the

1570s, the Spanish discovered gold and silver near Tegucigalpa. But the precious metals ran out, and Honduras became an agricultural backwater. Bananas grew as an export crop, but the profits went to the foreign owners of the companies. Only recently, with diversification, has the middle class of Honduras grown.

LITERATURE

A small population, widespread poverty, and a low literacy rate has hampered the development of literature in Honduras. It can also be difficult for writers to be apolitical. Writers who become political often fall afoul of the government. As Honduran writer and professor Roberto Sosa has noted, "For Central American writers, there is no road left but to be in favor of the oligarchies or against them."

Julio Escoto (1944–) has written books for both adults and children, as well as essays, articles, and stories. His most recent novel is *Bajo el almendro, junto al volcán,* published in 1988; it has not yet been translated into English. He is a founder of the Tegucigalpa publishing house Centro Editorial, one of the most important publishers in Honduras. He now lives in Costa Rica.

Roberto Sosa (1930–) is a professor of literature at the University of Honduras. He is best known for his poetry. His poetry collection *Un Mundo para todos dividido* (translated into English in 1983 as *The Difficult Days*) won Cuba's *Casa de las Américas* prize in 1971.

Horacio Castellanos Moya (1950–) is a Honduran-born writer of poetry and fiction who has spent much of his life in exile. After leaving Honduras he lived in El Salvador, Costa Rica, and Canada; he now lives in Mexico. His fiction often features political activists, both at home and in exile. Among his work is a 1987 collection of short stories entitled *Perfil de prófugo*. One story from that collection, "Encierro" (translated into English as "Confinement"), appears in the 1988 collection *And We Sold the Rain: Contemporary Fiction from Central America*.

LIGHTS! CAMERA! ACTION!

Honduras has not produced major, internationally distributed motion pictures. However, one American film has been set in Honduras:

The Mosquito Coast is based on Paul Theroux's 1981 novel of the same name. The film is like Swiss Family Robinson in reverse: Instead of coming together and thriving in isolation, this family comes apart. Harrison Ford turns in a haunting performance as an obsessed inventor who wants to take his family away from a corrupt USA. They flee into the jungle of Honduras' Caribbean Coast (a.k.a. Mosquito or Miskito Coast), where their dreams of a self-sufficient life turn into a nightmare. The late River Phoenix portrays the son who must protect his family from danger—which includes his increasingly demented father (1986, directed by Peter Weir).

LANGUAGE

The official language of Honduras is Spanish. English is often spoken as a second language by business executives. Due to the influence of the UK, English is still spoken on Honduras' Caribbean Coast. However, this English is a Caribbean patois, and may be unintelligible to foreign English speakers.

Linguists have categorized nine different languages spoken in modern Honduras—*Ethnologue: Languages of the World,* 12th Edition from their Web site at (http://www.sil.org/ethnologue/ethnologue.html).

BUSINESS IN HONDURAS

BUSINESS SUCCESS IN HONDURAS

> *Caveat: Despite the huge tracts of land formerly owned by foreign agricultural companies like United Fruit (now known as United Brands), the current Constitution of Honduras limits the amount of land that can be owned by a single foreign corporation. The law also demands that all foreign investment complements the needs of Honduras and its people. Foreign investment cannot substitute for local investment.*

Honduran law does not require that a foreign firm use a local agent. However, a local representative can be so useful that foregoing one is not recommended. At the very least, foreign companies should hire local legal representation.

As usual in Latin America, business in Honduras is based on personal relationships. Hondurans prefer doing business with people they know and like. Be aware that it is not unusual for a Honduran representative of a foreign company to also sell products made by a competitor.

The number of franchises in Honduras has grown in recent years. In 1992, the Honduran government changed its legal code to assist foreign investors, including franchise owners. The potential exists for expansion in the franchise market.

The 1992 legal code also removed the limits on the percentage of capital that can be owned by a foreigner. This allows a foreigner to own the controlling interest in a joint venture. (A few specific industries remain wherein majority control must be retained by a Honduran citizen. These exceptions include sectors of the agriculture, fishing, transportation, and media industries.) Joint ventures have been on the rise since 1992.

Price remains the single most important factor in whether or not Honduran consumers will buy goods and services. Affluent Hondurans have been known to purchase goods abroad if they can be gotten cheaper than within Honduras.

Customer service is also a consideration. Sales are lost due to lack of reliable local service.

Newspaper advertisements have traditionally been the most successful marketing technique. Deficiencies in Honduran telephone and mail services render direct mail problematical. Door-to-door sales have proven successful.

English is spoken by many (but not all) business executives. Nevertheless, all promotional materials should be translated into Spanish.

LEGAL AFFAIRS IN HONDURAS

Historically, the Honduran legal code has been deficient in providing legal deterrents toward violence against women. Most egregiously, the rape of a woman aged 13 and above is considered a private crime in Honduras. This means that, for prosecution to take place, the aggrieved party must hire her own prosecutor to pursue the case! Since hiring a prosecutor is an expensive undertaking, only the small, wealthy elite can afford justice. Furthermore, successful prosecution for rape is difficult, and the penalties for the crime are relatively light (usually from three to nine years).

Domestic violence is also a problem in Honduras. The court does not take action in domestic violence cases unless the victim is so badly injured as to be incapacitated for more than ten days.

As part of the shift from military oversight to civilian control, the Honduran secret police (the military-run National Investigation Unit) was disbanded in 1994. It was replaced by the civilian-run Criminal Investigations Unit, which began operations in 1995. This new unit was trained by the Israeli police and the US Federal Bureau of Investigation.

LEADING BUSINESSES IN HONDURAS

The following businesses are some of the largest employers in Honduras:

Banco Atlantida SA
Tegucigalpa.
National commercial bank. 610 employees.

Cerveceria Hondurena SA
San Pedro Sula, Cortes.
1,200 employees.

Compania Azucarera Chumbagua SA
San Pedro Sula, Cortes.
600 employees.

Compania Azucarera Hondurena SA
San Pedro Sula, Cortes.
566 employees.

Embotelladora la Reyna SA
Comayagüela.
350 employees.

Empresa Hondurena de Telecomunicaciones
Tegulcigalpa.
4,000 employees.

Empresa Nacional de Energia Electrica
Tegulcigalpa.
2,076 employees.

Lovable de Honduras SA de CV
San Pedro Sula, Cortes.
791 employees.

Quimicas Magna SA de CV
Tegucigalpa.
700 employees.

Tela Railroad Co
Lima Nueva La Lima, Cortes.
9,000 employees.

Textiles Maya SA de CV
San Pedro Sula, Cortes.
400 employees.
Worldwide Apparel Manufacturers SA de CV
Puerto Cortés Choloma.
360 employees.

The following are the largest print medium concerns in Honduras:

El Heraldo
Tegucigalpa.
Daily newspaper.
Honduras This Week
Tegucigalpa.
English-language weekly newspaper.
El Nuevo Dia
San Pedro Sula.
Daily newspaper.
La Prensa
San Pedro Sula, Cortes.
Daily newspaper.
La Tiempo
San Pedro Sula, Cortes.
Daily newspaper.
La Tribuna
Tegucigalpa.
Daily newspaper.

HONDURAN GEOGRAPHY

FLAG AND MAP OF HONDURAS

The flag of Honduras originated as the flag of the short-lived
Central American Federation (horizontal blue, white, and blue
stripes). In the center of the white stripe are five stars, symbolizing
the five Federation nations: Guatemala, Honduras, El Salvador,
Nicaragua, and Costa Rica.

HONDURAS

Size: 43,277 square miles
Population: 4,708,000
The second largest nation in Central America, Honduras lies between Guatemala, El Salvador, and Nicaragua. It has a long coast on the Caribbean and a very short one on the Pacific.

HONDURAN HISTORY

A.D. 900: The great Mayan cities of Honduras, including Copán, are abandoned.

900–1502: With the fall of the Mayans, several Amerindian civilizations share Honduras. No one tribe achieves dominance over the others. Most tribes seem to live a peaceful existence.

1502: Christopher Columbus leads the first European expedition to visit Honduras, on his fourth and final voyage to the New World. He lands first on one of the Bay Islands, then sails to the mainland. After landing around present-day Trujillo on 14 August 1902, he sails south. The sea is deep off this coast (which gives the country its name: Honduras is Spanish for "deep"). Waves are rougher in deep water, and after surviving a storm, Columbus names the next cape *Gracias a Dios* (Thanks be to God).

1525: Trujillo is founded by the Spanish. It becomes the first capital of Honduras, but it is hot and malaria-ridden.

1537: A new capital at Comayagua is established in the cooler interior highlands. In the same year, 30,000 Lenca warriors led by their chief Lempira nearly drive the Spanish out of Honduras. The Lenca are the only Amerindian tribe to mount a substantial opposition to the Spanish.

1538: The Spanish break the Lenca by inviting Lempira to a meeting, then slaying him. Within a year, the Lenca cease to be a threat. (Today, Lempira is a national hero in Honduras, and the country's currency is named after him.)

1549: Control of Honduras is given to Guatemala by the Spanish Crown.

1570s: Both gold and silver are discovered near Tegucigalpa. These mines prove to be the most productive south of Mexico and north of Peru. Until the ore runs out, Honduras is the wealthiest nation in Central America. Amerindians are enslaved to work the mines and plantations.

Early 1600s: English privateers find the Bay of Honduras a profitable area for attacking Spanish ships traveling between Mexico and Panama. They establish bases in northern Honduras, the Bay Islands, and Belize. Eventually, they diversify by logging local hardwoods for export.

1643: Honduran gold is shipped to Spain out of the port city of Trujillo. The port suffers frequent attacks from British and Dutch pirates. In 1643, the city is sacked and destroyed by Dutch privateers. Trujillo is not rebuilt until 1787.

1821: The Mexican Revolution eliminates Spanish authority in the region. All of Central America declares its independence from Spain.

1822: All of Central America is claimed by the Mexican Empire, but Mexican control never reaches as far south as Honduras.

1823: Central America breaks away from Mexico. Honduras joins the new Central American Federation, which is led by a Honduran, General Francisco Morazán. But the Federation is rent by factional disputes between conservatives and liberals.

1838: The Central American Federation dissolves, and Honduras declares its independence on 5 November 1838. Honduras becomes one of the five independent successor states of the Federation.

Factional fighting continues within Honduras, resulting in political instability for the next 50 years.

1860: The UK cedes the island of Ruatan to Honduras. US mercenary leader William Walker, who had previously conquered Nicaragua, attempts to capitalize on the situation by leading the Ruatan natives against Honduras. But UK warships thwart his scheme, so Walker decides to invade the Honduran mainland instead. He lands his small force of men at Trujillo and captures the Trujillo fort, but the UK lands marines and forces Walker to surrender. The British turn Walker over to the Hondurans, who execute him.

1876: Marco Aurelio Soto takes the office of president. His skill and ability bring relative peace to Honduras for the first time in the nation's independent existence. His successor, Luis Brográn, continues to modernize Honduras after being elected in 1883. But another period of violence breaks out in 1891.

1910: Sam (the Banana Man) Zemurray, a naturalized US citizen, buys 15,000 acres of Honduran land near the Caribbean coast. This marks the beginning of foreign agricultural domination of Honduras—the point at which Honduras becomes a "banana republic." The very next year, Zemurray helps to overthrow an unfriendly Liberal Honduran government. He hires mercenary Lee Christmas to enforce his will. Lee Christmas later becomes commander-in-chief of the entire Honduran Army.

1913: Bananas account for 66% of Honduran agricultural exports. Competing foreign-owned agricultural companies ally themselves with different Honduran political factions. The United Fruit Company (which eventually became United Brands) sides with the Honduran Nationalist Party. Zemurray's Cuyamel Fruit Company allies itself with the Liberal Party. When necessary, the owners prevail upon the United States to send troops to Honduras to protect their holdings. Zemurray's company is bought by United Fruit in 1929.

1933: General Tiburcio Carías Andino imposes peace on Honduras. Little progress is made toward solving Honduran problems during his 16-year dictatorship.

1949: The next president, Juan Manuel Gálvez, enacts moderate reforms. Some political freedoms are granted, despite the objections of the military and landowners.

1954: A general strike is called against the United Fruit Company. Some concessions are granted, but the strike's greater significance is in the unified opposition of Central Americans to the foreign corporations that have controlled their economies for decades.

1963: Colonel Osvaldo López Arrellano takes power in a military coup. During a second term in office, he is forced to resign in 1975 from the presidency over revelations that he has accepted $1.25 million in bribes from United Brands.

1969: Tensions between Honduras and El Salvador break out into the 100-hour "Soccer War." While the fighting quickly ends, the two countries do not sign a peace treaty until 1980.

1980s: Nicaragua and El Salvador suffer civil war, flooding Honduras with refugees. As a US ally, Honduras serves as a staging area for US-trained Contras.

1985: Honduras manages to hold elections. Instead of the winner, the second-place candidate, José Simeón Azcona del Hoyo, is installed as president.

1988: As the US continues to train Nicaraguan and Salvadoran troops in Honduras, many Hondurans become fed up with the US presence in their country. Huge anti-US demonstrations take place in Tegucigalpa and San Pedro Sula. President Azcona demands that foreign troops leave Honduras.

1990: Rafael Leonardo Callejas Romero becomes president. As the Nicaraguan war ends, the loss of US funds into Honduras results in economic dislocation in the region.

1994: Reform candidate Carlos Roberto Reina becomes president. He prosecutes his predecessor, President Callejas, for taking bribes. Anti-corruption measures are initiated, with mixed success.

HONDURAN BEHAVIOR

"LA LEY ES DURO, PERO ES LA LEY" ("The law is hard, but it is the law")

—A sign on the jail in Trujillo, Honduras.

On the character of Honduras' two business centers:

1. *Tegucigalpa*

   The largest city in Honduras, Tegucigalpa has been the country's capital since 1880. The name *Tegucigalpa* means "silver hill" in the local dialect; the city achieved prominence due to the gold and silver mines nearby. Most Hondurans shorten the capital's five-syllable name to *Tegus* (pronounced "TEY-goose"). Many Honduran corporations have their offices in Tegucigalpa.

   The streets tend to be narrow, resulting in daily traffic jams. The city is very noisy: Most buses do not have mufflers, and taxis summon riders by honking their horns.

   Across the river is the working-class suburb of Comayagüela.

2. *San Pedro Sula*

   The second-largest city in Honduras, San Pedro Sula is also the nation's business center. San Pedro Sula is the fastest-growing city in Central America. It also has the highest incidence of AIDS in Central America. The streets are based on a grid pattern, making it much easier to navigate than the maze of Tegucigalpa's streets.

Most large businesses not headquartered in Tegucigalpa are based in San Pedro Sula. The city is a true boom town, summoning the future while paying scant heed to the past.

Why are Hondurans the way they are?

Honduras has been dominated by foreign entities for most of its existence. The breakup of the Central American Federation did not protect Honduras from interference by its neighbors. Honduras suffered intervention from both Guatemala and Nicaragua. The Caribbean Coast of Honduras has often been dominated by outsiders. Even as the British retreated to British Honduras (which is now called Belize), US companies took over huge tracts of land for banana plantations. The plantation owners ran their lands as independent fiefdoms. They also made sure that Honduras had governments that favored the foreign countries. When necessary, they enforced their position with private mercenaries or by summoning the US marines.

It's no wonder that Hondurans see the Amerindian chief Lempira as a national hero, since he led 30,000 warriors against the Spanish in 1537.

Between foreign intervention and no tradition of self-determination, Honduras' chaotic political history is not surprising.

What do visitors notice about Honduras?

Most visitors notice two things—the country's poverty and its natural beauty. Many people expect Honduras to be the next big destination for ecotourism. Properly handled, this should help to enrich the Honduran poor.

HOW CAN I FIND MORE INFORMATION ABOUT HONDURAS?

Here are a few resources to start with:

Getting Through Customs' Web site at **http://www.getcustoms.com** tracks current holidays in Honduras. They also post Cultural I.Q. Quizzes, gift-giving guidelines, a demo of the PASSPORT database, and further international information. Telephone: (610) 353-9894; fax (610) 353-6994.

Embassy of Honduras
3007 Tilden Street NW
Washington, DC 20008
Telephone: (202) 966-7702

Honduras on the Internet—Internet resources about Honduras and its culture, businesses, government and economy. **http://www.latinworld.com/countries/honduras/**

The International Academy at Santa Barbara at **http://www.iasb.org/cwl** publishes *Current World Leaders,* an excellent resource for data on political leaders and parties in Honduras. Telephone: (800) 530-2682 or (805) 965-5010 for subscription information.

The Bureau of Consular Affairs at **http://travel.state.gov** can give you detailed information on obtaining passports, visa requirements, and consular affairs bulletins.

The Center for Disease Control at **http://www.cdc.gov/** provides valuable medical information, as well as information on any outbreaks of virulent infections in Honduras.

Like all Web sites, the preceding Internet addresses are subject to change, and there is no guarantee that they will continue to provide the data we list here.

Mexico

WHAT'S YOUR CULTURAL I.Q.?

1. TRUE or FALSE? The Aztecs are considered the oldest Amerindian civilization in Mexico.

   ANSWER: False. The Aztecs actually represent the last great Amerindian civilization. The Aztec Empire was predated by the Mayans, who in turn followed the Olmecs.

2. The Spanish conquistador Hernán Cortés, was assisted in his conquest of Mexico by which of the following?

   a. Superior military technology, including armor, guns, and the use of the horse

   b. The legend of the Aztec god-king Quetzalcóatl

   c. Political infighting between the Amerindian tribes

   d. Smallpox

   e. All of the above

   ANSWER: e. All of these factors helped. Certainly, the most surprising was the resemblance of Cortés to the mythological god-king Quetzalcóatl, who was expected to return in 1519—the very year Cortés arrived.

3. TRUE or FALSE? In the 18th century, the Philippines were nominally ruled by Mexico.

    ANSWER: True. Mexico (then known as the Viceregency of New Spain) exercised nominal control over a huge area, including all of Central America down to Panama, the southwestern United States (including California), several Caribbean islands, and the Spanish colony of the Philippines. In practice, however, Mexico was too distant for direct control of the Philippines.

4. The famous *Grito de Dolores* of 1810 is:

    a. A speech calling for Mexican independence

    b. The Mexican national dish

    c. The edict which Napoleon used to depose King Carlos IV of Spain

    d. The last words of Emperor Maximilian of Mexico

    ANSWER: a. Father Miguel Hildago, the parish priest of Dolores, Mexico, called for independence in a sermon given on 16 September 1810. This speech, known as the *Grito de Dolores* (Cry from Dolores), became one of the most famous speeches in Mexican history.

5. Military leader Antonio López de Santa Anna seized the presidency of Mexico no less than 11 times! TRUE or FALSE? Santa Anna is remembered as Mexico's greatest and most successful military leader.

    ANSWER: False. Actually, during Santa Anna's tenure, Mexico lost half its territory to the United States of America. Santa Anna first lost the Texas War of Independence, the US–Mexican War, and signed away southern Arizona and New Mexico in the Gadsden Purchase.

6. In October of 1861, a compact known as the Convention of London would have far-reaching effects on Mexico. What was the Convention of London?

   a. An agreement between the UK and Mexico
   to build a Mexican railway

b. An agreement between the UK, France, and Spain to seize Mexican
   import duties to pay for defaulted Mexican loans

   c. The first Shriner's convention in the UK

ANSWER: b. Mexico was bankrupt in 1861, so President Benito Juárez suspended payment of Mexico's foreign debt. The Convention of London was an agreement among the UK, France, and Spain to seize the Mexican customs house at the port of Veracruz until they collect their unpaid debts. But France went even further—French troops occupied Mexico City and installed Archduke Maximilian of Austria as Emperor of Mexico. Maximilian was deposed and executed in 1867.

7. The Mexican Revolution lasted from 1910 to 1920 and cost over a million Mexican lives. TRUE or FALSE? Opposing the Mexican Constitutional Government were radical leaders like Pancho Villa and Emiliano Zapata.

ANSWER: True. The USA supported the Constitutionalists, who had their capital at Veracruz, while Pancho Villa and Emiliano Zapata roamed the countryside and even occupied Mexico City. But the Constitutionalists eventually won.

8. Which of the following Mexican authors won a Nobel Prize for Literature?

a. Carlos Fuentes

b. Jorge Ibargüengoitia

c. Octavio Paz

d. Diego Rivera

e. None of the above

ANSWER: c. Octavio Paz won the 1990 Nobel Prize for Literature. Diego Rivera is not a writer; he was Mexico's most famous painter of murals. The other two men are renown Mexican authors.

9. TRUE or FALSE? Mexican businesspeople expect firm and extended eye contact from their business partners.

ANSWER: False. Actually, a steady gaze is considered an aggressive challenge in Mexico. Don't worry about "looking them in the eye" to appear trustworthy—use an intermittent gaze rather than a steady one.

10. *Gacetillas* are commissioned by the Mexican government, political parties, businesses, and even individuals. A *gacetilla* is:

a. A fiesta

b. A work of art, such as a painting or sculpture

c. An advertising campaign featuring a well-known celebrity

d. A favorable publicity piece disguised as a news story

ANSWER: d. The low wages paid to journalists and editors makes them susceptible to writing such publicity pieces. The Mexican government is the biggest buyer of *gacetillas*. The *gacetilla* is not illegal, even though it is disguised as a legitimate news story and runs alongside other stories—often on page one of a newspaper.

QUOTATIONS ABOUT MEXICO

"Poor Mexico—so far from God, so close to the United States."

—Attributed to Mexican Dictator Porfirio Díaz, who first came to power in 1876.

"In the thirty years of his widely censured reign, Porfirio Díaz built up a military establishment and an army three or four times the size of today's, which paraded every Independence Day to the cheers of the people. The officers went to France to learn le cran *and to Germany to learn whatever it was the Prussians knew in those days. At the conclusion of the Boer War, Díaz hired two or three of their generals . . . The Mexican infantry was the first to use an automatic rifle, the Swiss-made Mondragon . . .*

"All this collapsed with the Constitutional Revolution of 1913. The officers educated in France and Germany, the Boer generals, and the infantry with their shiny Mondragons—all were literally pulverized by a revolutionary army under Obregón, a farmer; under Pancho Villa, a cattle-rustler; under Venustiano Carranza, a politician; and I don't know what Pablo González was in real life, but he had every appearance of being a practicing notary public."

—From the "Explanatory Note" prefacing the novel *The Lightning of August* by Jorge Ibargüengoitia.

"Riding proudly on his horse, Demetrio felt like a new man. His eyes recovered their peculiar metallic brilliance, and the blood flowed, red and warm, through his coppery, pure-blooded Aztec cheeks.

"The men threw out their chests as if to breathe the widening horizon, the immensity of the sky, the blue from the mountains and the fresh air, redolent with the various odors of the sierra. They spurred their horses to a gallop as if in that mad race they laid claims of possession to the earth. What man among them now remembered the stern chief of police, the growling policeman, or the conceited cacique? What man remembered his pitiful hut where he slaved away, always under the eyes of the owner or the ruthless and sullen foreman, always forced to rise before dawn, and to take up his shovel, basket, or goad, wearing himself out to earn a mere pitcher of atole and a handful of beans?"

—From Mariano Azuela's classic novel of the Mexican Revolution, *The Underdogs.*

"The Holy Week Festival really begins on the Friday of Dolores, the Friday before Palm Sunday. To the villagers the word 'festival' signifies a certain easing of isolation and severity in their daily lives; work stops, special dishes are prepared, people spend the whole day in church or taking part in processions, visitors come from other villages, stalls are set up in front of the church and on street corners."

—From the novel *The Edge of the Storm* by Agustín Yáñez.

"Everything is slow in Mexico, but not because Mexicans cannot do things quickly. Everything is slow because the passage of time is less noticeable. Time is flat: too frequently nothing changes with time, and the sense of its going by—the reason for putting a premium on it—is absent.

From the simple and obvious explanation—much of Mexico is a region with no seasons, except when it rains and when it doesn't, and in the countryside the dry season is basically devoted to waiting for rain—to the more complex, time in Mexico is not what it is in the United States. Time divides our two countries, as much as any other single factor.

"One of the most obvious implications of this difference—which actually pertains to much of Latin America, particularly in those nations with a strong pre-Columbian heritage—is that immediate responses, rapid cause-and-effect relationships, are rare. Time lags, delayed reactions, an often incomprehensible patience, tend to be much more common. Quick causes are not always matched by equally quick effects. On many occasions, the effect is simply slow in coming: it will happen, in time."

—From *The Mexican Shock: Its Meaning for the United States* by political scientist Jorge G. Castañeda.

"Mexicans know that a party has been outstandingly successful if at the end of it there are at least a couple of clusters of longtime or first-time acquaintances leaning on each other against a wall, sobbing helplessly . . . A true celebrant of the Mexican fiesta will typically progress along a path that leads from compulsive joke-telling to stubborn argumentativeness to thick-tongued foolery, all in pursuit of a final, unchecked, absolving wash of tears . . . "

—From the essay collection *The Heart That Bleeds: Latin America Now* by Mexican author Alma Guillermoprieto.

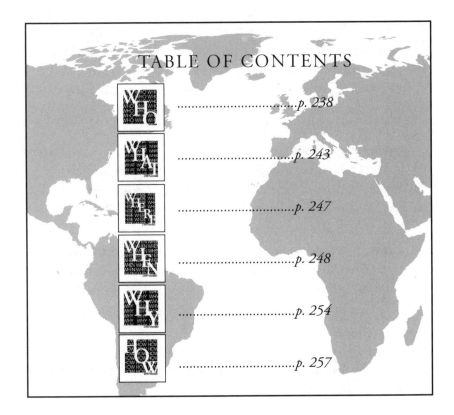

TABLE OF CONTENTS

THE MEXICANS

The majority of Mexicans have some degree of Amerindian ancestry. About 60.0% of Mexicans are mestizo (mixed Amerindian and European descent) and 30.0% are considered *indígenia* (Amerindian). Only some 9.0% of Mexicans are entirely of European descent, but they have traditionally made up the wealthiest and most powerful class. The remaining 1.0% encompasses a wide range of people, from blacks to Asians.

The difference between mestizo and *indígena* is often one of language and culture rather than genetics. Mexico's National Indigenous Institute (INI) recognizes less than 10% of Mexicans as *indígenas,* which they define as persons speaking an Amerindian language. However, many Mexicans who no longer speak an Amerindian language consider themselves *indígenas.* A 1991 amendment to the Mexican constitution declares the right of Mexico's indigenous peoples to preserve their languages and cultural traditions.

HOW TO TELL MEXICO AND THE MEXICANS FROM THEIR NEIGHBORS

Mexico is the most populous Spanish-speaking nation in Latin America. Only Portuguese-speaking Brazil has more people (or a larger Gross National Product).

1. Mexico is currently one of the three partners in the North American Free Trade Agreement, NAFTA. In a comparison of the three NAFTA nations, Mexico is the poorest nation, but it has more people than Canada (monetary figures in US dollars):

	Population (1995)	GNP (1993)	Per capita income (1993)
Mexico:	93,985,848	$324,950,000,000	$3,750
USA:	263,814,032	$6,385,320,000,000	$24,750
Canada:	28,434,545	$574,880,000,000	$20,670

2. Mexico shares a long border with the United States of America. To the south, Mexico borders Guatemala and Belize.

3. Historically, Mexico has had a dominant relationship over many other countries. After independence from Spain, the Mexican Empire claimed all of Central America down to the Panamanian border. In other words, Mexico briefly annexed Costa Rica, Nicaragua, Honduras, El Salvador, and Guatemala (which itself claimed remote Belize). However, Mexico's influence did not end there. The Spanish Empire ruled the remote Philippines through Mexico. And, of course, much of the southwestern USA was once part of Mexico.

LITERATURE

Mexico is now the leading producer of Spanish-language literature in the Americas. Mexico has a long and proud tradition of writers.

Rosario Castellanos (1925–74) grew up on her family estate near Mexico's border with Guatemala. Her fiction and poetry often examined the conflict between Mexico's Amerindian and Spanish heritage. Her first novel, *Bahún-Canán,* was published in 1957 (and was translated into English as *The Nine Guardians* in 1959). She worked with Mayans in the Chiapas region, and was so moved by them that she gave her family lands back to the Indians. She published more than 20 books in her long career. She was serving as Mexico's ambassador to Israel when she died, tragically, in an electrical accident in Tel Aviv.

Carlos Fuentes (1928–) is the son of a Mexican ambassador and grew up around the world. His first language was not Spanish but English, which he learned while his father was stationed in Washington, DC. After earning a degree in law in Mexico City, he opted instead for a career as a writer and educator. *La región más transparente,* his first novel, was published in 1958 (published in English in 1960 as *Where the Air is Clear*). Over a dozen of his books have been translated into English. His 1986 novel *Gringo viejo* (1986 English version: *The Old Gringo*) was made into a film in 1989 staring Gregory Peck and Jane Fonda. The recipient of many awards, Fuentes is one of the most successful writers in Latin America.

Jorge Ibargüengoitia (1928–83) was a renowned playwright and poet. His 1963 first novel (published in English as *The Lightning of August*) was a tremendously popular satire on the Mexican revolution. Out of favor with the Mexican authorities, he spent years teaching at universities in the United States before moving to Paris. He died in an airplane crash in 1983.

Octavio Paz (1914–) is Mexico's most honored living writer, having won the 1990 Nobel Prize for Literature. The son of a Mexico City lawyer, he first attracted attention for his antifascist articles written during the Spanish Civil War. Returning to Mexico, he then cofounded two leftist literary magazines. He has taught around the world and served as Mexico's ambassador to India from 1962 to 1968. While his writing encompasses a vast array of themes and topics, his poetry is primarily erotic. His 1950 essay, *El laberinto de la soledad* (translated into English in 1961 as *The Labyrinth of Solitude*), is still considered an important work on the Mexican character.

LIGHTS! CAMERA! ACTION!

Many films have been produced in Mexico, from expensive, internationally renown spectacles to low-budget monster films featuring masked wrestlers and an ambulatory Aztec mummy. The film studios in Mexico City are also used by foreign film companies (David Lynch's 1984 version of the science fiction classic *Dune* was filmed there).

1. **Like Water for Chocolate**   In this wildly successful *magical realism* comedy, Tita, the youngest daughter in a very traditional family, must forego her dreams to stay home and care for her aged mother. Tita sublimates her desires in her cooking, and finds that her food has a magical effect on those who eat it (1992, directed by Alfonso Arau).

2. **Mexican Bus Ride**   This film follows the surrealistic adventures of a naive young man on a mission—to fetch the family lawyer at the request of his dying mother. Also released under the English title *Ascent to Heaven* (1951, directed by Luis Bruñel).

3. **Old Gringo**   This is an English-language film rather than a Mexican one, but it is set in Revolutionary Mexico. The Old Gringo of the title is pioneering

writer-journalist Ambrose Bierce (portrayed by Gregory Peck), who vanished in Mexico in December 1913. Jimmy Smits plays Pancho Villa and Jane Fonda is a woman who becomes involved with both men. The film is based on the 1986 novel *Gringo viejo* by Carlos Fuentes (1989, directed by Luis Puenzo).

4. **Santa Sangre**   This bizarre offering is by the director of the violent cult classic *El Topo* (currently unavailable on video). *Santa Sangre* depicts the nightmarish upbringing of a young man in a Mexican circus. Driven mad by the violent acts of his parents, the young man escapes from an asylum and goes on a killing spree with his maimed mother. The director's hallucinogenic imagery has more of an impact than the confused plot (1990, directed by Alejandro Jodorowsky).

LANGUAGE

Ever since the conquistadores achieved supremacy in Mexico, the official language has been Spanish. However, for many years the Mexican ruling class affected French as the tongue of the cultured.

English is now the foreign language of choice among Mexican executives, and an English-speaker is usually close at hand in most urban business settings.

Indigenous languages are a political issue in Mexico, because the Mexican National Indigenous Institute (INI) uses language to designate a Mexican as an Amerindian. The indigenous languages of Mexico include Nahua (about 1.4 million speakers), Mayan, Yokokatane (an offshoot of Mayan), Zapotec, Mixtec, and others.

Linguists have categorized 243 different languages spoken in modern Mexico—*Ethnologue: Languages of the World,* 12th Edition from their Web site at (http://www.sil.org/ethnologue/ethnologue. html).

BUSINESS IN MEXICO

Mexico may be in NAFTA, but that doesn't mean that the business culture is the same in the USA and Mexico. One noticeable difference involves eye contact. US executives expect to make extended eye contact; someone who does not directly meet your gaze is suspected of being untrustworthy. Mexicans find continued, intense eye contact to be aggressive and threatening. Mexican business executives expect intermittent eye contact.

BUSINESS SUCCESS IN MEXICO

NAFTA

"The only thing that is not negotiable is the virginity of the Virgin of Guadalupe. That stays. Everything else is on the table."

—Attributed to a senior official in the Mexican Ministry of Finance, circa 1990.

The North American Free Trade Agreement (NAFTA) continues to facilitate trade between Mexico, the United States, and Canada. Despite difficult economic straits in Mexico, the US exported over $60 billion dollars worth of goods into Mexico in 1996.

Regulations for doing business in Mexico have become very similar to doing business in the USA. The main restriction placed on foreign firms is in selling to the Mexican government. Only Mexican firms may submit bids to the government (although Mexican subsidiaries of foreign-owned firms are permitted to bid).

All the standard methods for conducting business are present in Mexico, including franchising, joint ventures, local distribution, and outright foreign ownership of manufacturing and distribution outlets. Nevertheless, the use of a local representative is recommended.

Successful advertising campaigns take local cultural traditions into account. Furthermore, they must be designed specifically for Mexico. Without adaptation, campaigns cannot be successfully transferred from other markets, including such Spanish-speaking markets as Spain, Puerto Rico, or South America.

Despite the widespread knowledge of English among international business executives, all materials should be translated into Spanish.

NEGOTIATIONS IN MEXICO

Although some patterns of US-style business practices are becoming more common, Mexican business is still done on a personal basis. It can be difficult to get anything done without a network of contacts who trust and respect you. Courtesy is important, but remember that formal courtesy can conceal one's true feelings.

LEGAL AFFAIRS IN MEXICO

Revolutionary leader and former president of Mexico, Benito Juárez was one of the most important figures in the development of Mexican law. His judicial reforms were so extensive that they became known as the *Ley Juárez* (Law Juárez). Before his appointment as Justice Minister of Mexico, officials of both the Catholic Church and the military could not be tried for crimes in civil courts. By subjecting the Church to civil authority, he began the first of the reform laws that eventually removed the Church's privileged position in Mexico. Juárez is credited with the motto *El respeto al derecho ajeno es la paz* (Respect for the rights of others is peace).

Legal reforms have not changed the basic nature of the Mexican legal code, which is based on Napoleonic law. The fundamental difference between this and British law (on which most of the US legal system is based) is that under Napoleonic law, a person is considered guilty until proven innocent.

It is still recommended that US citizens do not drive in Mexico. In addition to problems of theft and vandalism, all participants in an automotive accident in Mexico are automatically arrested and held until all concerns about damages have been resolved.

It does not matter who is at fault—all parties are arrested. (For this reason, most Mexicans involved in an auto accident try to leave before the police arrive.)

THE GACETILLA

Journalists in Mexico have traditionally been paid low wages, and often supplement their income by being paid to write about their subjects. Newspapers do the same thing on a larger scale, accepting pay for running a story. Such stories are little more than a paid advertisement disguised as a news item. Such paid stories are called *gacetillas*. Clients are usually the government or political parties, but they are also bought by businesses and even individuals seeking to enhance their public profile. Most Mexican newspapers run a *gacetilla* on page one of every issue.

LEADING BUSINESSES IN MEXICO

The following businesses are some of the largest employers in Mexico:

Bachoco SA de CV
Celaya.
Hogs. 8,255 employees.
Bancomer SA
Mexico City.
National commercial bank. 25,700 employees.
Banco Nacional de Mexico SA
Mexico City.
National commercial bank. 31,797 employees.

CIA Nestle SA de CV
Mexico City.
Dry, condensed, and evaporated dairy products.
6,400 employees.

Cerveceria Moctezuma SA de CV
Mexico City.
Malt beverages. 5,300 employees.

Fibras Nacionales de Acrilico SA de CV
Naucalpan de Juarez.
Broadwoven fabric mills. 7,000 employees.

Grupo Embotellador de Mexico SA de CV
Mexico City.
Bottled and canned soft drinks. 12,250 employees.

ICA Construccion Urbana SA de CV
Mexico City.
Industrial building and warehouses. 5,220 employees.

Impulsora Cuenca del Papaloapan SA de CV
Papaloapan.
Sugarcane refining. 8,000 employees.

Impulsora de la Cuenca del Papaloapan SA de CV
Mexico City.
Sugarcane refining. 10,000 employees.

Industrias Bachoco SA de CV
Celaya.
Poultry slaughtering and processing. 7,700 employees.

Leche Industrializada Conasupo SA de CV
Naucalpan de Juarez.
Milk. 7,000 employees.

Sabritas SA de CV
Mexico City.
Potato chips and snacks. 8,000 employees.

Triturados Basalticos y Derivados SA de CV
Mexico City.
Highway and street construction. 6,000 employees.

The following are the largest print and broadcast media concerns in Mexico:

Emporium de Sonora SA de CV
Mexico City.
Radio broadcasting stations. 80 employees.

Grupo Acir Nacional SA de CV
Mexico City.
Radio broadcasting stations. 140 employees.

Radio Sistema Nacional SA de CV
Mexico City.
Radio broadcasting stations. 150 employees.

Televisa SA de CV
Mexico City.
Television broadcasting stations. 8,000 employees.

Television Azteca SA de CV
Mexico City.
Television broadcasting stations. 980 employees.

Televisora de Calimex SA de CV
Tijuana.
Television broadcasting stations. 305 employees.

MEXICAN GEOGRAPHY

FLAG AND MAP OF MEXICO

Mexico has used a green, white, and red tricolor flag (with vertical stripes) since its independence in 1821. However, the seal of Mexico in the center has often undergone alterations. The unchanging symbols in the seal derive from an Aztec mythological image—a snake, in the beak of an eagle, which is perched on a cactus, which grows on an island. This myth led the Aztecs to choose Mexico City as their capital (the city originally occupied an island in the middle of a lake).

MEXICO

Size: 756,066 square miles
Population: 93,985,848

Far larger than its Latin neighbors, Mexico lies between the United States (to the north) and Guatemala and Belize (to the south). Mexico has coasts on both the Caribbean and the Pacific Ocean.

MEXICAN HISTORY

Circa 800 B.C.: The Olmecs—the first identifiable civilization in Mexico—achieve supremacy in southern Mexico. Their calendar and works of art survive today.

Circa 200 B.C.: Pre-Columbian civilization reaches its "Golden Age" in Mesoamerica—an area stretching from the southern US to Nicaragua. The Mayans build large cities and temples, ruling Mesoamerica until around A.D. 900. This classic period of Amerindian development ends with the abandonment of many cities for reasons that are still unknown.

Before A.D. 1519: The tribes of Mesoamerica remain divided. Toltecs dominate the north; Mixtecs and Zapotecs fight for supremacy in the south. The central Valley of Mexico is home to several tribes, of which the Aztecs are the most fierce. The Aztecs build the city of Tenochtitlán, which will become the site of Mexico City.

1517: A Spanish expedition led by Francisco Hernández de Córdoba lands in Mexico but is driven off by hostile Amerindians. An expedition the following year is also repulsed.

1519: On orders of the governor of Cuba, Hernán Cortés leads the first European expedition to explore Mexico. After founding the settlement of Veracruz, he pursues a divide-and-conquer strategy among Amerindians tribes. Cortés is assisted by his lucky resemblance to the mythological god-king Quetzalcóatl, who is expected to return and reclaim his throne. Soon Cortés leads an army of 500 Spanish conquistadores and many thousand Totonac and Tlaxcalan warriors. The Aztec king, Moctezuma II, welcomes Cortés into Tenochtitlán, but the Aztecs soon resent the gold-hungry Spanish.

1520: After months of Spanish occupation of the island center of Tenochtitlán, the Aztecs finally attack. Moctezuma II, held hostage by the Spanish, is killed—perhaps by his own angry subjects. On 30 June 1520, the Spanish fight their way out along the causeways connecting the island to the mainland, an event commemorated as the *Noche Triste* (Sad Night). Many Spanish are slain.

1521: Leading a reinforced army of 900 Spanish and as many as 100,000 Amerindians, Cortés conquers Tenochtitlán, the seat of the Aztec Empire. The new colony, called *Nueva España* (New Spain), is organized. The Amerindians, now decimated by smallpox, are enslaved.

1528: King Charles V of Spain removes Cortés as governor. New Spain is governed by a council called an *audiencia,* led by a viceroy based in Mexico City. Spanish policy encourages mining and agriculture but forbids manufacturing, so that Mexico is forced to import manufactured goods from Spain.

1540s: Silver deposits are found to the north of Mexico City in Zacatecas. In the south, the Yucatán Peninsula is finally conquered.

1700: The Viceroyalty of New Spain reaches its largest extent. Its authority now encompasses all of Central America down to Panama, the southwestern US (including California), several Caribbean islands, and the Spanish colony of the Philippines. In practice, however, Mexico has only nominal control over such distant reaches.

1804: The Spanish government tries to check the immense influence of the Catholic Church in Mexico by demanding control over some Church funds. The Church calls upon Mexicans for more money, increasing discontent with both the Church and Spanish rule.

1808: Napoleon invades Spain and replaces King Carlos IV with his brother. Mexicans are divided on giving allegiance to the new king. Father Miguel Hildago, the parish priest of Dolores, Mexico, starts an independence movement. His call for independence, known as the *Grito de Dolores* (Cry from Dolores), delivered on 16 September 1810, is one of the most famous speeches in Mexican history. Hildago soon leads rebels against the Viceregal forces, but he is captured and executed in 1811.

1810–21: Mexican independence is achieved after 11 years of rebellion. But the new nation is not a republic but a monarchy, angering many of the rebels. A defector from the Spanish Viceregency, Colonel Augustín de Iturbide has himself inaugurated as first Emperor of Mexico in 1822. He is forced to abdicate by military leader Antonio López de Santa Anna after only nine months.

1824: A Mexican Constitution is approved, establishing the Republic of Mexico. Guadalupe Victoria becomes Mexico's first president. While the Empire of Mexico claimed all of Central America down to Panama, the Republic's southern border extends only as far as Guatemala.

1828: Santa Anna again intervenes in Mexico's leadership, forcing the acceptance of his candidate. Hailed as a military hero, Santa Anna himself seizes the presidency in 1833. During the next 22 years, Santa Anna occupies the presidency no less than 11 separate times.

1835–36: Texas successfully achieves independence from Mexico, after the defeat of Santa Anna's forces at the Battle of San Jacinto.

1840s: A revolt of Amerindians against their Mexican overlords in Yucatán almost drives the Mexicans out of the peninsula. The conflict becomes known as the War of the Castes.

1846–48: When Mexico protests the admission of Texas into the United States of America, the US Congress declares war. Mexico's forces are easily defeated, and the USA annexes the Mexican territory west of Texas. This Mexican territory now forms all or part of the states of California, Nevada, Utah, Colorado, Arizona, and New Mexico.

1853: To facilitate the building of a railroad, the USA purchases a slice of land from Mexico. Known as the Gadsden Purchase, this land is now part of southernmost Arizona and New Mexico. Anger over this final loss of Mexican land results in the final removal of Santa Anna from power in 1855.

1858–61: The conflict between conservatives and liberals erupts into civil war in Mexico. Known as the War of Reform, the liberals emerge as victors, enabling them to enforce the liberal constitution of 1857.

1861: Facing a bankrupt treasury, Mexican President Benito Juárez suspends payment of Mexico's foreign debt. In October 1861, England, France, and Spain sign the Convention of London, in which they agree to jointly occupy the Mexican customshouse at the port of Veracruz until they collect their unpaid debt.

1862: Under the ambitious Napoleon III, France decides to conquer all of Mexico. Napoleon restores the Mexican monarchy and places Archduke Maximilian of Austria on the throne. But French forces never defeat the Mexican rebels in the rural areas.

1866: After the USA's Civil War ends, it is again in a position to demand the removal of French forces from Mexico under the

Monroe Doctrine. As the French troops retreat, the unpopularity of Maximilian's rule becomes apparent, but he refuses to abdicate. The rebels, under Benito Juárez, defeat the remaining Imperial forces in May 1867. Maximilian is executed by firing squad the next month. Juárez returns to the presidency and continues his reforms.

1876–1911: Porfirio Díaz first comes to power in 1876. For the next 34 years, he rules Mexico either directly as president or indirectly through his proxies. This period, known as the *Porfiriato,* marked Mexico's entry into the industrial age. Railroads, telegraph, and telephone lines were built. But there was little political freedom under the "Order and Progress" of the *Porfiriato.*

1910: Opposition to the dictatorship of the *Porfiriato,* often organized in exile in the USA, erupts into strikes in 1910. Violent government suppression only leads to more violence. Díaz jails opposition candidate Francisco Madero during the 1910 presidential elections. Freed from jail, he reluctantly leads the growing rebellion, which officially begins on 20 November 1910. (This is now commemorated as the Revolution Day Holiday.)

1911: As the rebellion becomes widespread under such rebel leaders as Pancho Villa and Pascual Orozco, Díaz resigns and Madero is elected President. But Madero is unable to control the rebel factions, some of whom—like Emiliano Zapata—call for more radical solutions to Mexico's problems.

1913: Madero is assassinated in February 1913. His successors are no more successful at maintaining order. Mexico's leaders are divided into two camps: the Constitutionalists and the Radicals. The Constitutionalists hold Veracruz and are recognized by the US as Mexico's legitimate rulers. But the Radicals, such as Pancho Villa and Zapata, rule Mexico City and much of the countryside, where their demands for land redistribution are popular with the poor.

1917: Slowly, the Constitutionalists gain the upper hand. They write a new constitution (still in force today) and select Venustiano Carranza as president. Carranza is assassinated in 1920, but by then most of his rivals (including Zapata) have also been killed. The 10 years of Revolution between 1910 and 1920 cost the lives of almost one out of every eight Mexicans.

1920: President Alvaro Obregón initiates Mexico's reconstruction. In 1924 he is succeeded as president by Plutarco Elías Calles, who continues rebuilding Mexico. Calles' policies include opposition to the Catholic Church. He closes monasteries and deports foreign priests, leading to the Cristero Rebellion. This revolt by Catholic peasants is not subdued until 1929. After his term of office ends in 1928, Calles forms the first strong Mexican political party—the forerunner of today's ruling Institutional Revolutionary Party (PRI).

1934: Lázaro Cárdenas is elected president, and undertakes a massive land redistribution program. In 1938 he nationalizes all foreign oil interests in Mexico. These various oil companies are combined to create Petróleos Mexicanos, a.k.a. Pemex. This expropriation causes foreign investors to shun Mexico, but the economy booms with the advent of World War II.

1968: Mexico's postwar economic boom is accompanied by a population boom. As the nation's population doubles, the poor leave their small farms and move to the cities. They watch unhappily as millions are spent to host the 1968 Summer Olympics (the first ever held in a third-world country) in Mexico City. Shortly before the Olympics, a half-million people rally in Mexico City to protest worsening conditions and political oppression. Fearing that the protests will hinder the Olympics, the government sends troops to quell the protests. Several hundred protesters are killed.

1977: After suffering a stalled economy and a devaluation of the peso, the Arab oil boycott causes oil prices to rise. Oil-rich Mexico booms. But the government's spending far outstrips its income, and it borrows heavily from foreign lenders.

1981: The oil boom goes bust. Billions of dollars in debt, Mexico is forced to initiate an austerity program just when its economy is slumping.

1988: A Harvard-educated technocrat, Carlos Salinas de Gortari, is elected President in a disputed election. He quickly gains popularity with anti-corruption campaigns and reestablishing relations between Mexico and the Vatican. Privatization measures give a boost to the economy. Salinas also signs the North American Free Trade Agreement (NAFTA), which is known in Mexico as Tratado de Libre Comercio (TLC).

1994: The day that NAFTA goes into effect, some 2,000 Amerindian and Mestizo rebels attack in the southern state of Chiapas. Calling themselves the Zapatista National Liberation Army, they seize several towns. While they are soon driven out by the Mexican Army, their actions show that millions of Mexicans still feel disenfranchised. In an unrelated act of violence, Salinas' hand-picked successor, Luis Donaldo Colosio, is assassinated. His replacement, Ernesto Zedillo, barely wins the presidential election. Zedillo has barely taken office when, in December of 1994, the peso plummets and Mexico suffers a financial collapse.

1995: As both domestic and foreign capital flees from Mexico, the USA guarantees Mexico's loans up to $50 billion. But Mexico has to put up its oil revenues as collateral—a highly unpopular move. A depressed economy and austerity measures again impoverish millions of Mexicans.

1997: After 70 years of one-party rule, the PRI loses its majority in elections for the lower house of Congress. Also, in the first direct elections for mayor of Mexico City, voters chose Cuauhtemoc Cardenas Solorzano (a founding leader of the Party of the Democratic Action).

MEXICAN BEHAVIOR

"Mexico is the most Spanish country in Latin America; at the same time it is the most Indian."

—From *The Labyrinth of Solitude,* Octavio Paz's seminal study of the Mexican identity.

Octavio Paz notes several differences between Mexicans and Americans.

In the United States, the predominant cultural influence came from Protestant England, and included an evolving pattern of democracy. Furthermore, at the time of the founding of the United States, its Protestant sects had little or no tradition of converting Amerindians to their beliefs. The US's Amerindians were obstacles to be overcome, not potential converts or even slaves. Paz identifies the English tradition as exclusive; colonial America shunned the heathen Indians and avoided most of their traditions.

In Mexico, the predominant cultural influence is Catholic Spain. Spain had been under Moorish occupation for centuries. The last Moors were removed from Spain in 1492, the very year of Columbus' first voyage. Spain was a fragile new nation, united only by a strong monarchy which suppressed any opposition (democratic or otherwise). The Spanish colonizers came to Mexico with no democratic ideals, only a history of authoritarianism.

Spain was the seat of the Catholic Counter-Reformation. At the time, it was the most adamantly Catholic nation in the world. Conquest could only be legitimized in the eyes of the Spanish if it was accompanied by the conversion of the natives. Following this conversion, the conquistadores became susceptible to Amerindian traditions. Mexico City is built on the ruins of the Aztec capital of Tenochtitlán. Paz considers the Spanish tradition to be inclusive.

Whether this assessment is accurate or not, many Mexicans believe it. *The Labyrinth of Solitude* is considered a seminal work in defining what it is to be Mexican.

Why are Mexicans the way they are?

If the Poles cannot be explained without considering their relationship to the Russians, the Mexicans cannot be explained without considering their relationship to the United States.

Most Mexicans are ambivalent about the United States. Time and again, the US has humiliated and dominated Mexico. The US gobbled up half of Mexico's land, sent troops into Mexico several times, and still dominates Mexico economically. Yet the United States also represents a source of wealth and political stability.

Mexicans still cherish their connection to the land, even though only one-fourth of the population now works in agriculture. One of the obstacles facing Mexican agriculture is the determination of Mexican smallholders to keep their land at all costs—even though their plots of land are too small for efficient farming. Farmers resist attempts at creating more cost-effective communal or cooperative farms. The *Tierra y Libertad* (Land and Liberty) slogan of Mexican Revolutionary Emiliano Zapata still resonates for many farmers.

What are the origins of the animosity between Mexican classes?

Aside from the obvious class divisions with whites on top and slaves (black or Amerindian) on the bottom, the Viceregency of New Spain recognized two classes of whites. *Peninsulares* were born in Spain, and made up Mexico's highest class. The Mexican-born whites, called *criollos,* were accorded second place. The fact that birthplace was often the only difference between the classes infuriated many *criollos,* since a *peninsulare* did not have to be educated or of noble blood. In Mexico, the poorest Spanish-born peasant could be considered a member of the *peninsulares.*

Who are the Guadalupeños?

Although Mexico has a conflicted relationship with the Church, most Mexicans remain staunch Catholics. This tradition goes back a long way. In 1513, the Virgin Mary is said to have appeared three times to a poor Aztec boy named Juan Diego. A basilica was built on this site, and it is visited by more than one million pilgrims annually. The Virgin of Guadaloupe is seen as a symbol of unity between the Aztec and Spanish cultures, as well as a defining aspect of Mexican nationality. Many Mexicans consider themselves *Guadalupeños,* a nickname for those who believe in the miracle of Guadaloupe.

Why is nepotism so prevalent in Mexico?

The family is the single most important institution in Mexico. Nepotism is an accepted practice. Mexican executives generally put a higher importance on the best interest of their families than on the company they work for.

HOW CAN I FIND MORE INFORMATION ABOUT MEXICO?

Here are a few resources to start with:

Getting Through Customs' Web site at **http://www. getcustoms.com** tracks current holidays in Mexico. They also post Cultural I.Q. Quizzes, gift-giving guidelines, a demo of the PASSPORT database, and further international information. Telephone: (610) 353-9894; fax (610) 353-6994.

Embassy of Mexico
1911 Pennsylvania Avenue NW
Washington, DC 20006
Telephone: (202) 728-1600

The Mexican Consulate in New York City maintains a Web site:
http://quicklink.com/mexico/.

The United States Information Service (USIS) office in Mexico City has a Web site at:
http://www.usia.gov/posts/mexico_df.html.

Mexico Government Tourist Office
405 Park Ave., Suite 1401
New York, NY 10022
Telephone: (212) 755-7261; fax: (212) 753-2874

Mexico on the Internet—Informative site on Mexico. **http://www.latinworld.com/countries/mexico/**

The International Academy at Santa Barbara at **http://www.iasb.org/cwl** publishes *Current World Leaders,* an excellent resource for data on political leaders and parties in Mexico. Telephone: (800) 530-2682 or (805) 965-5010 for subscription information.

The Bureau of Consular Affairs at **http://travel.state.gov** can give you detailed information on obtaining passports, visa requirements, and consular affairs bulletins.

The Center for Disease Control at **http://www.cdc.gov/** provides valuable medical information, as well as information on any outbreaks of virulent infections in Mexico.

Like all Web sites, the preceding Internet addresses are subject to change, and there is no guarantee that they will continue to provide the data we list here.

Nicaragua

WHAT'S YOUR CULTURAL I.Q.?

1. TRUE or FALSE? In 1522, Gil González Dávila led the first European expedition into Nicaragua's interior. He discovers dense Amerindian populations around Lake Nicaragua. To pacify the area, González Dávila fought numerous bloody battles with the local Amerindians.

    ANSWER: False. The Amerindians proved to be peaceful and friendly—so much so that they voluntarily converted to Catholicism. The name Nicaragua came from their chief, Nicaro.

2. Francisco Hernández de Córdoba established Nicaragua's first two Spanish cities in 1524. These two cities later became rival centers, vying for control of Nicaragua. Which two cities are they?

    > a. Granada and Managua
    >
    > b. Managua and León
    >
    > c. León and Granada

    ANSWER: c. The rivalry between León, center of the liberals, and Granada, center of the conservatives, was so intense that it broke out into civil war several times.

3. Bluefields is a Nicaraguan port in the heart of Nicaragua's English-speaking region. TRUE or FALSE? The town of Bluefields was named after a Dutch pirate.

   ANSWER: True. The name "Bluefields" is an English corruption of "Blauvelt," a name it acquitted from a 17th-century Dutch pirate named Abraham Blauvelt. The British took control of the town in the following century.

4. The legendary US adventurer William Walker conquered Nicaragua in 1855 with a force of only 57 mercenaries. Which of the following is NOT true about Walker?

   a. He was a huge man, capable of intimidating opponents with feats of sheer strength

   b. He studied to become a physician

   c. He studied to become a lawyer

   d. He was a deeply religious man who never owned slaves, yet he made slavery legal in Nicaragua

   e. He declared himself president of Nicaragua

   ANSWER: a. Walker was many things (some of them contradictory), but he wasn't physically impressive. A slender man about 5'5" tall, he depended on his charisma and a total belief in the rightness of his cause.

5. William Walker and his men were driven out of Nicaragua in 1857. TRUE or FALSE? US financier Cornelius Vanderbilt financed the Central American forces that ousted Walker.

   ANSWER: True. Searching for funds to run Nicaragua, Walker made the mistake of taxing Cornelius Vanderbilt's Accessory Transit Company, which transported thousands of would-be prospectors across Nicaragua en route to the California gold fields. Outraged, Vanderbilt financed Conservative forces in neighboring countries, allowing a Costa Rican army to defeat Walker in 1857.

6. In an attempt to defuse the conflict between León and Granada, a new capital city was selected in 1857. The new capital, Managua, was midway between the two rival cities. What major drawback did Managua share with León?

>   a. Both cities were in seismically active zones

>   b. Both cities were uncomfortably close to the British-controlled Caribbean Coast

>   c. Unlike the rest of Catholic Nicaragua, both cities were centers of the Moravian Church

    ANSWER: a. Earthquakes virtually destroyed both cities. León was leveled in 1610, and Managua was severely damaged in 1931 and 1972. Granada, not León or Managua, was the city made wealthy by trade. And all three cities are near the Pacific, far away from the British-controlled, Moravian-dominated, Caribbean coast.

7. Both Nicaragua and Panama were considered as sites for the US-built canal. TRUE or FALSE? The US Congress voted for Panama because a Nicaraguan canal would have needed more costly digging of channels.

    ANSWER: False. In 1902, the Congress voted against Nicaragua because they were afraid of Nicaragua's volcanoes. (Nicaragua's Mount Momotombo had a major eruption before the vote.) Actually, the Nicaraguan route would have needed less digging than Panama, not more. Most of the proposed Nicaraguan route used existing rivers and lakes, so only 16 miles of channels needed to be excavated.

8. Nicaragua has had one long-lasting political dynasty, which ruled the country from 1937 to 1979. Which president founded this dynasty?

   a. Adolfo Díaz

   b. Augusto César

   c. Anastasio Somoza Garcia

   d. Daniel Ortega

   ANSWER: c. The dynasty founded by Anastasio Somoza Garcia would rule Nicaragua for 42 years. Two of his sons would become president as well, and the family amassed a huge fortune.

9. The USA has intervened in Nicaraguan affairs many times, most recently in the 1980s. TRUE or FALSE? During the administration of Ronald Reagan, the United States financed the Sandinista guerrillas in their battle with the Contras.

   ANSWER: False. It was the other way around. The United States financed the Contras against the Marxist Sandinista government.

10. Despite the country's poverty and unstable leadership, Nicaragua maintains a vibrant cultural life. What is the nickname of Nicaragua?

    a. The Land of Painters

    b. The Land of Singers

    c. The Land of Poets

ANSWER: c. Nicaraguans claim to have more poets per capita than any other nation in the world.

QUOTATIONS ABOUT NICARAGUA

"When General Walker decided to destroy Granada, yes, I was there with him. At the time, I accepted the decision just as I accepted nearly everything else he did. I had nothing to compare him with, you see. When you're young, and in a war, very little you've been taught holds, because you have nothing in life to compare to what you're doing.

"Here's how the decision came about. Every day then was confusion, and brought us a new rumor and a new panic. Granada became a pest house. Cholera, malaria, breakbone fever, and diseases even the surgeon hadn't heard of moved in. The hospital turned into a rat hole, in spite of everything Guy Sartain did to keep it together. He told the general that in another six weeks every American in Granada would be dead. The Rangers were raiding the countryside for any food they could get hold of. But the peasants shot at them, or joined the Allies and took their food with them.

"It seemed to me that the better part of the people I had known were gone away or dead. And to make it worse, the damned Costa Ricans settled their rebellion in the south and got into the fight again. They came up and took the town of Rivas back, which left us totally surrounded.

—From *The Nation Thief* by Robert Houston. Houston's novel is a fictionalized version of William Walker's invasion of Nicaragua (with just 57 mercenaries) from 1855 to 1857.

"The American Falange was marching down the road. No. I don't want to see them. What am I going to buy

tomorrow at the market? With the shortages . . . *But the mercenaries recruited in New Orleans, Charleston or Mobile continued to march under the morning sun in their pretentious uniforms. Banners were waving above the stages erected in the plaza . . . The feeble voice of William Walker drifted out over the heads of the spectators gathered in the plaza.* Why do I have to listen to him! *She covered her ears with her hands. The waves from the lake roared without muffling his voice. Speaking in English, he accepted the duties as President of Nicaragua.* To think that he came barely a year ago, in the service of the 'democrats.' And now they are the 'legitimate' ones who are in the saddle. Please explain that to me! . . . It is the 2nd of August, 1856. The second of August, 1856. The second of August!, *she repeated desperately. She wanted to hold onto the date as onto a life jacket."*

—A depiction of Walker's invasion from the point of view of a resident of Granada, from the short story "The Dog" by Nicaraguan author Lyzandro Chávez Alfaro.

> *"There's no place as bad as Puerto Cabezas in the rainstorms, when the streets turn to muddy fields. On Sunday mornings we had to leap the puddles on our way to service at the Moravian Church, set in a deserted square lined with bare oaks, clouds of mosquitoes swarming around the wooden spire. The sea is warm and oily, full of coconut tree branches swept along by the currents together with kerosene cans, broken chairs, the sea a garbage dump, one day the spongy corpse of a drowned man floated beyond the bushes . . . "*

—From the story *A Bed of Bauxite in Weipa* by Sergio Ramírez. (Puerto Cabezas is a town on the Caribbean coast—one of the few places in Nicaragua where the Moravian Church has more followers than the Catholic Church.)

> "... *There were only twenty-three people alive who could still speak it [the language of Nicaragua's Rama tribe]; the other Ramas had already lost their tongue. A French linguist had spent months with the aging twenty-three, to record the structure and phoenetics of the language before it disappeared. 'She came up against quite a problem,' Cathy told me. 'Most of the old Ramas had lost their teeth, so they couldn't pronounce some of the words properly ...' False teeth were much too expensive to be an option. Dental costs could therefore deliver the final blow to a tiny, dying language. Nicaragua is a land of small tragedies as well as large ones.*"

—From *The Jaguar Smile: A Nicaraguan Journey* by Salman Rushdie.

> "*One of the first things you notice in the port of El Bluff, three miles across the lagoon from Bluefields, is a stranded wrecked freighter painted with Ortega's campaign slogan* TODO SERÁ MEJOR. *That says it all.*
>
> "*Bluefields began in the seventeenth century as a buccaneer haven dominated by a Dutch pirate named Abraham Blauvelt. Along with Gracias a Dios and Black River in Honduras, it had become by the early eighteenth century one of the main settlements for planters and loggers from British Jamaica on the prowl for cheap acreage.*"

—From *The Fever Coast Log* by Gordon Chaplin. (The ironic campaign slogan of Daniel Ortega—the last of the Sandinista presidents—translates as "Everything will be better.")

> "*Managua, Nicaragua's capital, was a beaten-up city with seedy buildings and bullet holes. No glitz here, no*

glamour, nothing. The war had worn out everybody and everything—people, buildings, environment.

"Here was a country with 3.9 million people that had been superpowered to death, and for no decent reason."

—From *Investment Biker: Around the World with Jim Rogers* by Jim Rogers.

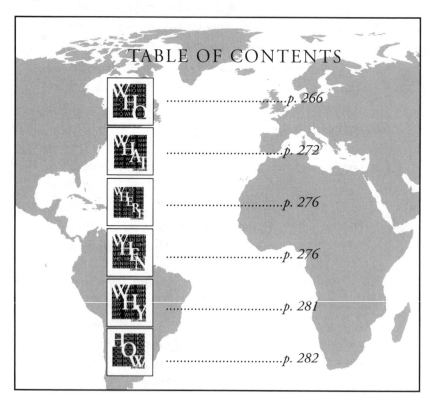

TABLE OF CONTENTS

THE NICARAGUANS

The mestizos—persons of mixed Spanish and Amerindian blood—make up the bulk of Nicaraguans at 69.0%. Some 17.0% of Nicaraguans identify themselves as being solely of European descent. About 9.0% are listed as black and 5.0% are Amerindian, but these populations are isolated from the mainstream of Nicaraguan life.

The Nicaraguans call themselves *nicas* or *pinolleros*. Other commonly used terms are *costeños* (coastal dwellers—usually referring to residents of the Atlantic coast of Nicaragua); *evangélico* (Protestant—not necessarily a member of an evangelical or charismatic sect); and *pañas* (Spaniards, from *españoles* —referring to the Spanish-descended minority that rules Nicaragua).

Under the Chamorro administration, the use of the Sandinista form of address *compañero* (comrade) was banned among government personnel. Officials were to be addressed as *señor* or *señora* (or Doctor, for those with a degree).

HOW TO TELL NICARAGUA AND THE NICARAGUANS FROM THEIR NEIGHBORS

Fiercely patriotic and enamored of debate, Nicaraguans hate being mistaken for any of their neighbors—especially their prosperous neighbors to the south, the Costa Ricans.

1. Most Nicaraguans are informal. Greetings and introductions tend to be casual. The people dress informally—suits and ties are rarely seen on men, and high heels are uncommon on women. Casual dress is appropriate for Nicaragua's climate, which is uncomfortably hot all year long.

2. Nicaraguan Spanish has many local words used only in Nicaragua. Some Nicaraguans also seem to take pride in their use of obscenities. Such words even appear on billboards and are uttered by the broadcast media.

3. Central America has frequently seen intervention by the USA's military. But only Nicaragua has suffered

occupation at the hands of a private mercenary army from the USA. The bizarre invasion of Nicaragua by William Walker is unique in Central America.

LITERATURE

Despite years of political upheaval, Nicaragua has a vibrant cultural life, spanning writing, art, and theater. Many of Nicaragua's writers have spent years away from their home country, either in exile or to seek broader opportunities. Poetry is especially popular—Nicaraguans often claim that their country has more poets (per capita) than any country in the world.

Claribél Alegría (1924–) has published 14 volumes of poetry, in addition to her fiction and nonfiction work. Always supportive of revolutionary change in Nicaragua, her work chronicles the hardships of people caught up in violence and repression. In 1987, she published *They Won't Take Me Alive,* a testimonial to the life of a Salvadoran guerrilla who was killed fighting the government. She is married to North American author Darwin J. Flakoll; they divide their time between Nicaragua and Spain.

Ernesto Cardineal (1925–) is known as Nicaragua's poet-priest, and served as Minister of Culture for the Sandinista regime. After studying in Mexico City and at Columbia University in New York, he entered a Catholic monastery in 1956 and was ordained as a Jesuit priest in 1965. (He was expelled from the Jesuits in 1984 for taking a political office.) On a visit to Cuba in 1970, he underwent a "second conversion" as a Communist. His collections—many of which have been translated into English—include *Apocalypse and Other Poems* (1977) and *Zero Hour and Other Documentary Poems* (1980).

Pablo Antonio Caruda (1916?–) is considered a contender for the Nobel Prize for Literature. While he supported the overthrow of Somoza, he soon broke with the Sandinistas. As such, he became one of the few nationally known Nicaraguan poets to oppose the Sandinista regime. His works include *The Jaguar and the Moon* (1959) and *The Promised Land* (1952).

Lyzandro Chávez Alfaro (1929–) is Nicaragua's best-known proponent of the Central American literary style known as the new narrative, which he pioneered in his first novel, *Trágame tierra,* published in 1969. This novel won Spain's Seix Barral prize. His work includes essays, fiction, and poetry. He has served as Nicaragua's ambassador to Hungary.

Rubén Darío (1867–1916) is one of the best-known Latin American poets. He began a lifelong series of travels in 1886, when he left Nicaragua for Chile. It was in Chile that he adopted the modernist style, gaining his fame as one of the most innovative poets of his time. His 1888 work *Azul (Blue)* revolutionized Latin American poetry. Continuing his travels, he visited Europe before settling in Argentina, where he published the shocking *Prosas profanas* in 1896 (translated into English as *Profane Prose* in 1922). He returned to Nicaragua several times, and died there in June of 1916. He is revered as Nicaragua's greatest poet.

Sergio Ramírez (1942–) is Nicaragua's foremost living writer of fiction. He was awarded a degree in law in 1964, then lived in exile in Costa Rica and Germany. In addition to several collections of short stories, he published a novel in 1982 entitled *¿Te dió medio la sangre?* (translated into English in 1985 as *To Bury Our Fathers*). In 1986, he provided a rare sympathetic depiction of homosexuality in Nicaragua in the short story "The Siege." Political oppression and the domination of Central America by the USA are his most enduring themes. He served as vice president of Nicaragua during the Sandinista regime.

Carlos Martínez Rivas (1924–) is considered one of the most innovative poets in Central America. However, little of his work has been translated into English. It has been said of Rivas that he hates being translated, and that he feels translation is a form of assassination. He has been a rival of poet Ernesto Cardineal for many years.

Leonel Rugama (1949–70) was a promising young author whose life and career were cut short by Nicaragua's political violence. While he wrote both prose and poetry, he is best known for a work called *The Student and the Revolution,* a manifesto he wrote at age 19. He was only 20 years old when he was killed in Managua while he was preparing to join the guerrillas in the mountains. His work is collected into a single volume, published in Nicaragua in 1978, and translated into English in 1985 as *The Earth Is a Satellite of the Moon.*

INVITATION TO THE DANCE

The Caribbean coast of Nicaragua is culturally different from the rest of the country—a fact reflected in their music. *Costeña* music is based on West Indian rhythms, which themselves are traceable to African musical traditions. *Costeña* songs are sung in a Caribbean dialect of English.

LIGHTS! CAMERA! ACTION!

Although Nicaragua itself does not have an active, major film industry, Nicaragua's stormy history has made it the focus of several motion pictures, all of them directed by foreigners.

1. **Alsino and the Condor**   This film relates the story of a young boy, Alsino, who is kidnapped from his Nicaraguan village. Alan Esquivel does a marvelous job portraying the young Alsino, caught up in Nicaragua's civil war. This film won first-place awards at film festivals in Los Angeles and Moscow (1982, directed by Miguel Littin).

2. **Pictures from a Revolution—A Memoir of the Nicaraguan Conflict**   This documentary compares

two Nicaraguas, a decade apart. A photojournalist for *The New York Times* covers Nicaragua at war in 1981, then returns a decade later to post-revolutionary Nicaragua. In the process, the film examines the entire history of the Sandinista Revolution (1991, directed by Susan Meidelas, Richard P. Rogers, and Alfred Guzzetti).

3. **The Uprising** This film depicts a young man's change from soldier to guerrilla. The protagonist, a member of Somoza's National Guard, rebels against his government's brutality and joins the Sandinistas. Filmed using actual peasants and soldiers, the film lies somewhere between documentary and cinéma vérité (1980, directed by Peter Lilienthal).

4. **Walker** This is the film version of the life of William Walker, the US mercenary leader who invaded Central America several times and declared himself President of Nicaragua in 1855. As Walker, Ed Harris imbues the central character with a mythic presence—as well as considerably more height than the real Walker, who was only 5'5" tall (1987, directed by Alex Cox).

LANGUAGE

The official language of Nicaragua is Spanish. English is the most common second language. During the Communist Sandinista regime, many foreign teachers came to Nicaragua—but since most of them were Spanish-speaking Cubans, no new languages were taught.

Linguists have categorized seven different languages spoken in modern Nicaragua—*Ethnologue: Languages in the World,* 12th Edition from their Web site at (http://www.sil.org/ethnologue/ethnologue.html).

BUSINESS IN NICARAGUA

THE KLEPTOCRACY OF NICARAGUA

Sadly, Nicaragua has a long history of corruption in high places. For much of this century, being in power meant having a license to steal—a twisted form of government sometimes known as a *kleptocracy*. After decades of legalized theft, the Somoza regime finally stepped over the line in its outrageous theft of international aid funds following the devastating 1972 earthquake. That action brought some idealistic Communist rebels, the Sandinistas, to power. Yet when the Sandinistas lost the 1990 elections, before handing over the reins of government, they looted Nicaragua's remaining assets in a spree that came to be known as the *piñata*.

BUSINESS SUCCESS IN NICARAGUA

Caveat: After over a decade of guerrilla war and instability, Nicaragua has nowhere to go but up. At the present, however, the market is small and few people have the money to purchase consumer products.

On the other hand, many of the Nicaraguans who fled their country during the 1980s have returned. They became familiar with brand-name products while in exile (especially those who lived in the United States). Returning Nicaraguans would like to purchase these brand-name products once again.

Most foreign products are currently distributed by local representatives. Nicaraguan law provides considerable protections for local agents and distributors. These protections make it difficult and expensive to switch local representatives.

Nicaragua is underserved in many types of franchises, especially in the area of fast food. Pizza Hut, Budget Rent-a-Car, and Hertz are among franchises currently operating in the country. The so-called *Nicas Ricas* (Nicaraguans who earned US dollars in the Miami area) are good target markets for US-style fast-food franchises. Nicaragua has no laws specifically regulating franchises.

Similarly, there is no current law regulating direct marketing. However, numerous obstacles to successful direct marketing exist, including a chaotic postal system and other infrastructure problems.

Nicaragua's general commercial code covers joint ventures and direct licensing agreements. Business investors may wish to register under Nicaragua's Foreign Investment Law. This law provides several benefits, notably guarantees allowing net profits to be taken out of the country. Tax abatements are negotiated on a case-by-case basis.

After years of economic stagnation, business advertising has returned to Nicaragua. (There were plenty of posters and billboards during the Sandinista years, but they were primarily political propaganda.) Billboards, along with radio and newspaper ads, are the primary media for promotion.

All business and promotional materials should be translated into Spanish for use in Nicaragua. The only exception is the Caribbean coast, where much of the population speaks a Creole dialect of English.

FREE TRADE ZONES

A free trade zone was set up outside the Managua Airport in 1991. Incentives are offered to export industries that are located in this zone. Pharmaceutical, clothing, electronics, and sporting goods industries are especially suitable to the zone.

LEGAL AFFAIRS IN NICARAGUA

Issues over property rights remain problematical in Nicaragua. Redistribution of land was a major tenet of the Sandinista regime. Furthermore, as part of the peace agreement, demobilized Sandinista guerrillas were promised land. This promise has not been fully met, causing some former guerrillas to take up arms again.

In an effort to deal with the land problem, the government evicted squatters from about 200 farms in June of 1992.

Now the new government of President Arnoldo Aleman faces the land problem from the other side. Many of Aleman's right-wing supporters are Nicaragua's former landowners. They are pressuring him for full compensation for property seized by the Sandinistas. But even if Aleman wants to offer such compensation, it is doubtful whether the Nicaraguan Congress will allow him to do so.

LEADING BUSINESSES IN NICARAGUA

The following businesses are some of the largest employers in Nicaragua:

Banco Nacional de Desarrollo
Managua.
National commercial bank. 1,200 employees.
Desarrollo Cafetalero SA
Jinotega.
Agriculture distribution. 357 employees.
Industrial Cevecera SA
Managua.
350 employees.
Instituto Nicaraguense de Telecomunicaciones y Correos
Managua.
3,492 employees.
Mena Marenco Frank
Managua.
1,100 employees.

Nicaragua Sugar Estate Ltda
Chinandega.
4,500 employees.
Pellas & Cia Sociedad General Comercial de Comercio SA F Alfredo
Managua.
300 employees.
Servico Agricola Gurdain SA
Leon.
230 employees.
Teran G Division Fotografica SA Robert
Managua.
360 employees.

The following are the largest newspapers in Nicaragua:

La Prensa
Managua.
Daily circulation: 26,000.
La Prensa is owned by the family of President Violetta Chamorro.

El Nuevo Diario
Managua.
Daily circulation: 35,000.
El Nuevo Diario is the leading independent newspaper; it tends toward sensationalism and is pro-Sandinista.

Barricada
Managua.
Daily circulation: 18,000.
Barricada is the official Sandinista newspaper.

La Tribuna
Managua.
Daily circulation: 15,000.
La Tribuna is pro-business and conservative.

NICARAGUAN GEOGRAPHY

NICARAGUA

FLAG AND MAP OF NICARAGUA

The current flag of Nicaragua originated as the flag of the short-lived Central American Federation, which featured horizontal blue, white, and blue stripes. The national arms of Nicaragua are often (but not always) added to the central white stripe. The arms encompass a volcano, a rainbow (symbolic of peace), and the Cap of Liberty within a triangle.

Size: 50,838 square miles

Population: 4,206,357

Nicaragua is the largest nation in Central America (Mexico is considered part of North America). Nicaragua lies between Honduras and Costa Rica. It has coasts on both the Caribbean and the Pacific.

NICARAGUAN HISTORY

Until 1502: Several groups of Amerindians made Nicaragua their home. They range from technologically unsophisticated groups like the Miskito, to highly organized Aztecs encroaching into Nicaragua from the north. Agriculture flourishes in Nicaragua's fertile lowlands.

1502: On his fourth and final voyage to the New World, Christopher Columbus leads the first known European expedition to land in Nicaragua.

1522: Gil González Dávila leads the first Spanish expedition to Nicaragua. Heading north from Panama, they encounter the Amerindians settled around Lake Nicaragua. This interaction is peaceful, and the indigenous peoples voluntarily convert to Christianity—an unusual event in Spanish-Amerindian relations. The region is named Nicaragua, after a local chieftain named Nicarao. No permanent Spanish settlement is established.

1524: The first Spanish settlements are established by Francisco Hernández de Córdoba at Granada and León. The Spanish enslave the local Amerindians and force them to mine for gold. The modest local gold reserves are soon exhausted, and Nicaragua attracts relatively few Spanish colonists. Granada, in a fertile agricultural region, becomes a conservative trading center.

1610: León is destroyed in an earthquake. The city is rebuilt nearby. Despite being poorer than wealthy Granada, León is made the capital of the Nicaraguan province. The city becomes a center for liberal ideals, which is unusual for a capital city. Overall control of Central America is based in distant Guatemala.

1600s: British and Dutch privateers establish outposts on Nicaragua's Caribbean coast. Eventually, the British claim the area, but they do not contest Spanish control of the interior.

1821: All of Central America declares its independence from Spain. Far from the center of power in Guatemala, Nicaragua plays no part in the revolution.

1822: All of Central America is claimed by the Mexican Empire. Mexican troops never reach Nicaragua.

1823: Central America breaks away from Mexico. Nicaragua becomes part of the new Central American Federation.

1833: US troops are sent, briefly, to Nicaragua, the first of many US interventions.

1838: The Central American Federation dissolves, and Nicaragua is one of the five independent successor states. The old feud between

Nicaragua's two major cities, liberal-dominated León and conservative Granada, breaks out into violence as each struggles to control the new country.

1848: Thousands of would-be prospectors traverse Central America, en route to the California gold fields. Nicaragua and Panama both become convenient points for the cross-oceanic trade. US financier Cornelius Vanderbilt establishes the Accessory Transit Company, which transports people and goods from the British-owned Caribbean port of Graytown to the Pacific port of San Juan del Sur (most of this journey is via boat, up rivers and across Lake Nicaragua). Both the United States and Great Britain consider building a Nicaraguan canal.

1855: The Liberals in León, still fighting the Conservatives in Granada, decide to seek outside help. They invite the aid of US adventurer William Walker, who is already infamous for a failed attempt to capture Baja California from Mexico. With only 57 troops, Walker captures Granada. Walker declares himself President of Nicaragua, but makes the mistake of seizing Vanderbilt's Transit Company. Vanderbilt finances Conservative forces in neighboring countries, and a Costa Rican army ousts Walker in 1857.

1857: In an attempt at compromise, a new capital is established at Managua, midway between León and Granada. The choice of Managua is unfortunate, as it is in a seismically active zone. Earthquakes level much of Managua in 1931 and 1972. Nor does the new capital settle the Liberal-Conservative conflict, which erupts into civil war several times.

1893: Liberal leader José Santos Zelaya seizes power from a Conservative President. Santos Zelaya rules Nicaragua as Dictator for the next 12 years.

1902: Nicaragua's volcanic Mount Momotombo erupts. The event frightens the US Congress into deciding on a Panamanian route for their proposed canal, even though a Nicaraguan route (most of it through rivers and lakes) would require only 16 miles of channels to be dug.

1905: Under the terms of the Harrison-Altamirano Treaty, the UK relinquishes its claim to Nicaragua's Caribbean Coast. The Treaty grants protections to the Coast's English-speaking Miskito and Creole populations.

1909: After President Santos Zelaya taxes US banana growers and invites a German company to build a canal in Nicaragua, the United States forces his resignation.

1910: Faced with another Liberal president, US troops are sent to Nicaragua to force the appointment of a Conservative.

1912: After continued instability, US Marines occupy Nicaragua for 20 years. The troops are referred to as an "embassy guard."

1925: Civil war again breaks out in Nicaragua.

1926: The Caribbean coast is occupied by thousands of US Marines. In the interior, the US recognizes Adolfo Díaz, a Conservative, as the legitimate president. But Liberal leader General Augusto César Sandino refuses to accept Díaz as president, and conducts a guerrilla war in the interior.

1933: General Sandino ends his revolt after US troops are withdrawn. When he arrives in Managua for negotiations with the Conservatives, he is assassinated. The orders for Sandino's murder were given by the National Guard commander, Anastasio Somoza Garcia.

1937: Running unopposed, Anastasio Somoza Garcia is elected president. The Somoza family will rule Nicaragua for the next 42 years, either in person or through their proxies. By rewriting the Nicaraguan Constitution four times, they manage to maintain a fiction of democracy while holding on to power. The Somoza family runs Nicaragua as their personal fiefdom; their landholdings approach the size of El Salvador!

1956: Anastasio Somoza Garcia is assassinated by a young journalist, Rigoberto López Pérez. Anastasio's son, Luis Somoza Debayle, takes power.

1967: After Luis' death, his younger brother Anastasio Somoza Debayle becomes president.

1972: A major earthquake levels most of Managua. Some 6,000 people are killed and 300,000 are left homeless. International aid pours in. Much of that aid is appropriated by the Somoza family and their allies, outraging both Nicaraguans and international opinion. Opposition activity increases.

1974: A Marxist guerrilla organization, the FSLN (Frente Sandinista de Liberación Nacional, a.k.a. Sandinistas), grows in strength. They kidnap and hold for ransom many members of the Somoza family. The Somoza regime responds with brutal crackdowns on dissidents.

1978: Pedro Joaquín Chamorro, an opposition leader and publisher of the newspaper *La Prensa,* is assassinated. A general strike is called. The FSLN (a.k.a. Sandinistas) control many areas of Nicaragua.

1979: The victorious Sandinistas march into Managua, forcing Somoza to resign. The new Sandinista government initially has the support of most Nicaraguans.

1981: Daniel Ortega emerges as the leader of the Sandinista government. Several prominent intellectuals, including Violetta Chamorro, stop supporting the Sandinistas. Meanwhile, the administration of US President Ronald Reagan budgets $19 million to destabilize the Sandinistas and support the anti-Communist Contra guerrillas.

1986: Tens of thousands of people die or flee Nicaragua due to the fighting between the Sandinistas and the Contras. US aid to the Contras peaks at $100 million, listed as "humanitarian" aid. The Iran-Contra scandal comes to light in November of 1986.

1987: The Central American Peace Accord (Esquipulas II) is signed by five Central American nations, including Nicaragua. The President of Costa Rica, Oscar Arias, receives the 1987 Nobel Peace Prize for his work in negotiating this peace plan.

1990: After protracted negotiations between the Sandinistas and the Contras, a free election is held. Despite polls showing that Sandinista President Daniel Ortega has a slight lead, opposition candidate Violetta Barrios de Chamorro is elected president. Following the elections, the US lifts its trade embargo against Nicaragua.

1996: Right-wing candidate Arnoldo Aleman, a former mayor of Managua, is elected president. Nicaragua celebrates its second peaceful election in a row. Defeated once again in his bid for the presidency, Daniel Ortega demands a recount. Some irregularities are noted but the outcome of the election is indisputable.

NICARAGUAN BEHAVIOR

"The Atlantic coast minorities—African Caribbeans, who speak English, and indigenous peoples, who speak Miskito or English and occasionally Sumo, Rama, or Garífuna—are not part of national Nicaraguan culture. Historically colonized by Britain and geographically isolated from the Spanish traditions of the majority sector, they remain both remote and distinct from the mestizo Pacific."

—From *Life Is Hard: Machismo, Danger, and the Intimacy of Power in Nicaragua* by Roger N. Lancaster.

What is the central (nonpolitical) occupation of Nicaraguan life?

Baseball—Nicaraguans love the game. Organized leagues abound, and informal baseball games spring up anywhere there is a field. The careers of Nicaraguans who play in the US Major Leagues are avidly followed.

Why are Nicaraguans the way they are?

In his book *El Nicaraguense (The Nicaraguan)*, poet Pablo Antonio Cuadra describes his countrymen this way:

"The Nicaraguan is an imaginative, fantastic individual who frequently achieves baroque extravagance. But when faced with real life . . . he displays a disconcerting sobriety.

> *"The Nica, in singular terms, is a braggart. In plural, he's self-critical, and his self-criticism is expressed with a great deal of mockery."*

The latter characteristic is very evident. Mockery and humor are widespread in Nicaragua. The pretentious and self-important are lampooned and deflated.

Some observers consider this mockery a national defense mechanism. Faced with poverty, war, natural disasters, and rapacious leaders, the Nicaraguan's only recourse is to laugh.

HOW CAN I FIND MORE INFORMATION ABOUT NICARAGUA?

Here are a few resources to start with:

Getting Through Customs' Web site at **http://www. getcustoms.com** tracks current holidays in Nicaragua. They also post Cultural I.Q. Quizzes, gift-giving guidelines, a demo of the PASSPORT database, and further international information. Telephone: (610) 353-9894; fax (610) 353-6994.

Embassy of Nicaragua
1627 New Hampshire Avenue NW
Washington, DC 20009
Telephone: (202) 939-6570

Nicaragua on the Internet—Comprehensive, informative site on Nicaragua.
http://www.latinworld.com/countries/nicaragua/

The International Academy at Santa Barbara at **http://www.iasb.org/cwl** publishes *Current World Leaders,* an excellent resource for data on political leaders and parties in Nicaragua. Telephone: (800) 530-2682 or (805) 965-5010 for subscription information.

The Bureau of Consular Affairs at **http://travel.state.gov** can give you detailed information on obtaining passports, visa requirements, and consular affairs bulletins.

The Center for Disease Control at **http://www.cdc.gov/** provides valuable medical information, as well as information on any outbreaks of virulent infections in Nicaragua.

Like all Web sites, the preceding Internet addresses are subject to change, and there is no guarantee that they will continue to provide the data we list here.

Panama

WHAT'S YOUR CULTURAL I.Q.?

1. TRUE or FALSE? In 1501, Christopher Columbus led the first European expedition to reach Panama.

    ANSWER: False. It was Spanish navigator Rodrigo de Bastidas who was the first known European to reach Panama in 1501. Christopher Columbus arrived a year later, on his fourth and final voyage to the New World.

2. Vasco Núñez de Balboa helped establish the first European settlement in Panama in 1510. Which town was this?

    a. Panama City

    b. Colón

    c. David

    d. Darién

    ANSWER: d. Balboa founded Darién. The town's full name is Santa María la Antigua del Darién. Panama City, the capital and largest city, was founded in 1519. David and Colón are Panama's second and third largest cities.

3. TRUE or FALSE? Vasco Núñez de Balboa discovered the Pacific Ocean.

   ANSWER: False. Not only did many indigenous people already know of the existence of the Pacific Ocean (Balboa was guided by Amerindians across the Isthmus of Panama), but Europeans had already reached the Pacific on the Asian side. Balboa was simply the first known European to find the Pacific on the far side of the New World.

4. Panama suffered from the attacks of British, French, and Dutch privateers. Which of these privateers was responsible for the infamous 1671 looting and burning of Panama City?

   a. Sir Francis Drake

   b. Sir Henry Morgan

   c. Sir John Hawkins

   d. Captain William Kidd

   ANSWER: b. It was Welsh buccaneer Sir Henry Morgan who looted and destroyed Panama City in 1671, although Sir Francis Drake was also active in Panama. Morgan later became governor of Jamaica.

5. TRUE or FALSE? It took a foreign discovery to bring renewed prosperity to Panama in 1848.

   ANSWER: True. Panama's importance declined when Spain lost her colonies in South and Central America. But the discovery of gold in California revived Panama's wealth, as thousands of Americans traveled to California via Panama (rather than making the long, dangerous land journey across the United States).

6. Although Venezuela and Ecuador broke away from Colombia in 1830, most Panamanians were content to remain. Which event is usually given for the birth of Panamanian separatist sentiment?

   a. The US Gold Rush of 1848

   b. The completion of the trans-isthmus Panama Railroad in 1855

   c. Colombia's granting of local autonomy to Panama in 1855

   d. The reorganization of the Republic of Colombia in 1886

   ANSWER: d. Panama, which had been an autonomous province of Colombia since 1855, lost its autonomy when Colombia was reorganized in 1886.

7. US President Teddy Roosevelt was determined to secure Panamanian independence so that he could get a more favorable canal treaty than Colombia would grant. TRUE or FALSE? The US used "gunboat diplomacy" to assist the cause of Panamanian independence.

   ANSWER: True. The US posted a warship off Colón, Panama on 3 November 1903. Panama declared its independence from Colombia the very next day.

8. Which of the following are popular sports in Panama?

   a. Soccer

   b. Baseball

   c. Cock fighting

   d. Boxing

   e. All of the above

   ANSWER: e. Soccer, baseball, and cock fighting are popular throughout Central America, but Panamanians are noted for their interest in boxing.

Panama has produced 14 world boxing champions, including Roberto Duran.

9. TRUE or FALSE? You want to avoid dealing with any member of the *rabiblancos* while in Panama.

ANSWER: False. You won't get much done without them. *Los rabiblancos* (whitetails) is the nickname for the wealthy, English-speaking, European-descended oligarchy that holds most of the money and power in Panama. Most (if not all) decision-makers in business will be members of this group.

10. General Omar Torrijos was the most influential Panamanian leader of modern times. Which of the following did he accomplish in his 21 years as Panama's leader?

a. He was the first president to come to power via democratic elections

b. He renegotiated the Panama Canal Treaty to give Panama immediate control of the Canal and the Canal Zone

c. He changed the banking laws, making Panama into the "Switzerland of Central America"

d. He made Panama into an open and free society, with complete freedom of expression

ANSWER: c. Torrijos did indeed make Panama a world banking center, although many of the deposits came from narcotics traffickers. But Torrijos was a dictator who seized control from democratically elected President Arias in 1968. His 1977 renegotiation of the Panama Canal Treaty withholds control from Panama until the year 2000. He was never much on civil liberties, and critics of his regime were often harassed or jailed. He died in an airplane crash in 1981, and was succeeded by General Manuel Noriega.

QUOTATIONS ABOUT PANAMA

"At Colon they drove in a cab, at evening, along the esplanade. Whitish, like a vast fish's eye, the sea lay as though dead. Against a picture postcard of sunset the immoderately tall thin pines were the emblems of a resigned hopelessness, and in the nostrils the hot air was like a vapor of wool."

—From the novel *Eyeless in Gaza* by Aldous Huxley.

". . . it was the Sandinistas who arranged for me to visit Hollywood, the slum lying on the edge of the American Zone. A visit, they told me, was unsafe without an escort of an inhabitant, but one of their number knew of one who would insure our safety.

"Hollywood proved to be a horrifying huddle of wooden houses sunk in rain water like scuttled boats and of communal lavatories which stank to heaven and leaked into the water around."

—A visit to the Hollywood slum outside the American Zone, from *Getting to Know the General* by Graham Greene.

"Twenty-one years elapsed between Torrijos's rise and Noriega's fall. The civilians who are back in power now refer to that time as La Dictadura, but that isn't what they called it then. By and large, the business class had a tolerant view of Torrijos, who dominated Panama's political landscape until he died, in a plane crash, in 1981. Torrijos rewrote the banking laws so they were like Switzerland's, and turned Panama into a major financial center. He also negotiated, in 1977, an alternative to the onerous in-perpetuity Canal Treaty that Teddy Roosevelt had imposed on Panama when he instigated its revolution

*and secession from Colombia, in 1903 . . . He signifi-
cantly reduced illiteracy and child-mortality rates, and
made a lot of Panamanians proud of his role as a major
player in the turbulent regional politics of the time."*

—From the collection *The Heart That Bleeds: Latin America Now* by
Alma Guillermoprieto.

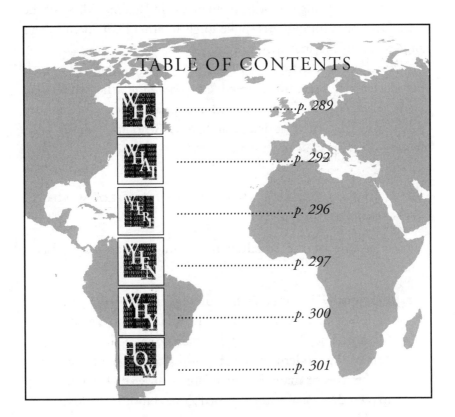

THE PANAMANIANS

Mestizos make up the bulk of Panama's population at 64.0%.
Blacks and mulattos account for 14.0%, whites for 10.0%,
Amerindians for 8.0%, and Asians for 4.0%. The Chinese are the
most numerous Asian group.

Panama was an important trans-shipment point for African slaves being sent to South America, and the country has a substantial black population today. This segment of the black population has lived in Panama for hundreds of years; they speak Spanish and are culturally Hispanicized. A second population of blacks came from the Caribbean Islands to work on large projects, especially the railroad and the Canal. Their origin in the Antilles led to the nickname *antillanos* being extended to all blacks in Panama. Many of the black Caribbean immigrants spoke English rather than Spanish, and some retain this characteristic.

Urban white Panamanians hold most of the country's wealth and power. They are nicknamed *los rabiblancos* (the whitetails). Many of them speak English as well as Spanish. They are a separate group from the rural agricultural barons, who have never been major political players in Panama.

HOW TO TELL PANAMA AND PANAMANIANS FROM THEIR NEIGHBORS

Panama is one of the smallest and youngest nations in Latin America.

1. Obviously, Panama is the only Central American nation with a canal linking the Atlantic and Pacific Oceans. The Panama Canal remains one of the wonders of the modern world. It is also a central obsession in the lives of many Panamanians, who want Panama to own the Canal and the Canal Zone, but fear the loss of US expertise and money.

2. Panama borders Costa Rica to the north and Colombia to the south. Panama broke away from Colombia (with considerable US assistance and prodding) in 1903.

3. Most Panamanians seem to have nicknames. Even powerful politicians are referred to by their nicknames.

Dictator Manuel Antonio Noriega was known as *la Piña* (the Pineapple) due to his pock-marked complexion; his successor as President, the pleasant and rotund Guillermo Endara, was called *Pan de Dulce* (Honey Bun)!

4. The powerful families in Panama (nicknamed the *rabiblancos*) are urban rather than rural. Since the early days of Spanish colonization, Panama has gained wealth as a trans-shipment center and trading post. The Panama Canal continued this trend. Agriculture has generally been an afterthought. (In fact, for much of its history, Panama has not even been self-sufficient in food.) Although a class of wealthy rural ranchers eventually developed, they never achieved the political influence that is characteristic of agricultural barons elsewhere in Central America.

5. Although the distribution of wealth is unequal, Panama remains the wealthiest Central American nation.

LITERATURE

There are some of Panama's writers who have had their works translated into English.

Carlos Fuentes (1928–) was born in Panama City while his father was Mexico's Ambassador to Panama. One of Latin America's most famous authors, Fuentes is considered Mexican rather than Panamanian. (For more information, see the Mexico chapter.)

Bertalica Peralta (1939–) has published 14 books of poetry. Her work—which includes journalism, fiction, and children's stories—has won numerous awards. Her 1973 short story "Guayacán de Marzo" (English translation: "A March Guayacan") was awarded the Premio Literario from the National Institute of Culture in Panama. She is now the Director of Information and Public Relations at the University of Panama.

Pedro Rivera (1939–) is a poet and fiction writer better known for his work in film. He has made more than 30 documentaries and edits the film magazine *Cine Formato 16*. Most of his writings have not been translated into English, but his story "Tarantulas of Honey" is collected in *And We Sold the Rain: Contemporary Fiction from Central America* (published by Four Walls Eight Windows, NY, 1988).

Panamanian writers who have not been translated into English include Demetrio Korsi, Ricardo Miró, Tito del Moral, and Rogelio Sinán.

LANGUAGE

The official language of Panama is Spanish. Because of the presence of the US-run Canal Zone, many Panamanians in Panama City and Colón speak English as well.

Almost half of Panama's black population came from English-speaking areas of the Caribbean, and some of them retain their idiosyncratic English. (As in Belize, US citizens should note that they might not be able to understand this local dialect of English.)

Linguists have categorized 13 different languages spoken in modern Panama—*Ethnologue: Languages of the World,* 12th Edition from their Web site at http://www.sil.org/ethnologue/ethnologue. html).

BUSINESS IN PANAMA

Panama is dominated by an English-speaking, well-educated elite. They are often referred to as *los rabiblancos* (the whitetails). The majority of your business dealings will be done with members of this group. Many of them are highly concerned about their lineage, which prestige demands be totally European. Never imply that a *rabiblanco* might have African or Amerindian ancestry.

Get yourself a nickname, if you don't have one already. If you don't have one, the Panamanians will give you one (and it may not be to your liking). Even powerful politicians are addressed by their peers by nicknames. Former president Arnulfo Arias was nick-named *Fufo;* Second Vice President Guillermo Ford calls himself *Billy.* Women also have nicknames: the mayor of Panama City, Omaria Correa, was known as *Mayín.* President Guillermo Endara didn't have a nickname, so people began calling him—although not to his face—*Pan de Dulce* (Honey Bun), an allusion to his sweet demeanor and dumpy physique.

Panama's liberal business climate has resulted in the registration of hundreds of US companies in Panama—many of which exist only on paper. Estimates of the number of US nonproductive investments (that is, that have no physical operations in Panama) in Panamanian banks range as high as two-thirds!

Sing Us a Song, Mr. President

Ever since the success of Alberto Fujimori in Peru, many Panamanians have looked around for a similar savior—a man with no political obligations who comes out of nowhere to win the presidential election and then reforms the nation. The name usually floated about for this white-knight role is Panamanian musician Rubén Blades, who has founded a political party called Papa Egoró. The name means Mother Earth, but not in Spanish—it is in Embrá, an indigenous Amerindian language. But Blades did not manage to put together a serious candidacy in the 1994 elections, leaving his political future in doubt.

BUSINESS SUCCESS IN PANAMA

> *Caveat: The Colon Free Zone (CFZ) offers both opportunity and risk for foreign businesspeople. Operating in the CFZ offers clear financial advantages, and the local infrastructure is generally good. However, the CFZ also has a reputation for piracy of intellectual property, not to mention narcotrafficking and money laundering.*

The long-standing presence of US citizens has influenced business practices in Panama. As in the United States of America, business dealings are usually direct and straightforward. Although Panamanians prefer doing business with people they know and like, many are willing to dispense with the lengthy relationship-building process that characterizes business elsewhere in Latin America.

A number of foreign franchises have been successful in Panama. Note that Panamanian law mandates that retail outlets are owned by Panamanian citizens only. Registered licensing agreements are not required by law, but foreign firms often use them to protect their registered trademarks.

Joint ventures remain rare in Panama. The potential exists for expansion in Panama of all three techniques: franchises, licensing agreements, and joint ventures.

Affluent Panamanians are trendy and status-conscious. Vigorous marketing techniques are required to influence this group. The advertising market is competitive and sophisticated. In addition to ad campaigns in the newspapers, television advertisements are needed to succeed in Panama City. Outside Panama City, radio advertisements are often sufficient—radio is the only medium that reaches every village and outpost in Panama.

LEADING BUSINESSES IN PANAMA

The following businesses are some of the largest employers in Panama:

Azucarera Nacional SA
Panama City.
2,600 employees.

Banco Nacional de Panama
Panama City.
National commercial bank. 2,000 employees.

Cerveceria Nacional SA
Panama.
1,200 employees.

Chiriqui Land Co
Panama City.
14,500 employees.

Compania Azucarera la Estrella SA
Panama City.
1,200 employees.

Direccion de Aeronautica Civil
Panama City.
2,000 employees.

Hospital Santo Thomas
Panama City.
2,000 employees.

Instituto de Recursos Hidraulicos y Electrificacion
Panama City.
5,000 employees.

Instituto Nacional de Telecomunicaciones
Panama City.
3,960 employees.

Panama Canal Commission
Panama City.
9,000 employees.

Varela Hermanos SA
Panama City.
4,350 employees.
The following are the largest print and broadcast media concerns in Panama:

El Panama America
Panama City.
Newspapers. Daily circulation: 22,000.
La Estrella de Panama
Panama City.
Newspapers. Daily circulation: 20,000.
La Prensa
Panama City.
Newspapers. Daily circulation: 35,000.

PANAMANIAN GEOGRAPHY

FLAG AND MAP OF PANAMA

The Panama has a distinctive red, white, and blue flag. This color selection may have been intended to honor the United States of America for its assistance in Panama's independence. An alternate explanation states that the white stands for peace, the red for law, and the blue for civic virtue.

Size: 29,157 square miles
Population: 2,680,903

One of the smallest nations in Latin America, Panama lies at the juncture of Central and South America. (Or, since Central America is considered geographically a part of North America, Panama is at the juncture of North and South America.)

PANAMA

PANAMANIAN HISTORY

Until 1501: Panama is home to several groups of Amerindians, including the Guaymi and Cuna tribes. Little is known of them, as they did not build cities like the Maya to the north or the Inca to the south.

1501: Spanish navigator Rodrigo de Bastidas becomes the first known European to explore Panama. In 1502, Christopher Columbus also visits Panama on his fourth and final voyage to the New World.

1510: Bastidas' shipmate, Vasco Núñez de Balboa, helps establish the first European settlement in Panama, Darién. (The town's full title is Santa María la Antigua del Darién. Guided by Indian allies, Balboa crosses the Isthmus of Panama and "discovers" the Pacific Ocean.

1519: Panama City, Spain's first Pacific outpost in the Americas, is founded by Pedro Arias de Avila, the first governor of Panama. It prospers as the departure point for the Spanish conquest of Peru. Panama is eventually ruled from Lima as part of the Viceroyalty of Peru.

1671: Welsh buccaneer Sir Henry Morgan loots and burns Panama City, which has become wealthy as a trans-shipment point for Peruvian gold and silver. Sir Francis Drake also loots Panamanian ports, as do various French and Dutch buccaneers.

1717: The Viceroyalty of Peru is split up. Panama now comes under the control of the Viceroyalty of New Granada.

1821: The Viceroyalty of New Granada declares its independence from Spain, and becomes the Confederation of Gran Colombia.

1830: Venezuela and Ecuador withdraw from the Confederation, but Panama remains part of Gran Colombia.

1848: With South America now independent from Spain, Panama's prosperity as a trans-shipment port declines. But the discovery of gold in California revives Panama's wealth, as thousands of east-coast Americans travel to California via Panama.

1855: Panama is granted local autonomy. The Panama Railroad is built to cross the isthmus, marking the first major US investment in Panama.

1856: US troops land in Panama to protect the Panama Railroad. This is the first of many US interventions on Panamanian soil.

1886: Gran Colombia is reorganized as The Republic of Colombia, and Panama's autonomy is revoked. The beginnings of Panamanian separatist sentiment are traced to this loss of autonomy.

1880s: A French company tries and fails to build a canal across Panama.

1903: Convinced by the 1898 Spanish-American War that a canal is necessary, the United States encourages Panama to declare independence from Colombia. The sequence of events is:

> **3 November 1903:** A US warship is posted off of Colón, Panama.

4 November 1903: Panama declares independence from Colombia.

6 November 1903: The USA becomes the first nation to recognize Panamanian independence.

18 November 1903: The USA and Panama sign the Hay-Bunau Varilla Treaty, which allows the US to build the Canal and rent (in perpetuity) the Canal Zone for a payment to Panama of $250,000 per year.

1904: Manuel Amador Guerrero is elected the first president of Panama.

1908: US troops are sent to Panama, under the auspices of the Hay-Bunau Varilla Treaty, which gives the US the authority to intervene "to reestablish public peace and constitutional order."

1914: The Canal opens, and the first ship passes through.

1936: The payment from the US for rent on the Panama Canal is raised to $430,000 per year.

1941: President Arnulfo Arias introduces a new Panamanian constitution. He will serve three separate terms as president, but each time will be ousted by a military coup.

1955: The payment from the US for rent on the Panama Canal is raised to $1,930,000 per year, but Panamanians now want full control of the Canal.

1964: Twenty-one Panamanians are killed in protests over US presence in Panama. For a short time, Panama breaks off diplomatic relations with the US.

1968: General Omar Torrijos ousts President Arias, which marks the beginning of 21 years of military rule.

1977: General Torrijos and US President Jimmy Carter agree to return the Canal Zone to Panama by the year 2000.

1981: General Torrijos is killed in an airplane crash. General Manuel Noriega now becomes dictator of Panama.

1989: Using vote fraud and armed thugs (who are photographed beating opponents, including opposition politician Guillermo Ford), General Noriega manages to "steal" the election. His puppet candidates ensure that he remains in power.

1990: Accusing him of narcotics trafficking, the USA invades Panama and arrests General Noriega. Some 300 Panamanian civilians are slain in the action, and the wooden houses of Panama City's Chorrillo neighborhood are burnt down. The US Agency for International Development (USAID) later funds the rebuilding of Chorrillo.

1994: Ernesto Pérez Balladares is elected president.

PANAMANIAN BEHAVIOR

Why are Panamanians the way they are?

More than any other Latin American country, Panama has become dependent upon the largess of the United States of America, which is known informally as *El Gigante del Norte* (the Giant to the North). The Great Liberator himself, Simón Bolívar, wanted Panama to be part of his Confederation of Gran Colombia. Even though Ecuador and Venezuela left Gran Colombia in 1830, Panama was content to stay with Colombia. Were it not for the US, Panama might still be part of Colombia.

As elsewhere in Latin America, Panamanian society is highly stratified. Panama's underclass remain poor, while banking and narcotrafficking have brought new wealth to a relative few.

Panamanians of all types often display a reluctance to become agitated. "Take it easy" is an slogan commonly heard in Panama.

Panamanians call themselves *panameños*.

What occupies the thoughts of many Panamanians? (Aside from the Canal, of course.)

Sports. In addition to soccer and baseball, cockfighting is a national obsession. Boxing is also extremely popular—Panama has produced 14 world boxing champions, including Roberto Duran. Panama has also given the world many top jockeys, and horse racing is popular. Affluent Panamanians enjoy golf and yachting.

Why are all those Americans in Panama?

In addition to the US employees who operate the Panama Canal and US citizens who have retired to Panama, this is the home base of the US Southern Command (SOUTHCOM). The US military is divided into four Commands: Atlantic, European, Pacific, and Southern, which is by far the smallest of the four. Now that Latin America is becoming more peaceful (that is, requiring less US military intervention), SOUTHCOM's mission has been extended to combat narcotrafficking. SOUTHCOM must also remain ready for disaster relief—a constant threat in the tectonically active Pacific coast of Latin America.

How do Panamanians dress?

Panama tends to be very hot and often humid. Conservative business attire is expected, but ties are often dispensed with.

HOW CAN I FIND MORE INFORMATION ABOUT PANAMA?

Here are a few resources to start with:

> **Getting Through Customs'** Web site at **http://www. getcustoms.com** tracks current holidays in Panama. They also post Cultural I.Q. Quizzes, gift-giving guidelines, a demo of the PASSPORT database, and further international information. Telephone: (610) 353-9894; fax (610) 353-6994.

> **Embassy of the Republic of Panama**
> 2862 McGill Terrace NW
> Washington, DC 20008
> Telephone: (202) 483-1407

IPAT (The Panama Tourist Bureau)
P.O. Box 4421
Zone 5
The Republic of Panama
Telephone: (507) 226-7000 or (507) 226-3544;
fax: (507) 226-3483 or (507) 226-6856

Official Guide To Panama—includes information on investment opportunities, emerging markets, tourism, eco-tourism, industry, privitization, shipping, finance, banking, and more.
http://www.panamainfo.com/

The International Academy at Santa Barbara at **http://www.iasb.org/cwl** publishes *Current World Leaders,* an excellent resource for data on political leaders and parties in Panama. Telephone: (800) 530-2682 or (805) 965-5010 for subscription information.

The Bureau of Consular Affairs at **http://travel.state.gov** can give you detailed information on obtaining passports, visa requirements, and consular affairs bulletins.

The Center for Disease Control at **http://www.cdc.gov/** provides valuable medical information, as well as information on any outbreaks of virulent infections in Panama.

Like all Web sites, the preceding Internet addresses are subject to change, and there is no guarantee that they will continue to provide the data we list here.

Paraguay

WHAT'S YOUR CULTURAL I.Q.?

1. TRUE or FALSE? The 35-year reign of recently deposed Paraguayan Dictator General Alfredo Stroessner was the longest in the 20th century.

   ANSWER: False. Actually, North Korea's late Kim Il Sung beat him by 11 years.

2. The long rule of General Stroessner was ended via a coup by General Andrés Rodríguez. What relation to Stroessner is Rodríguez?

   > a. Stroessner's grandson
   >
   > b. Stroessner's son-in-law
   >
   > c. Stroessner's evil twin

   ANSWER: b.

3. Paraguay is one of the two landlocked countries in South America. TRUE or FALSE? Paraguay has no navigable rivers.

   ANSWER: False. Fortunately, the Rio Paraguay offers a connection to Uruguay, Argentina, and the Atlantic Ocean.

4. The 1986 movie *The Mission* depicted the establishment and destruction of the most famous religious settlements in Paraguay. Which religious order founded these missions?

   a. The Franciscans

   b. The Jesuits

   c. The Trappists

   d. The Mennonites

   ANSWER: b. The Jesuits established missions (called *reducciónes*) throughout Upper Paraguay. Jealous plantation owners wanted the Mission Indians as slaves, so these missions were destroyed in 1767. In modern Paraguay, most of the religious colonies are run by Mennonites rather than by a Catholic order of monks (such as the Jesuits, Franciscans, or Trappists). However, the Mennonite colonies have relatively few Amerindian converts.

5. TRUE or FALSE? Soon after winning independence from Spain in 1810, Dictator José Gaspar Rodríguez de Francia sealed Paraguay's borders from outside influences.

   ANSWER: True. Under Rodríguez de Francia, who ruled from 1814 to 1840, Paraguay became self-sufficient as its contact with the outside world diminished.

6. What percentage of modern Paraguayans are mestizos (persons of mixed European and Amerindian descent)?

   a. About 45%

   b. About 75%

   c. About 90%

ANSWER: c. Isolated and overwhelmingly outnumbered, the original Spanish colonists immediately interbred with the indigenous population. Today, the vast majority (90.8%) of Paraguayans are mestizo, of combined European and Guaraní Indian descent.

7. During the War of the Triple Alliance, fought from 1864 to 1870, Paraguay simultaneously fought Argentina, Brazil, and Uruguay. TRUE or FALSE? Paraguay is said to have lost half its population as a result of this war, including most of its men.

ANSWER: True. In the War of the Triple Alliance, Paraguay made the mistake of warring against its three most powerful neighbors. By the end of the war, Paraguay had lost a huge amount of its population and much of its land as well (including its border with Uruguay).

8. Paraguay made out a little better when it fought the Chaco War (1932 to 1935) for control of the Chaco Desert. With whom did Paraguay fight?

a. Bolivia

b. Brazil

c. Argentina

ANSWER: a. The Chaco War between Bolivia and Paraguay ended in a mili tary stalemate. Arbitration by the United States gave three-quarters of the Chaco to Paraguay.

9. TRUE or FALSE? The sole official language of modern Paraguay is Spanish.

   ANSWER: False. Paraguay is the only nation in all of South America with two official languages: Spanish and the Amerindian language Guaraní.

10. Paraguay is a member of the Mercosur Customs Trade Union. Which of the following is NOT a fellow Mercosur member?

   a. Argentina

   b. Bolivia

   c. Brazil

   d. Chile

   ANSWER: b. Bolivia is not currently a member of Mercosur.

QUOTATIONS ABOUT PARAGUAY

"Paraguay had the reputation of being the darkest country on the planet...This was the place where deposed dictators found a new home (Somoza from Nicaragua, Perón from Argentina). This was the place where fugitive Nazis received a hearty welcome—Eduard Roschmann, 'the Butcher of Riga,' allegedly died here; Josef Mengele, 'the Angel of Death,' was a Paraguayan citizen for much of the time he was the world's most wanted war criminal; and

Martin Bormann lived just across the border. This was also the place where Italian neo-Fascists gave lectures, Croatian thugs trained security details, Chinese tong kings picked up tips, and the new president himself—the 'clean' one—was associated with drug kingpins who'd made $145 million in shipping heroin."

—Pico Iyre, "Up for Sale, or Adoption," collected in *Falling Off the Map.*

"In spite of the dirt and fumes of old cars the air was sweet with orange blossoms...

"Soldiers were goose-stepping in front of the cathedral, and a very early tank stood on a plinth up on the green sward...

"Except for the skyscraper of a new hotel, it was a very Victorian town."

—From *Travels With My Aunt,* by Graham Greene.

"'So you have already been to Paraguay?' said Candide.

"'Indeed I have,' replied Cacambo. 'I was once a servant in the College of the Assumption, so I know how the reverend fathers govern...' 'The reverend fathers own the whole lot, and the people own nothing: that's what I call a masterpiece of reason and justice.'"

—From *Candide* by Voltaire, in which Cacambo gives his satirical view of the Jesuit Missions in Paraguay.

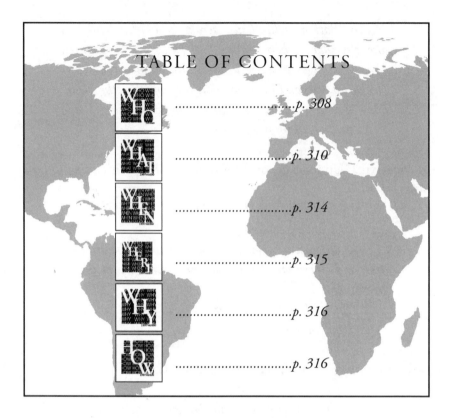

TABLE OF CONTENTS

THE PARAGUAYANS

The vast majority (90.8%) of Paraguayans are mestizo, of combined European and Guaraní descent. Amerindians account for 3.0%. The largest immigrant group not of mixed blood is German (1.7%), although the percentage of Koreans and other Asians is growing. The remainder (4.5%) are of various groups.

The original immigrants to Paraguay during the colonial period were Spanish. But these settlers were so few—and Paraguay so remote—that all the Spanish men took multiple Amerindian wives.

HOW TO TELL PARAGUAY AND THE PARAGUAYANS FROM THEIR NEIGHBORS

Paraguay and its inhabitants are fairly unique on the continent, so it shouldn't be difficult identifying them. Some facts:

1. If the country has a coastline, it's not Paraguay. (Paraguay is one of two landlocked nations in South America. Bolivia is the other one.) However, Paraguay does have a considerable amount of river traffic.

2. Paraguay is the only South American nation to make an Amerindian language co-official with Spanish. So if everybody seems to speak Guaraní, it's Paraguay.

3. Paraguay borders Bolivia, Brazil, and Argentina. It used to border Uruguay as well, but it lost much of its territory in the War of the Triple Alliance.

4. Paraguay is known as the smuggling capital of South America. Huge amounts of counterfeit goods—worth as much as $10 billion US—enter the continent via Paraguay! Much of the smuggling goes through Paraguay's *Ciudad del Este* Free Trade Zone.

LITERATURE

One author of international renown stands out in Paraguay.

Augusto Roa Bastos (1917–) is Paraguay's most famous author. His ambitious 1974 novel *Yo el supremo,* published in English in 1986 as *I, the Supreme,* examines the life of a Paraguayan dictator. Bastos is a veteran of the Chaco War, and has written about the war in his short stories. Since his writings blend the past with the present, and Christianity with Indian beliefs, he is usually categorized as a *magic realism* stylist. He was awarded the 1989 Miguel de Cervantes Prize for Spanish Literature.

LIGHTS! CAMERA! ACTION!

Paraguay does not have a major indigenous film industry, but one internationally distributed film has been shot about the Jesuit missions:

The Mission features Jeremy Irons as a Jesuit priest who founds a peaceful and prosperous mission among the Guaraní people. He is joined in this task by a repentant soldier, played by Robert de Niro. When the Jesuits are ordered out of Paraguay, the protagonists stay to defend their mission. Beautifully photographed (although little was filmed in present-day Paraguay), the film was nominated for an Academy Award as Best Picture. Political activist Daniel Berrigan, a Jesuit, served as technical advisor for the film, and wrote about the experience in his book *The Mission: A Film Journal. Unforgettable moment:* De Niro climbing a mountain (as a self-inflicted penance) with his late brother's metal armor tied to him, dragging him down (1986, directed by Roland Joffé).

LANGUAGE

As noted above, Paraguayans are unique in that they have two official languages, Spanish and Guaraní. Both languages have influenced the other, making Paraguayan Spanish full of Guaraní terms.

Linguists have categorized 21 different languages spoken in modern Paraguay—*Ethnologue: Languages of the World,* 12th Edition from their Web site at (http://ww.sil.org/ethnologue/ethnologue.html).

BUSINESS IN PARAGUAY

As in other countries where the military takes an active role, business in Paraguay must be approved by the military leaders. In Paraguay, General Andrés Rodríguez, the president, is a partner to many business scenarios.

BUSINESS SUCCESS IN PARAGUAY

Caveat: Trademark and copyright infringement continues to be a major problem in Paraguay. Counterfeits of many brand-name products are produced and sold. Lawsuits on trademark issues can take from 10 to 15 years to resolve. Next to El Salvador, Paraguay has the highest rate of software piracy in Latin America.

Paraguayans know that they are a long way from foreign manufacturers, and they are wary of purchasing anything that cannot be serviced locally. In most industries, it is vital to provide extensive after-sale support and service within Paraguay. This is especially true due to the proliferation of substandard counterfeit products in Paraguay.

The most popular method of producing consumer goods in Paraguay is via local licensing agreements. Joint ventures and franchises are occasionally used as well.

The Paraguayan government accounts for a large portion of business, but local firms are given major advantages over foreign ones. A public bid is required for government purchases over $60,000.

LEGAL AFFAIRS IN PARAGUAY

The Republic of Paraguay has sued the Governor and Attorney General of the State of Virginia (among other officials) over the planned execution of a Paraguayan national. Angel Francisco Breard was sentenced to death in 1993 for the rape and murder of a woman in Arlington, Virginia. Breard is a citizen of both Paraguay and Argentina. The complaint stems from Virginia's failure to notify the Paraguayan Consulate of Breard's arrest, which is required under such international treaties as the Vienna Convention. The case has received heavy media play in Paraguay. In a Paraguayan court, Breard could have expected leniency for confessing to his crime. However, in Virginia, his confession only guaranteed a death sentence.

Since President Stroessner was deposed in 1989, Paraguayan law has changed to facilitate the adoption of Paraguayan orphans by foreign nationals. Paraguay has been a leading supplier of children for adoption by baby-hungry US citizens. Over 400 Paraguayan children were adopted by US citizens in 1995. The adopting parents pay several thousand US dollars in fees to various facilitating organizations. However, when the demand for children exceeded the supply, some Paraguayans utilized illegal methods. There have been numerous reports of babies being stolen or coerced from impoverished, rural parents. Even worse, there are allegations that some doctors and hospitals have conspired to steal newborn infants from their mothers. As a result of these abuses, the Paraguayan government suspended all new adoption applications in September of 1996. The US Embassy makes the following recommendation to persons wishing to adopt: Insist on a DNA test to verify the identity of any woman claiming to be the mother of an infant up for adoption.

LEADING BUSINESSES IN PARAGUAY

The following companies are some of the largest employers in Paraguay:

Cerveceria Paraguaya SA
Asuncion.
Malt beverages. 902 employees.

Consorcio de Ingenieria Electromecanica Sociedad Anonima
Asuncion.
Electrometallurgical products. 1,200 employees.
Fenix Sociedad Anonima
Asuncion.
Men's and boy's clothing. 1,800 employees.
Industrializadora Guarani SA
Asuncion.
Bottled and canned soft drinks. 1,300 employees.
Industria Nacional del Cemento
Asuncion.
Cement and hydraulic. 800 employees.
Manufactura de Pilar SA
Asuncion.
Broadwoven fabric mills. 1,380 employees.
Paraguay Refrescos Sociedad Anonima
Barcequillo.
Bottled and canned soft drinks. 1,045 employees.

The following are the largest print and broadcast media concerns in Paraguay:

Editorial Azeta SA
Asuncion.
Newspapers. 500 employees.
Editorial El Pais SA
Asuncion.
Newspapers. 317 employees.
La Opinion SA
Asuncion.
Newspapers. 130 employees.
Teledifusora Paraguaya Sociedad Anonima
Lambare.
Television broadcasting stations. 150 employees.

PARAGUAYAN HISTORY

Until 1524: Paraguay is on the fringes of the powerful Inca Empire. Several other Amerindian tribes occupy most of present-day Paraguay.

1524: Alejo García leads the first party of Europeans to enter Paraguay.

1537: Asunción is founded by a small party of some 350 Spaniards. Settling among friendly Guaraní, they intermarry and are virtually absorbed into the native culture. Soon after, the Jesuits begin establishing their highly successful missions (known as *reducciónes*) in southern (upper) Paraguay.

1720: Friction between Paraguayans and the Jesuits results in the Comunero Revolt. The Paraguayans (who want to enslave the Amerindians under Jesuit protection) oust their pro-Jesuit governor. This is considered the first revolt against Colonial Spain in the New World.

1767: Madrid orders the Jesuits ousted from the New World. The so-called "Jesuit Republic" is destroyed.

1810: The Paraguayans again fight for independence, this time successfully.

1811: The Paraguayans drive off an invading Argentine army, securing Paraguay as an independent state.

1814–40: Paraguay is ruled by "El Supremo," the dictator José Gaspar Rodríguez de Francia, who seals Paraguay's borders from outside influences.

1864–70: In the War of the Triple Alliance, Paraguay battles its three most powerful neighbors: Argentina, Brazil, and Uruguay. Paraguay loses land (including its border with Uruguay) and half its population, including most of its men.

1932–35: Paraguay and Bolivia fight the Chaco War for control of the (virtually worthless) Chaco Desert. Outside arbitration awards three-quarters of the Chaco to Paraguay.

1947: Civil war erupts in Paraguay.

1949–89: General Alfredo Stroessner seizes power and rules Paraguay for 35 years.

1989: Stroessner is deposed by his son-in-law, General Andrés Rodríguez, who is elected president.

1991: General Rodríguez is reelected president.

PARAGUAYAN GEOGRAPHY

PARAGUAY

PARAGUAY

Asuncion

FLAG AND MAP OF PARAGUAY

Paraguay uses the popular red, white, and blue tricolor as a flag, with a national seal in the center. It is unique among national flags in that the two sides are not identical: One side has the National Seal, the other the Treasury Seal.

Size: 157,048 square miles

Population: 5,538,198

Paraguay has lost a large amount of land over the years. Even part of the land encompassing the Jesuit *reducciónes*—sometimes called the "Jesuit Republic"—has been lost to its neighbors. (The beautiful falls depicted in the beginning of the film *The Mission* are the *Cataratas del Iguazú,* they now belong to Argentina.)

Paraguay is one of the smaller countries of the Southern Cone of South America. It is also a member of the Mercosur Customs Trade Union. The other Mercosur members are Argentina, Brazil, Chile, and Uruguay. Collectively, Mercosur represents a population of 213,611,000.

PARAGUAYAN BEHAVIOR

Why are Paraguayans the way they are?

Paraguay's isolation is the usual explanation. Enforced by such leaders as Dictator José Gaspar Rodríguez de Francia, Paraguay sealed itself off from the outside world after achieving independence. Paraguay became very self-reliant—and, through interbreeding, very Indian.

Either because of its Amerindian heritage or because of its hot climate, Paraguayans are not typically known for being energetic. Even commerce is conducted at a languid pace, and businesses often close early. Some visitors find the Paraguayan character to be refreshingly straightforward, relaxed, and unpretentious.

How do Paraguayans dress?

Rather conservatively, but the heat is taken into account. Paraguay is one of the hottest nations in the Americas. But since clothes and cosmetics are quite cheap in Paraguay (compared to the prices in neighboring countries), some people dress fashionably. In addition to imports, Paraguay's artisans produce fine textiles (especially lace), leather goods, and accessories.

HOW CAN I FIND MORE INFORMATION ABOUT PARAGUAY?

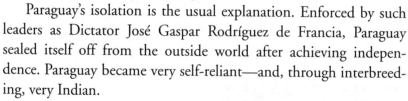

Here are a few resources to start with:

Getting Through Customs' Web site at **http://www. getcustoms.com** tracks current holidays in Paraguay. They also post Cultural I.Q. Quizzes, gift-giving guidelines, a demo of the PASSPORT database, and further international information. Telephone: (610) 353-9894; fax (610) 353-6994.

Embassy of Paraguay
2400 Massachusetts Avenue NW
Washington, DC 20008
Telephone: (202) 483-6960

The United States Information Service (USIS) office in Asuncion has a Web site: **http://www.usia.gov/posts/asuncion.html**.

Paraguay Index—site with extensive information on Paraguay.
http://lanic.utexas.edu/la/sa/paraguay/

The International Academy at Santa Barbara at **http://www.iasb.org/cwl** publishes *Current World Leaders*, an excellent resource for data on political leaders and parties in Paraguay. Telephone: (800) 530-2682 or (805) 965-5010 for subscription information.

The Bureau of Consular Affairs at **http://travel.state.gov** can give you detailed information on obtaining passports, visa requirements, and consular affairs bulletins.

The Center for Disease Control at **http://www.cdc.gov/** provides valuable medical information, as well as information on any outbreaks of virulent infections in Paraguay.

Like all Web sites, the preceding Internet addresses are subject to change, and there is no guarantee that they will continue to provide the data we list here.

Peru

WHAT'S YOUR CULTURAL I.Q.?

1. TRUE or FALSE? The magnificent ruins called Machu Picchu were built (and later abandoned) by the Aztecs before the Spanish reached Peru.

   ANSWER: False. Yes, Machu Picchu was abandoned, but it was built by the Incas, not the Aztecs. Often called "The Lost City of the Incas," it was unknown to the Spanish. US explorer Hiram Bingham discovered the ruins in 1911.

2. The Spanish made Peru the seat of Spanish South America because:

   a. It was the location of South America's biggest silver mine

   b. It was free from earthquakes

   c. It was the seat of the Inca Empire

   d. Its flat expanses made for easy travel

   ANSWER: c. Peru was the center of *Tahuantinsuyo*, which was what the Incas called their empire (the name means "four corners"). Peru also ruled Bolivia (where the great silver mine of Potosí is located). Peru is certainly not free of earthquakes; a 1971 quake measuring

7.7 on the Richter scale killed some 70,000 Peruvians. And, except for the coast, Peru is not at all flat—much of it is mountainous and difficult to traverse. The easternmost interior is flat, but this is part of the *montaña,* the dense Amazon jungle.

3. TRUE or FALSE? Tupac Amaru led the last major Inca rebellion against the Spanish in Peru.

   ANSWER: True. But that 1572 rebellion was not the last time the name of Tupac Amaru spread fear among Peru's overlords. Much later, in 1780, another Indian rebellion was led by someone claiming to be Tupac Amaru. And, in modern times, Peru's second largest terrorist organization is known as the *Movimiento Revolucionario Túpac Amaru.* This group grabbed international attention when its members seized the Japanese embassy in Lima, holding it for four months from December 1996 to April 1997.

4. Which of these is Peru's greatest unexploited natural resource? (Hint: ask any science fiction fan for the answer.)

   a. Peru's height and location

   b. The secrets of Peru's Inca ruins

   c. The extraterrestrial maps on the plains at Nazca

   ANSWER: a. Peru has the world's highest plains near the equator. It is easier to boost a spacecraft into orbit (or beyond) from earth's equator than from anywhere else (including Cape Canaveral). It also helps to start from a high launching site. Peru has high, dry plains near the equator. Science fiction writers often locate future spaceports in Peru. (By the way, although the odd lines at Nazca can best be viewed by airplane, that's not considered proof that the lines are the work of extraterrestrials.)

5. TRUE or FALSE? When the first Europeans arrived in Peru in 1532, the mighty Inca Empire had just been weakened by a five-year civil war.

ANSWER: True. The previous emperor had unwisely divided his empire between two sons, who battled for supremacy after their father died. Atahualpa defeated his brother and became the 13th Emperor of the Incas, but his victory was short-lived. The Spanish imprisoned him, collected a huge ransom for his release, and then killed him anyway.

6. Which of the following men declared Peru to be independent from Spain?

   a. Francisco Pizarro

   b. Diego de Almagro

   c. José de San Martín

   d. Simón Bolívar

ANSWER: c. Argentine freedom fighter José de San Martín chased the Spanish out of Lima and declared Peru independent in 1821. He left the mopping up to fellow rebel leader Simón Bolívar, who did not defeat the remaining Spanish troops until 1826. The other two men, Francisco Pizarro and Diego de Almagro, were two of the original conquistadores who conquered Peru for Spain. Both were killed by their quarrelsome fellow Spaniards.

7. TRUE or FALSE? After Peru's modest reserves of gold and silver were exhausted, and long before petroleum

was discovered, Peru's most valuable mineral resource was guano.

ANSWER: True. The guano in Peru's southern provinces became so valuable as a fertilizer that Chile fought two wars with Peru to gain control of it. Chile won both times.

8. TRUE or FALSE? At one time, the Spanish ruled all of South America from Lima, the capital of the Vice-royalty of Peru.

ANSWER: True. Francisco Pizarro founded Lima in 1535, where the Spanish administered their Vice-royalty until the colonial population grew too large and cumbersome. The northwest region, including Ecuador, was split off around 1739, and other regional divisions followed.

9. Today, which of these ethnic groups are the most pop-ulous in Peru?

a. The mestizos (people of mixed European and Amerindian descent)

b. The Aymara Indians

c. The Quechua Indians

d. The whites (people of European descent)

ANSWER: c. The Quechua alone make up almost half of all Peruvians. They are followed by the mestizos, the whites, and the Aymara.

10. TRUE or FALSE? The noted Peruvian author Mario Vargas Llosa was elected President of Peru in 1990.

ANSWER: False. Vargas Llosa ran for president in 1990, but came in second. The winner was Alberto Fujimori, the only South American head of state who is of Japanese descent.

QUOTATIONS ABOUT PERU

"High reef of the human dawn.
Spade buried in primordial sand.
This was the habitation, this is the site:
here the fat grains of maize grew high
to fall again like red hail.
The fleece of the vicuña was carded here
to clothe men's loves in gold, their tombs and mothers,
the king, the prayers, the warriors."

—From "The Heights of Macchu Picchu," by Chilean poet Pablo Neruda, who visited the Peruvian ruins in 1943.

"Through the prism of the mist, the heat of the low jungle sky seemed to focus on this wretched spot, where tarantulas and scorpions and stinging ants accompanied the mosquito and the biting fly into the huts, where the vampire bats, defecating even as they fed, would fasten on exposed toes at night, where one could never be certain that a bushmaster or fer-de-lance had not formed its cold coil in a dark corner. In the river, piranhas swam among the stingrays and candirus and the large crocodilians called lagartos; in adjacent swamps and forest lived the anaconda and the jaguar. But at Remate de Males such creatures were but irritants . . . "

—A description of *Remate de Males* (Spanish for *Culmination of Evils*), a jungle settlement near the Peruvian-Brazilian border, from Peter Matthiessen's pessimistic novel *At Play in the Fields of the Lord*.

"As in all rural houses of the Peruvian sierras, which almost always have a stone seat built-in next to the door, there was one leaning back by the threshold I had just

crossed. Doubtless it was the same ancient bench of my childhood, filled in and plastered numerous times."

—The homecoming of César Vallejo, from his autobiographical story *On The Other Side of Life and Death.*

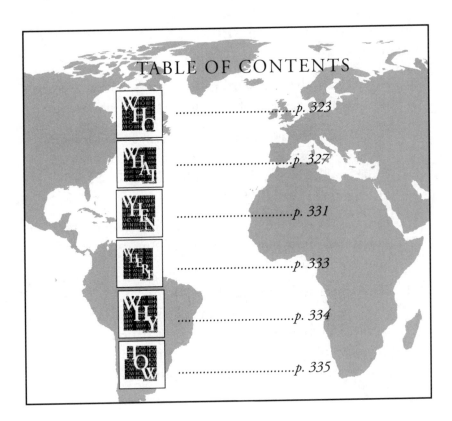

TABLE OF CONTENTS

THE PERUVIANS

Peru has always been a highly stratified society, with a wealthy oligarchy ruling over poor mestizos and even poorer Indians. The Amerindians constitute the largest group, with the Quechua numbering 47.1%, the Aymara making up 5.4%, and other Indian groups at 1.7%. Mestizos make up 32.0%, and whites account for only 12.0%. The remaining 1.8% includes the Japanese immigrants, from whom President Alberto Fujimori has descended.

The original immigrants to Peru during the colonial period were Spanish. Many of them intermarried with Amerindian populations, resulting in Peru's mestizo class.

HOW TO TELL PERU AND THE PERUVIANS FROM THEIR NEIGHBORS

Peru's borders have changed in the past 150 years, but there are several easily identifiable aspects of the country and its inhabitants:

1. Peru borders Ecuador, Colombia, Brazil, Bolivia, and Chile. Peru lost control of some southern territory to Chile, and its border dispute with Ecuador broke out into fighting in early 1995.

2. Peru was the center of Latin America's Inca Empire, the largest and most powerful group of Amerindians in South America.

3. While there are Asians in other Latin American countries (such as the South Koreans in Paraguay or the Japanese in Brazil), Peru is the only nation in the Americas to elect a president of Japanese descent. Alberto Fujimori was first elected to the presidency in 1989.

LITERATURE

Peru has produced several authors of note, including one with a world-wide reputation. They include:

Ciro Alegría (1909–67) sided with Peru's Indians against his fellow Hispanic Peruvians. His 1935 novel *La serpiente de oro* (English version published in 1943 as *The Golden Serpent*) celebrated the lives of Indians, setting the pattern for his later works. After two terms of imprisonment by Peruvian authorities, he fled into exile. In exile, he lived in Chile, Cuba, and the United States.

José María Arguedas (1911–69) also took the Indians of Peru as a recurring theme. A linguist and professor, he incorporated aspects of the Quechua language into his Spanish-language writings. The wandering narrator of his 1958 novel, *Los ríos profundos* (translated into English in 1978 as *Deep Rivers*) relates to nature but not to people. Arguedas also wrote poetry in Quechua. He killed himself in Lima in 1969.

Ricardo Palma (1833–1919) is the person most responsible for preserving Peruvian tradition and literature. His life's work was the six-volume *Tradiciones peruanas,* in which he took Peruvian tales dating from colonial times and recorded them in a complex, playful style, full of puns and metaphors. (In 1945, portions of the *Tradiciones* were translated into English as *The Knights of the Cape and 37 Other Selections from the Tradiciones peruanas.*) During the Chilean occupation of the War of the Pacific, both Palma's extensive personal library and the National Library of Peru were destroyed. After the war, he rebuilt the National Library's collection until it was once again one of the finest in South America.

César Vallejo (1892–1938) was born into a mestizo family in the Andean sierra. His childhood was happy until the death of his mother, which he recounted in his autobiographical story *On The Other Side of Life and Death.* In 1922 he wrote *Trilce* (English edition published in 1973), a collection of poems written after his wrongful imprisonment. The collection contains some of the finest poetry in the Spanish language. He left Peru in 1923, never to return. He worked as a journalist in Paris, became a Communist in Moscow, and helped to establish the Communist Party in Spain. Sickly for many years, he died in Paris in 1938.

Mario Vargas Llosa (1936–) is Peru's most famous celebrity, and one of the best-known authors in Latin America. No stranger to controversy, his first novel, *La ciudad y los perros* (1962, published in English in 1966 as *The Time of the Hero*), was publicly burned for its scathing treatment of life in a Peruvian military academy. His 1977 work, *La tía Julia y el escribidor,* published in English in 1982 as

Aunt Julia and the Scriptwriter, inspired the 1990 film *Tune In Tomorrow* (with the locale moved from Peru to New Orleans). Vargas Llosa is also a playwright and journalist. He ran for President of Peru in 1990, but was defeated by Alberto Fujimori. Note that, unlike most Latin Americans, he uses both his surnames in everyday usage. Thus his surname is alphabetized under **v,** not **ll** (**ll** being a separate letter in traditional Spanish).

LIGHTS! CAMERA! ACTION!

Peru has a nascent film industry, which has produced several movies to date. They include:

1. **La Boca del Lobo (The Mouth of the Wolf)** This film focuses on the guerilla war in Peru (eerily reminiscent of the Vietnam War). Set in a poor Indian village in the Andes, an army patrol searches for guerilla activity. But the guerillas are elusive; they attack only isolated soldiers, never the full patrol. When a new commanding officer decides that all the townspeople are renegades, a young soldier must decide whether to follow his conscience or his horrific orders. *Unforgettable moment:* The soldiers awake to find that, during the night, the guerillas have stolen their Peruvian flag and replaced it with a Marxist flag (1988, directed by Francisco J. Lombardi).

2. **The Green Wall** This film is an autobiographical story of a family who abandons urban life in Lima for the splendor of the Peruvian jungle (the "Green Wall" of the title). The jungle is presented as both idyllic and unforgiving. An interesting look at trading one set of problems for another (1969, directed by Armando Robles Godoy).

LANGUAGE

Peru now has three official languages: Spanish, plus the Amerindian languages Quechua and Aymara. All of your business contacts will speak Spanish, and some will speak English as well. Many Peruvian Indians are bilingual in Spanish and their native language. Only in the most remote areas are the Indians unfamiliar with Spanish.

Linguists have categorized 91 different languages spoken in modern Peru—*Ethnologue: Languages of the World,* 12th Edition from their Web site at (http://ww.sil.org/ethnologue/ethnologue.html).

BUSINESS SUCCESS IN PERU

Many foreign businesses become successful by appointing a local agent or representative in Peru. However, Peruvian law does not require a local representative to sell to the private sector. Foreign businesses may sell directly to Peruvian consumers.

Fast-food franchises have expanded in Peru in recent years. There is no law specifically governing franchises. Areas not yet serviced by franchises at this writing include automotive repair, fitness centers, clothing, pharmacies, hotels, and motels.

Joint ventures and licensing agreements are possible. Joint ventures in textiles have experienced strong growth. Items that can be assembled or finished in Peru have potential, especially when such locally finished goods are cheaper than imports (which are subject to import duties and high shipping costs).

Direct marketing is well developed in Peru, and telemarketing firms are available. Data bases of potential customers exist but are expensive to acquire.

Peruvian consumers tend to distrust the quality of items sold by mail. Traditionally, such products have had problems with warranties and after-sale service. As a result, Peruvians make relatively few purchases through catalogs.

Inexpensive goods from Asia (especially South Korea and Taiwan) have acquired a major share of the Peruvian market. Products from Europe and North America can best compete with Asian goods by emphasizing quality and after-sale service.

Advertising expenditures in Peru have grown by around 20% per year in the 1990s. Radio enjoys the widest audience, reaching Peruvians even in the most remote and rugged areas. Television is popular, but not all Peruvians possess television receivers. The newspaper market is important but fractured; no less than 15 papers compete on a national basis.

LEGAL AFFAIRS IN PERU

Terrorist groups such as the Shining Path and the Túpac Amaru Revolutionary Movement receive worldwide publicity, but their actions do not generally affect the international business traveler. The cocaine industry has more influence on international business, due to its high profitability, inherent violence, and the government efforts to limit it. Two-thirds of the world's coca crop is grown in Peru. The law enforcement agencies of many nations monitor the Peruvian drug traffic. Consequently, innocent business travelers to Peru may find police attention focused on them.

Human rights are still a concern in Peru, although the situation has improved. Extralegal activities by the government still occur, and suspected guerrillas have been seized and killed. In 1992, a professor and nine students were abducted and slain by the military. The Peruvian leadership passed a decree preventing civilian courts from investigating this incident. Such a decree seems to be in violation of the Constitution.

LEADING BUSINESSES IN PERU

The following businesses are some of the largest employers in Peru:

Banco Credito del Peru
Lima.
National commercial bank. 5,500 employees

Cooperativa Agraria Azucarera Casa Grande Ltda
La Liberta.
Sugarcane and sugar beets. 4,500 employees.
CPT-Telefonica del Peru SA
Lima.
Telephone communications. 9,000 employees.
Empresa Minera del Centro del Peru SA
Lima.
Copper ores. 8,500 employees.
Empresa Nacional de Telecomunicaciones del Peru SA
Lima.
Communication services. 9,000 employees.
Empresa Nacional de Transporte Urbano del Peru SA
Lima.
Local passenger transportation. 5,000 employees.
Petroleos del Peru SA
Lima.
Crude petroleum and natural gas. 5,580 employees.
Southern Peru Copper Corp
Lima.
Copper ores. 5,570 employees.

The following are some of the largest newspaper publishers in Peru:

Empresa Editorial El Comercio SA
Lima.
700 employees.
Publisher of *El Comercio,* Peru's oldest and largest national daily newspaper.
Editoria La República SA
Lima.
360 employees.
Publisher of *La República,* Peru's leading Leftist daily newspaper.
Empresa Periodistica Nacional SA
Lima.
420 employees.

Empresa Peruana de Servicios Editoriales SA
Lima.
338 employees.

PERUVIAN LEADERS

President Alberto Fujimori has almost single-handedly remade Peru. When he was elected in 1989 (using a slogan of "Honesty, Technology, and Work"), Peru was suffering massive inflation and only one in five Peruvians had a steady full-time job. Twelve days after taking office, Fujimori instituted an economic reform package that included slashing subsidies on food and fuel. Many Peruvians suffered, but the economy gradually recovered. In 1992, Fujimori took it upon himself to dissolve the Peruvian congress and suspend the constitution—a highly illegal act that evoked protests from the USA and other democracies. Yet the gambit succeeded; without the obstructionist (and unpopular) congress, Fujimori was able to institute massive reforms.

Interestingly, before he was first elected, Fujimori was affectionately known to the Peruvians as *El Chinito* (the little Chinaman), despite the fact that he is of Japanese ancestry. Once he became president and established his authority, the diminutive was dropped and his nickname became *El Chino*.

Vladimiro Montesinos, an intelligence consultant, is sometimes considered the second most powerful man in Peru. He is a close advisor to President Fujimori, yet he holds no official job or title. Montesinos is believed to have planned Fujimori's 1992 "coup," and helped to cripple the Shining Path guerillas. But Montesinos' days of glory may be numbered—in the summer of 1996, one of Peru's biggest drug traffickers, Demetrio Chávez Peñaherrera testified that he paid Montesinos $50,000 per month to facilitate cocaine shipments. Although Chávez later recanted his testimony, Montesinos remains under suspicion.

Carlos Abimael Guzmán, a.k.a. Presidente Gonzalo, a.k.a. The Fourth Sword of Marxism, was the leader of the Communist Party of Peru, better known as the *Sendero Luminoso* (Shining Path). At their peak, his guerillas controlled about half of Peru's rural areas. He was captured in 1992, after which thousands of his *Senderos* were arrested. Although crippled, the organization made a resurgence in mid-1996 under the command of Oscar Ramirez Durand, known as *Comrade Feliciano.*

PERUVIAN HISTORY

Before 1438: Several Amerindian cultures rise and fall, including the Chavín, the Mochinca, and the Nazca. Later, the Tiahuanaco of Bolivia expands into Peru. When they retreat, the Chimu achieve supremacy in Peru, and build large cities. The Inca at this time are restricted to southern coastal areas.

1438–1532: The Incans become the preeminent Amerindian people in Peru, establishing an empire that encompasses Ecuador, Peru, and Bolivia, and reaching into parts of Argentina and Chile.

1532: The Incan Empire is rocked by a civil war. After Emperor Atahualpa emerges as the victor, the first Europeans arrive. An expedition led by Francisco Pizarro captures Atahualpa and executes him. The Spaniards make great headway toward conquering the now-leaderless Inca. Pizarro founds Lima in 1535.

1537: The Spanish victors fight among themselves and Pizarro is slain.

1548: Representatives of the Spanish crown defeat the rebel conquistadores, and consolidate their hold on what is now the Viceroyalty of Peru.

1739: As the colonial population grows, administration of the Viceroyalty from Lima becomes more difficult. The northwest, including Ecuador, is split off as part of the Viceroyalty of New Granada. Later, Argentina and Bolivia are placed into the new Viceroyalty of La Plata.

1780–83: The remaining Incas make a last stand, led by Tupac Amaru.

1820: As one of Spain's oldest colonies, Peru remains loyal while other South American countries rebel. Argentine rebel José de San Martín leads his army from Chile into Peru.

1821: The Spanish troops withdraw from Lima. José de San Martín declares Peru independent on 28 July 1821. He then withdraws and leaves Peru to fellow rebel leader Simón Bolívar. The remaining Spanish troops are not defeated until 1826.

1823: José de la Riva Agüero becomes the first president of Peru. But the Peruvian congress soon invites Simón Bolívar to become dictator. Bolívar intends to unite Peru and the Confederation of Gran Colombia. He leaves Peru in 1827 when Gran Columbia experiences instability.

1836–39: Peru and Bolivia join in a brief union. The union is split up by invading armies from Chile. Peru then suffers from civil war.

1845: Army leader Ramón Castilla becomes president for the first time. In two nonsuccessive terms of office, he unites Peru's factions and institutes many reforms, including the abolishing of slavery.

1866: Spain attempts to reconquer Peru. Ecuador, Peru, Bolivia, and Chile unite to beat back the Spanish attack. Spain finally recognizes Peru's independence in 1879.

1879–81: The War of the Pacific pits Peru and Bolivia against Chile. Chile wins again, occupying Lima in 1881. Peru cedes its southernmost province of Tarapacá—with its valuable nitrate deposits—to Chile. Territorial disputes with Chile are not finally settled until 1929.

1932: Peru and Colombia almost go to war over a border dispute.

1939: After years of dictatorship, constitutional leadership is reestablished when Manuel Prado is elected president. He brings Peru into the Second World War on the Allied side in 1945.

1968–80: A military dictatorship once again rules Peru.

1989: After a decade of economic decline in Peru, Alberto Fujimori is elected president. He makes radical changes to the Peruvian economy. In 1992, he dissolves congress and suspends the constitution, after which he institutes further reforms. Peru's economy begins to recover.

1995: In January, military forces from Ecuador and Peru fight over the disputed border in the Cordillera del Cóndor region. Thanks to better positioning and superior weapons, the Ecuadorians get the better of the exchange. But neither side wins an outright victory, and the border remains undelineated.

1996: On 17 December, some 20 members of the Túpac Amaru Revolutionary Movement seize the Japanese Embassy in Lima. Over 400 guests are held hostage, although this number is eventually reduced to 72. The rebels demand the release of some 400 imprisoned members of their group; President Fujimori refuses to comply.

1997: In April, Peruvian forces storm the Japanese Embassy, killing all of the 14 Túpac Amaru terrorists. Only one of the 72 hostages dies, and all of the Japanese nationals are released unharmed. President Fujumori's popularity soars.

PERUVIAN GEOGRAPHY

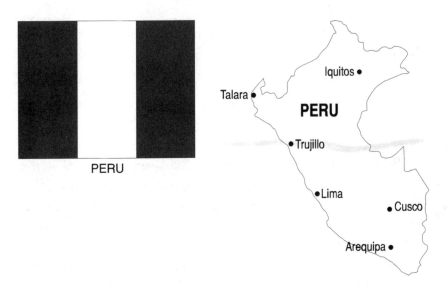

FLAG AND MAP OF PERU

The white in the Peruvian flag is meant to represent justice and peace. The red stands for the blood of those who fought for Peru's independence from Spain. Legend has it that the colors were chosen by General José de San Martín, the liberator of Peru, who was inspired by some flamingos that flew over his victorious troops.

Size: 496,225 square miles

Population: 24,087,372

What the Aztecs were to Mexico, the Incas were to Peru. Peru was the center of the Incan Empire, which the Incans called *Tahuantinsuyo* (Four Corners).

Peru's premier tourist attraction, Machu Picchu, is the most impressive Amerindian site in South America. Built by the Incas, it was abandoned for an unknown reason and remained unknown to the Spanish colonizers. Only in 1911 was it discovered, by a US adventurer named Hiram Bingham. Bingham was actually searching for Vilcabamba, a different Inca site. Vilcabamba was the location of the Inca's last stand—the final fortress to be held by the Incas against the invading Spaniards. Bingham thought he'd found it when he stumbled onto Machu Picchu, but Vilcabamba was later identified as the modern-day Espíritu Pampa.

No visitor to Peru should pass up the chance to visit Machu Picchu.

PERUVIAN BEHAVIOR

Why are Peruvians the way they are?

Peru's social stratification permeates all facets of life. Unlike the Latin American nations to the south, Peru has a large Amerindian population—far too large to be ignored. These Indians have been marginalized economically, and make up some of the poorest people in South America.

The Amerindians constitute the lowest strata of Peruvian society. Many of them live in conditions that have scarcely changed for hundreds of years.

Mestizos make up the next level. While often oppressed by the ruling class, it was the mestizos who elected Alberto Fujimori (a fellow outcast) as president in 1990.

Like all ruling classes, the white Peruvians fight to retain their hold on power. Most business dealings will be with members of this class.

What do you call Peru's Amerindians?

The term *indios* is now considered insulting. *Indigenas* is acceptable. However, most Peruvians call them *campesinos*, or peasants. Of course, in Peru's class-conscious society, most mestizos (persons of mixed Spanish and Indian ancestry) would be insulted if they were mistaken for Amerindians—even though some mestizos are no better off than many campesinos.

How do Peruvians dress?

Peruvians tend to be more formal than North Americans, and dress is considered an important indicator of a person's status. Conservative business attire is expected.

What's the greatest hazard in Peru for foreign travelers?

Cholera outbreaks, terrorism, and earthquakes get the publicity, but the traveler's greatest risk in Peru is from altitude sickness. Lima is near sea level, but other popular destinations (such as Cuzco and the area around Lake Titicaca) are high enough for this illness.

Anyone can be struck by altitude sickness, and rest is the only sure cure. Be aware that Peruvian folk remedies for the sickness usually contain coca leaves. (Coca leaves, which are chewed by many Amerindians, are legal in Peru. Cocaine itself is highly illegal.)

HOW CAN I FIND MORE INFORMATION ABOUT PERU?

Here are a few resources to start with:

Getting Through Customs' Web site at **http://www. getcustoms.com** tracks current holidays in Peru. They also post Cultural I.Q. Quizzes, gift-giving guidelines, a demo of the PASSPORT database, and further international information. Telephone: (610) 353-9894; fax (610) 353-6994.

Embassy of Peru
1700 Massachusetts Avenue NW
Washington, DC 20036
Telephone: (202) 833-9860

The Ministry of Foreign Affairs of Peru has a Web site at: **http://www.rree.gob.pe/i-defaul.htm**.

Commission for the Promotion of Peru
PROMPERU
Calle 1 Oeste s/n, Urb. Córpac—Lima 27
Telephone: 224-3408 / 224-3396
Telefax: 224-3396
http://www.foptur.gob.pe

Peru on the Internet
http://www.latinworld.com/countries/peru/

The International Academy at Santa Barbara at **http://www.iasb.org/cwl** publishes *Current World Leaders,* an excellent resource for data on political leaders and parties in Peru. Telephone (800) 530-2682 or (805) 965-5010 for subscription information.

The Bureau of Consular Affairs at **http://travel.state.gov** can give you detailed information on obtaining passports, visa requirements, and consular affairs bulletins.

The Center for Disease Control at **http://www.cdc.gov/** provides valuable medical information, as well as information on any outbreaks of virulent infections in Peru.

Like all Web sites, the preceding Internet addresses are subject to change, and there is no guarantee that they will continue to provide the data we list here.

Uruguay

WHAT'S YOUR CULTURAL I.Q.?

1. Which of the following are the original inhabitants of Uruguay?

   a. The Aztec

   b. The Charrúa

   c. The Guaraní

   d. The Inca

   ANSWER: b. The Charrúa Indians, who were also known as the Querandí. They killed the first European explorers who arrived in Uruguay in 1516.

2. TRUE or FALSE? The Portuguese were the first Europeans to establish a permanent settlement on Uruguayan soil.

   ANSWER: True. The Portuguese fortress at Colonia was the first, built in 1680.

3. The Uruguayans expelled the Spanish from their country in 1811, only to be occupied by another power. Who was this second occupier?

a. Argentina

b. Brazil

c. The Charrúa

d. Portugal

ANSWER: b. Brazil was not removed from Uruguay until 1828.

4. TRUE or FALSE? The Uruguayans finally achieved independence with the help of the United States of America.

ANSWER: False. It was the UK, not the USA, that helped broker Uruguayan independence.

5. TRUE or FALSE? In 1970, a US adviser named Dan Mitrione was kidnapped in Montevideo and killed by the Communist Tupamaro Movement.

ANSWER: True. The true nature of Dan Mitrione's job has never been proven. The US and Uruguayan governments claimed he was an innocent adviser for the Agency for International Development (USAID). The *Tupamaros* maintain he was a CIA agent, teaching torture and interrogation techniques to the Uruguayan police. The incident was fictionalized in the 1973 Costa-Gavras film *State of Siege*.

6. The military junta that ruled Uruguay from 1973 to 1980 classified every adult Uruguayan using a system of letters. Which of the following letters was NOT used in this notorious classification system?

a. A

b. B

c. C

d. X

ANSWER: d. Only the first three letters of the alphabet were used. Under this classification, *A* meant *Reliable*, *B* stood for *Questionable*, and *C* was *Subversive*.

7. The military junta ruled Uruguay with an iron hand during the 1970s. Peace was restored at the cost of human rights. TRUE or FALSE? Thousands of Uruguayans were slain by the junta.

ANSWER: False. Although Uruguay suffered through one of the most brutal regimes ever seen in Latin America, relatively few citizens were killed. However, thousands were imprisoned or fled into exile.

8. Which of the following superlatives is NOT true about Uruguay?

a. Uruguay has the strongest economy in Latin America

b. More of Uruguay's population lives in urban areas (mostly Montevideo) than any other people in Latin America

c. Uruguay boasts the most literate population in South America

d. About 86% of Uruguayans are direct descendants of European immigrants—the highest proportion in South America

ANSWER: a. Uruguay has a lot to boast about, but its economy has been sluggish for decades.

9. TRUE or FALSE? The tax structure in Uruguay encourages its citizens to save.

ANSWER: False. Just the opposite—Uruguayans who save are penalized. The current taxes encourage Uruguayans to spend their income.

10. Uruguayans enjoy a drink called yerba mate, which is also known as Paraguayan tea. Which of the following is NOT part of the yerba drinking ritual?

    a. The yerba mate leaf is packed into a gourd

    b. The cebador (server) pours hot water into the gourd

    c. The first drinker drains the gourd, after which it is refilled with hot water for the next drinker

    d. The drinkers spit the yerba mate leafs in the general direction of Paraguay

ANSWER: d. The tea is drunk through a silver straw which has a screen on the bottom end (to keep the yerba mate leaves from being sucked into the mouth).

QUOTATIONS ABOUT URUGUAY

"The scenery is very uninteresting; there is scarcely a house, an enclosed piece of ground, or even a tree, to give it an air of cheerfulness."

—Charles Darwin, exploring the desolate country north of the Plata.

"Through such 'armed propaganda' and guerrilla theater, the Tupamaros generated a growing public following. They'd break into illicit money-laundering operations in the middle of the night...embarrassing mainstream politicians and business leaders. They bombed a number of subsidiaries of American corporations, but again, always late at night, never intending to maim or kill, and usually with explosive charges far more noisy than destructive. They'd leave behind a spray of pamphlets. The posh Montevideo Country Club was spread atop a lovely hill, overlooking the gleaming blue sea and surrounded by a

*lazily undulating green golf course—all on public land,
though land arbitrarily closed to virtually everyone in
Montevideo, except club members, every day of the week
except Sunday. Late one weeknight, the Tupamaros blew
the clubhouse to smithereens, and the next morning virtually everyone in Montevideo, except club members, had
trouble restraining a smile. Once, in the wee hours of
another morning, they ransacked an exclusive high-class
nightclub, scrawling the walls with perhaps their most
memorable slogan: O BAILAN TODOS O NO BAILAN
NADIE—Either everybody dances or nobody dances."*

—From *A Miracle, A Universe: Settling Accounts with Torturers,* a
study of dictatorial regimes by US writer Lawrence Weschler. The
escalating actions of the Communist Tupamaros in the 1960s led
first to a draconian government crackdown, and then to the military
dictatorship of 1972–81.

*"It's really very curious how people repeat Vain
Endeavours. However, their subsequent attempts aren't
included in the catalog: they'd take up too much space.
One man made seven attempts to fly, each time equipped
with different apparatus; several prostitutes wanted to
find alternative employment; a woman wanted to paint a
picture; someone struggled to lose his sense of fear; almost
everyone was trying to be immortal or at least lived as if
they were.*

*"The attendant assures me that only a tiny percent-
age of all the Vain Endeavours undertaken actually get
into the museum."*

—From the short story "The Museum of Vain Endeavours" by
Uruguayan writer Christina Peri Rossi.

*"We 'took maté' with them and the gauchos... 'tomar maté'
is the idiom, literally 'to take the pot' but it means to drink*

yerba herb tea through a silver pipe from a gourd pot called a maté. Socially it means even more; it is the Uruguayan symbol of hospitality.

"Custom requires that all in the same circle of friendliness drink from the same pot and the same silver pipe.... There is a belief that germs cannot live on the hot silver pipe, that it is self sterilizing. I hope that the belief is true, for the rite is as unavoidable as kissing the bride.

"Maté is not unpleasant, being much like green tea, but it is an acquired taste. Uruguayans and Argentinos set much store by it and believe that it is food, drink, and vitamins all wrapped in the same package. There is a story of a besieged garrison that lived for weeks on maté alone. The story is almost certainly true but I would find it a thin diet."

—From *Tramp Royale*, Robert A. Heinlein's travel memoir. The gauchos are the cowboys of Uruguay and Argentina.

"He was born here, on the coast. The river, the sand, and the countryside have isolated and nullified him for fifty years, while the mailboat maintains his illusion of being in touch with the faraway events he considers history. His isn't a person; like all the inhabitants of this side of the river, he is a certain intensity of existence that occupies, or takes the shape of his personal mania, his personal idiocy. Because around here we only differ from one another in the type of self-negation we choose or which is imposed on us. A little joke of a country, from the coast to the rails that limit Colonia, where each one of us grows up in his role and plays it badly."

—From *Body Snatcher* by Uruguayan author Juan Carlos Onetti.

"In a few months the Season will be here again. The international golf, polo, fishing, yachting, tennis, bridge. Above

all: the social contest. Three months of it, ending in a hys-teria of carnival. Then everyone pours away, because that also is the done thing."

—Gordon Meyer, describing the tourist town of Punta del Este in *Summer at High Altitude.*

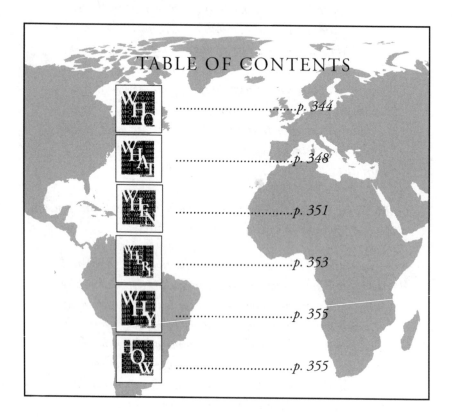

THE URUGUAYANS

 Uruguay has the most ethnically European population in Latin America: 86.0% of Uruguayans are direct descendants of European immigrants. Mestizos make up only 8.0%, and blacks around 6.0%.

Immigrants to Uruguay came from all over Europe, but Spanish and Italians predominate. Other substantial populations included Germans, English, Slavs, and Eastern European Jews.

Eighty-seven percent of Uruguayans live in urban zones; this is the highest per capita urban population in Latin America.

URUGUAYAN CULTURE

LITERATURE

For such a small country, Uruguay has been blessed with numerous authors and playwrights. Uruguay is the most literate country in South America. Only Argentina has a greater per capita consumption of newspapers.

Uruguay's most noted authors include:

Mario Benedetti (1920–) writes in many different genres: He is a poet, a novelist, an essayist, playwright, and literary critic. His fiction often depicts the lives of middle class denizens of large urban areas. He fled the military dictatorship in Uruguay, traveling to Argentina, Peru (from where he was deported), and Cuba. Most of his work has not been translated into English.

José Enrique Rodó is Uruguay's most famous author. *Ariel,* his classic novel, is one of the few Uruguayan works available in English.

Eduardo Galeano is a historian and essayist. No one is spared in Galeano's caustic writing. His *Open Veins of Latin America: Five Centuries of the Pillage of a Continent* begins with this:

> *"The division of labor among nations is that some specialize in winning and others in losing. Our part of the world, known today as Latin America, was precocious: it has specialized in losing ever since those remote times when Renaissance Europeans ventured across the ocean*

and buried their teeth in the throats of the Indian civilizations."

Juan Carlos Onetti (1909–94), a novelist, was one of Uruguay's best-known contemporary writers. After working as a journalist in Argentina, he returned to Uruguay and began publishing fiction. His first novel, *El pozo (The Pit),* published in 1939, was eventually hailed as the forerunner of a new trend in Latin American literature. His works are characteristically bleak, focusing on middle-aged men leading despairing lives. His 1950 novel *Una Vida Breve* (published in English in 1976 as *A Brief Life*) was set in a fictional city of Santa María, which resembles his native Montevideo. Many of his later works used this fictional locale. In 1974, he was arrested by the military junta for writing "pornography." Upon his release, he fled to exile in Spain, where he lived until his death in Madrid in 1994. His son, Jorge Onetti, is also a novelist.

Pablo Vierci (1950–) was born in Montevideo and continues to write in Spanish, but he has lived in Portuguese-speaking Brazil since 1974. His comic first novel, *Los Tramoyistas,* was published in English in 1979 as *The Impostors: The Truth and the Lies about Their Travels in the Amazon.*

Juan Zorilla de San Martín is considered by many to be South America's finest romantic poet. His son, José Luis Zorilla de San Martín, is well known as a sculptor.

One of the best accounts of Uruguay under the dictatorship is by US writer Lawrence Weschler, in his book *A Miracle, A Universe: Settling Accounts with Torturers.*

INVITATION TO THE DANCE

Like the Argentines, the Uruguayans are big fans of the tango. And, as in Argentina, there is the same division between *tangueros* (tango aficionados). Older fans tend to prefer the traditional (pre-1950s) tango; the younger people tend to enjoy the tango variations pioneered by Astor Piazzolla, the Argentine tango composer.

Remember that tango refers to a style of music, not just a dance. There are plenty of tango works that are not meant to be danced to.

The tango is not the only style of indigenous music in Uruguay. Although Uruguay has a minuscule black population, a style of Afro-Uruguayan music and dance called *candombe* has evolved.

LIGHTS! CAMERA! ACTION!

Uruguay does not have a major indigenous film industry. However, a few movies have been made using Uruguay as a locale. They include:

1. **El Muerto** A Latin American version of a Western, complete with cowboys (gauchos) and rustlers. The time is the late 19th century (in fact, the film climaxes on New Year's Eve, 1899). A young man kills another in a street fight in Buenos Aires, and must flee Argentina to avoid arrest. He soon finds work with an elderly Uruguayan rancher and gunrunner. The old outlaw has everything the young man wants: a ranch, a gang, money, and a beautiful mistress. Can he successfully supplant the old chief? *Unforgettable moment:* The cocky young man uses a horse he doesn't own as collateral on a bet! Based on a short story by Jorge Luis Borges (1979, directed by Hector Olivera).

2. **State of Siege** In 1970, the Uruguayan *Tupamaros* (Communist Underground) kidnapped a US adviser named Dan Mitrione in Montevideo. The Tupamaros claimed that Mitrione was teaching torture and interrogation techniques to the Uruguayan police. The US and Uruguayan governments denied this; they claimed Mitrione was just an advisor from the US Agency for International Development. The Tupamaros executed Mitrione, setting the stage for the years of brutal

repression by the Uruguayan government. *State of Siege* is Constantin Costa-Gavras' fictionalized version of the Mitrione kidnapping, starring Yves Montand as the kidnapped American. *Unforgettable moment:* The *Túpamaros'* leader meeting various members on a bus, where they vote for or against executing the American. Costa-Gavras would later explore the military coup in Chile in his film *Missing* (1973, directed by Constantin Costa-Gavras).

LANGUAGE

The official language of Uruguay is Spanish, but as in Argentina, the Uruguayans speak a very distinct dialect of Spanish. There were so many immigrants from Italy that the Uruguayan Spanish absorbed many Italian words. However, if you speak formal Spanish, you will be able to make yourself understood.

Furthermore, near the border with Brazil, some Uruguayans speak a mixture of Spanish and Portuguese. This hybrid is called *fronterizo*.

BUSINESS IN URUGUAY

BUSINESS SUCCESS IN URUGUAY

Caveat: Uruguay has no income tax. Instead, citizens are taxed on their net worth. This method of taxation is inimical to saving—the Uruguayan who lives from paycheck to paycheck, never putting anything aside, comes out ahead under this scheme. It should come as no surprise that Uruguayans tend to have low amounts of savings.

Thus far, franchises in Uruguay have been limited to a few areas, such as food and garments. The fast-food franchises have shown rapid growth.

Joint ventures and licensing agreements are common in Uruguay. Direct marketing has not been found to be cost effective, in part because of Uruguay's small size.

Many of Uruguay's industries have not had the resources to upgrade their technologies. This has made Uruguay a good market for used and/or obsolete machinery. This also minimizes difficulties with incompatible technologies. If something works, Uruguayans are happy to use it, even if a newer version is available.

The lack of capital has made financing a major factor in sales in Uruguay. A foreign firm that offers reliable (but not necessarily state-of-the-art) goods via creative financing methods will succeed in Uruguay.

Advertising rates are currently affordable in Uruguay. Television and newspapers are the most popular venues. Uruguayans are conservative by nature, and new products can take a long time to gain acceptance.

LEGAL AFFAIRS IN URUGUAY

Many countries with limited freedom of speech restrict what can be said about the government. But Uruguay also limits speech about the heads of state of other countries.

In May of 1996, two Uruguayan journalists were sentenced by Uruguayan courts to two years of imprisonment for reporting on the corrupt activities of the President of Paraguay. Uruguayan law makes it a crime to question the honor of a foreign head of state.

LEADING BUSINESSES IN URUGUAY

The following businesses are some of the largest employers in Uruguay:

Administracion Nacional de Combustibles Alcohol y Portland
Montevideo.
Cane sugar refining. 4,653 employees.

Administracion Nacional de Telecomunicaciones
Montevideo.
Telephone communications. 7,062 employees.

Administracion Nacional de Usinas y Trasmisiones Electricas
Montevideo.
Electric services. 9,934 employees.

Banco de la Republica Oriental de Uruguay
Montevideo.
State commercial bank. 6,300 employees.

Compania Sudamericana de Empresas Electricas Mecanicas
Montevideo.
Residential construction. 1,973 employees.

Cooperativa Nacional de Productores de Leche
Montevideo.
Creamery butter. 2,576 employees.

Metzen y Sena SA
Montevideo.
Pottery products. 1,800 employees.

The following are some of the largest newspapers in Uruguay:

El Pais Sociedad Anonima
Montevideo.
650 employees.

Reg Sociedad Anonima
Montevideo.
300 employees.

URUGUYAN HISTORY

Until 1516: Uruguay is home to a small tribe called the Charrua (sometimes called the Querandí), the original indigenous inhabitants of Uruguay.

1516: Spanish explorer Juan Díaz de Solís leads the first known expedition to Uruguay. He and most of his party are slain by the Charrua. (Later, the Charrua were themselves wiped out of existence by the colonizers.)

1680: The Portuguese found Uruguay's first permanent outpost, the fortress of Colonia, directly across the Rio de la Plata from Buenos Aires.

1726: The Spanish found Montevideo, largely to contest Portuguese domination of Uruguay. Many of Montevideo's first residents are brought from the Canary Islands. Montevideo has a good harbor and becomes a valued port of call to ships of all nations.

1777: Portugal cedes Colonia to Spain. The Spanish add Uruguay to the new Viceroyalty of Rio de la Plata.

1811: Under the leadership of José Gervasio Aritgas (later hailed as the Father of Uruguay), the Uruguayans fight for independence from Spain. They succeed, only to be occupied by troops from newly independent Brazil in 1821.

1825: A group of patriots (who become known as the Thirty-three Immortals), led by Juan Antonio Lavalleja, battle the Brazilians for control of Uruguay. The British intercede on the side of the Uruguayans, forcing the Brazilians out.

1828: Uruguayan independence is recognized by Brazil. Uruguay is allowed to exist as a buffer state between Brazil and Argentina.

1839–51: The Uruguayan Civil War is fought between the Colorados (Reds) and the Blancos (Whites). The two sides will continue to jockey for power.

1865–70: Uruguay joins Brazil and Argentina to pummel Paraguay in the War of the Triple Alliance.

1903–7: José Batlle y Ordóñez of the Colorados is elected president for the first time. A well-educated journalist, Batlle brings peace and stability to Uruguay. When he returns to the Presidency in 1911, he establishes social welfare legislation that is far in advance of any other Latin American country. Uruguay comes to be known as "the Switzerland of South America." Beef exports bring prosperity to Uruguay.

1950s: Uruguay's prosperity begins to wane. A boycott imposed by Argentine dictator Juan Perón damages the Uruguayan beef industry.

1960s: Uruguay's extensive social welfare system begins to bankrupt the country. Social unrest increases. The Communist National Liberation Movement, known as the *Tupamaros,* begin an urban guerrilla war.

1972: Unable to deal with increasing social unrest, Colorado president Juan Bordaberry turns to the Uruguayan military for help.

1973–80: A military junta takes control of Uruguay, imposing peace through one of the most brutal regimes seen in Latin America. While few citizens are killed, thousands are imprisoned or flee into exile. Every adult Uruguayan is classified as either A (Reliable), B (Questionable), or C (Subversive).

1981: Uruguay returns to civilian rule, although the military remains in the background.

URUGUAYAN GEOGRAPHY

URUGUAY

URUGUAY

FLAG AND MAP OF URUGUAY

Inspired by the successful revolution of the United States of America, the flag of Uruguay was chosen to resemble the Stars and Stripes. The nine alternating blue/white stripes represent Uruguay's nine original provinces. The sun symbol is called the Sun of May. This symbol dates back to the first demonstration of Uruguayans against their Spanish colonial overlords in May of 1810. During the demonstration, sunlight (the Sun of May) broke through the clouds, and was interpreted as God's favor shining on the demonstrators.

Size: 176,215 square miles

Population: 2,955,241

Uruguay is the smallest country of the Southern Cone of South America. Uruguay is a charter member of the Mercosur Customs Trade Union. The other Mercosur members are Argentina, Brazil, Paraguay, and (most recently) Chile. Collectively, Mercosur represents a population of 213,611,000.

Is There Anything There Besides Montevideo?

By far Uruguay's largest city, Montevideo is home to 1.3 million people—almost half of Uruguay's population. Montevideo dominates Uruguay even more than Buenos Aires dominates Argentina.

For tourists, Uruguay might as well consist of just Montevideo, its environs, and the Atlantic Resorts like Punta del Este. Unless you have business with the ranchers in the Uruguayan hinterlands, it will be the same for you.

Like all big cities, Montevideo has its share of problems, which are exacerbated by a poor economy. Montevideo has enough run-down neighborhoods to acquire the local appellation of un necrópolis de sueños rotos—*a dead city of broken dreams.*

continues

> *But the disappointments of the city's inhabitants are not the concern of most visitors, and Montevideo continues to draw thousands of tourists each year.*

HOW TO TELL URUGUAY AND THE URUGUAYANS FROM THEIR NEIGHBORS

Here are a few ways to differentiate Uruguay from its neighboring countries:

1. Uruguay is tiny. It is the smallest of the Spanish-speaking countries of South America. It's even smaller than the former colony of Guyana (formerly British Guiana). Only Suriname (formerly Dutch Guiana) and French Guiana are smaller than Uruguay.

2. Uruguay borders just two countries, Argentina and Brazil—the two largest nations in South America. In fact, Uruguay owes its existence to the fact that it serves as a buffer nation between these two aggressive giants.

3. In terms of behavioral styles, you can draw a line northward from Argentina through Uruguay into Brazil. At one end are the conservative Argentines, who dress formally and seem to be serious even when they're having fun. At the other end are the hedonistic Brazilians (notably the residents of Rio de Janeiro). The Uruguayans are in the middle. Although they are linguistically and ethnically closer to the Argentines, Uruguayans are more relaxed and informal. But Uruguayans are not quite as uninhibited as Brazilians.

URUGUAYAN BEHAVIOR

What is mate and why does everyone drink it?

Mate (pronounced "mah-tay") is a drink prepared from the yerba mate leaf (*Ilex paraguayensis*), and is also known as Paraguayan tea. Uruguayans of every social and economic class drink it. It is not alcoholic, but, like coffee and tea, it contains caffeine.

The ritual surrounding mate drinking approaches the complexity of the Japanese tea ceremony. Mate is drunk in groups, but only one container is used. This container, called a gourd, looks like a cone with the top point lopped off—not unlike some travel coffee mugs that have wide bases for stability. The mate gourd can be a simple wooden cup or a fancy silver vessel, depending on the owner's wealth. The cebador (server) fills the gourd with chopped yerba leaves, then pours not-quite-boiling water into the gourd. A skillful cebador pours the water such that it produces a good froth. The gourd is then handed to the first drinker, who sips the mixture through a silver straw. After the gourd is drained, it is returned to the cebador, who then refills it with hot water and hands the gourd to the next drinker.

How do Uruguayans dress?

The Uruguayans are somewhat less formal than their neighboring Argentines. Nevertheless, business attire is formal.

HOW CAN I FIND MORE INFORMATION ABOUT URUGUAY?

Here are a few resources to start with:

Getting Through Customs' Web site at **http://www. getcustoms.com** tracks current holidays in Uruguay. They also post Cultural I.Q. Quizzes, gift-giving guidelines, a demo of the PASSPORT database, and further international information. Telephone: (610) 353-9894; fax (610) 353-6994.

Embassy of Uruguay
3rd Floor
2715 M Street, N.W.
Washington, DC 20007
Telephone: (202) 331-1313; fax: (202) 331-8142
http://www.embassy.org/uruguay/

Uruguayan Office of Tourism
541 Lexington Avenue
New York, NY 10022
Telephone: (212) 755-1200, ext. 346

Nexo Uruguay—cultural, medical, business, and tourist
information. Sponsored by the Uruguayan Ministry of
Tourism.
http://www.nexo.com.uy/

Uruguay on the Internet
http://www.latinworld.com/countries/uruguay/

The International Academy at Santa Barbara at
http://www.iasb.org/cwl publishes *Current World Leaders*,
an excellent resource for data on political leaders and parties in Uruguay. Telephone: (800) 530-2682 or (805)
965-5010 for subscription information.

The Bureau of Consular Affairs at **http://travel.state.gov**
can give you detailed information on obtaining passports,
visa requirements, and consular affairs bulletins.

The Center for Disease Control at **http://www.cdc.gov/**
provides valuable medical information, as well as information on any outbreaks of virulent infections in Uruguay.

Like all Web sites, the preceding Internet addresses are subject to
change, and there is no guarantee that they will continue to provide
the data we list here.

Venezuela

WHAT'S YOUR CULTURAL I.Q.?

1. TRUE or FALSE? Christopher Columbus, the first European to arrive in Venezuela, named it Tierra de Gracia (the Land of Grace).

   ANSWER: True. On his third journey to the New World in 1489, Columbus became the first known European to land in Venezuela. His name for Venezuela didn't stick.

2. Hoping that Venezuela was the home of the El Dorado (the lost city of gold), the Spanish quickly explored and conquered the country. But they found few mineral resources and turned to farming instead. Obviously, they failed to discover Venezuela's oil, but what other mineral resources did they miss?

   a. Iron

   b. Coal

   c. Gold

   d. Diamonds

   e. All of the above

ANSWER: e. Yes, Venezuela has significant deposits of all of these resources.

3. TRUE or FALSE? The name Venezuela comes from the name of the first Amerindian tribe encountered there by Europeans.

    ANSWER: False. On a 1499 expedition led by explorer Alonso de Ojeda, the houses of Venezuelan Amerindians (built on stilts above shallow water) were adjudged to be reminiscent of the city of Venice. Venezuela means "Little Venice." Some claim that the ship's navigator, Amerigo Vespucci, named Venezuela; most sources attribute it to de Ojeda himself.

4. Venezuela is the most Caribbean of the South American nations, both geographically and psychologically. Which of the following Caribbean islands does NOT lie just off of Venezuela's coastline?

    a. Grenada

    b. Turks and Caicos Islands

    c. Trinidad and Tobago

    d. The Netherlands Antilles

    ANSWER: b. The Turks and Caicos Islands are north of Haiti, southeast of Florida. The other islands are all within 100 miles of mainland Venezuela. Trinidad is important in Venezuelan history; the British supported the Venezuelan independence movement from there.

5. TRUE or FALSE? Venezuela was once a German colony.

    ANSWER: True. The financially challenged King Charles I of Spain signed over Venezuela to his creditors, the German banking house called Wesler. From 1527 to 1546, the Weslers frantically explored Venezuela, searching for anything of value. They failed. The Germans left little trace of their occupation, and Venezuela reverted to the Spanish Crown.

6. After defeating the Spanish in the northern part of South America in 1819, Venezuelan freedom fighter Simón Bolívar, attempted to combine which of the following countries into his Confederation of Gran Colombia?

> a. Colombia and Panama
>
> b. Ecuador and Venezuela
>
> c. Peru and Bolivia
>
> d. All of the above

ANSWER: d. And he failed. Only Colombia and Panama remained together within a few years of the death of El Libertador in 1830.

7. Today, Simón Bolívar is Venezuela's national hero. TRUE or FALSE? By the time of his death in 1830, he was a wealthy and venerated leader in Venezuela.

ANSWER: False. Bolívar died in poverty, after being banned from Venezuela. Whatever his talents as a military hero, he was not a skilled politician. He ruled as a dictator, and when the Venezuelans had enough of him they forced him into exile.

8. TRUE or FALSE? In 1902, after Venezuela refused to pay its foreign debt, warships from the United States blockaded Venezuelan ports.

ANSWER: False. Actually, the warships blockading Venezuelan ports were European. It was the USA, invoking the Monroe Doctrine, that secured an end to the blockade in 1903.

9. Venezuela did not have a democratically elected president until 1947, when Rómulo Gallegos took office in 1948, but he was ousted by military coup after a few months. Aside from his short presidency, Gallegos is best known for which of the following:

    a. He was a staunch anti-Communist

    b. He sired over 80 children

    c. During his rule, Venezuela became the world's top oil exporting nation

    d. He wrote ten novels

    e. All of the above

ANSWER: d. See the following section for an excerpt from Gallegos' most famous novel, his 1935 book *Canaima*. The military justified their coup by claiming that Gallegos was a Communist. It was a previous Venezuelan leader, the dictator Cipriano Castro, who had more than 80 children.

10. TRUE or FALSE? Venezuela has a distinctive, unique flag, quite unlike the flags of neighboring nations.

ANSWER: False. Except for the addition of an arc of seven white stars (one for each of Venezuela's provinces) the Venezuelan flag is very similar to the flags of Ecuador and Colombia. All three use the same color scheme of yellow, blue, and red.

QUOTATIONS ABOUT VENEZUELA

(He learned:) "The course of the large Guyana rivers and the way to pass from one to the other through the labyrinth of the tributaries, caños, and canoe-towing paths connecting them, the scarcely passable roads through intricate forests and uninhabited savannas, the uncertain course, known only by the Indians and just marked by the arestín growing along the old friar's road to reach Rionegro, avoiding the great Orinoco rapids and all the courses the natives know how to draw across that immense wilderness, and who of those Indians were the best rubber tappers, who were good tapioca makers, and where they lived."

—From *Canaima* by Rómulo Gallegos, a novel set in Venezuela's Orinoco Delta.

"Before Puerto Cabello was built, the nearest town was Borburata, on the coast between the savanna of Santa Lucía and the beach called Gañango. Although it was a prosperous village, it was destined to survive only a short time. When Lope de Aguirre invaded the country the townspeople moved out, and the whole area was almost completely deserted. Some time later the Guipuzcoana Company was formed; this was a Spanish investment firm interested in exploiting the agricultural riches of Venezuela. That was the beginning of Puerto Cabello; the company, to protect its interests, built warehouses, walls and forts, a church, and a shipyard there. As for the Indians, we know hardly anything about them. It is generally believed that the people of Borburata and the employees of the Guipuzcoana Company were the first settlers, but that is not true: the Negroes had arrived before them."

—From *Cumboto,* a novel exploring Venezuelan race relations by Ramón Díaz Sánchez.

"...what seems to be an isolated patch of blue mist floats lightly on the glare of the horizon. This is the peninsula of Azuera, a wild chaos of sharp rocks and stony levels cut about by vertical ravines...Utterly waterless, for the rainfall runs off at once on all sides into the sea, it has not soil enough—it is said—to grow a single blade of grass, as if were blighted by a curse. The poor, associating by an obscure instinct of consolation the ideas of evil and wealth, will tell you that it is deadly because of its forbidden treasures. The common folk of the neighborhood...are well aware that heaps of shining gold lie in the gloom of the deep precipices cleaving the stony levels of Azuera."

—From Joseph Conrad's novel *Nostromo;* his fictional Azuera is based on Venezuela.

TABLE OF CONTENTS

THE VENEZUELANS

Venezuela has achieved a high level of homogeneity via interbreeding. Mestizos (persons of mixed white and Amerindian descent) account for a full 67% of the populations. Whites, among whom the wealth is concentrated, make up 21%. Of the remainder, 10% of Venezuelans are black and just 2% are Amerindian.

HOW TO TELL VENEZUELA AND THE VENEZUELANS FROM THEIR NEIGHBORS

Venezuela is where South America meets the Caribbean. While many of its people remain poor, decades of oil exports have given a significant percentage of Venezuelans a high standard of living.

1. Venezuela borders Guyana (the former British Guiana), Brazil, and Colombia. In the Caribbean, off Venezuela's coast, lies Grenada, Trinidad and Tobago, plus the Colonial Islands of the Netherlands Antilles.

2. After the Spanish were thrown out of South America, Venezuela was united with three adjacent nations (Ecuador, Colombia, and Panama) as the Confederation of Gran Colombia. Venezuela and Ecuador left the Confederation in 1830.

3. Venezuela is proud to be the homeland of freedom fighter Simón Bolívar. Would South America ever have declared independence from Spain without El Libertador? (Yes, but don't say that in front of a Venezuelan.)

4. Venezuela is the most Caribbean of the South American Spanish-speaking nations, both in geography and in attitude. Venezuelans display an easy-going enjoyment of life.

LITERATURE

Venezuela has a significant literary tradition. Thanks to its oil wealth, the country has been able to support well-funded newspapers and a state publishing house, Monte Avila. Venezuela's authors include:

Luis Britto García (1940–) is a novelist and playwright from Caracas. He first gained attention with a 1964 collection called *Fugitivos.* He is best known for his massive novel *Abrapalabra,* which was published in 1980. Most of his work has not yet been translated into English.

Rómulo Gallegos (1884–1969) worked as a lawyer, a politician and teacher as well as a writer. Of his 10 novels, his 1929 work *Doña Bárbara* (published under the same name in English in 1931) is notable for its unflinching description of the Venezuelan character. His 1935 novel *Canaima* (published in English in 1984) includes detailed descriptions of the flora and fauna of the Venezuelan jungle. He served as president of Venezuela in 1948, but was ousted by the military after less than a year in office. He spent the next 10 years in exile. After his death, Venezuela's biggest literary prize was named for Gallegos.

Ramón Díaz Sánchez (1903–68) began writing as a journalist. His masterpiece is the 1950 novel *Cumboto, cuento de siete lenguas* (published in English in 1969 as *Cumboto*), which deftly examines the relationship between blacks and whites in Venezuela. He also served as Venezuela's Director of Culture and Fine Arts.

LIGHTS! CAMERA! ACTION!

Venezuela has co-produced some films with other countries. They include:

1. **Oriane** A *magic realism* romance, this film tells the story of a young woman and her relationship with her

late aunt. After inheriting her Aunt Oriane's remote villa, young Marie deciphers the family secret that has been haunting her. Co-produced with France, the film was a great success for first-time director Fina Torres (1984, directed by Fina Torres).

2. **Simón Bolívar** This film is about the life of the man known as the Liberator of South America, who was also a native of Venezuela. This international epic (co-produced with Italy) stars an over-the-top Maximilian Schell as El Liberator (1972, directed by Alessandro Blasetti).

LANGUAGE

The official language of Venezuela is Spanish (which is called *castellano*, not *español*).

English is not generally spoken, although international executives may speak it.

Linguists have categorized 40 different languages spoken in modern Venezuela—*Ethnologue: Languages of the World*, 12th Edition from their Web site at (http://www.sil.org/ethnologue/ethnologue.html).

BUSINESS IN VENEZUELA

THE PRIVATIZATION MINISTERS' GAME OF MUSICAL CHAIRS

Former Venezuelan President Carlos Andres Perez set up a much-needed post of Privatization Minister (which the Venezuelans call Planning Minister) in 1991. But the two coup attempts in 1992 frightened off foreign investors. New President Rafael Caldera is soft on privatization, and he has run through four Privatization Ministers since he took office in 1994. The latest one, Teodoro Petkoff, has been unable to sell the government's interest in Banco de Venezuela (the country's second-largest bank) due to a current court investigation of the bank. Also up for sale is the government's 49% interest in CANTV, the national telecom company.

BUSINESS SUCCESS IN VENEZUELA

> *Caveat: Venezuela's labor laws make it expensive to fire an employee or agent. Because of this, foreign firms often prefer to use commissioned agents rather than hired agents. (In most cases, a commissioned agent is not considered an employee.)*

Foreign companies wishing to do business in Venezuela frequently establish a joint venture. This can be done by creating a new company in Venezuela or by buying into an existing local firm. The services of a competent Venezuelan lawyer are vital. Venezuelan law applies equally to joint ventures and wholly owned subsidiaries of foreign firms.

Franchises are possible, but must be registered with the Superintendent of Foreign Investment. Once a franchise agreement is registered, it may not be renegotiated.

Newspapers are the primary medium for advertising. Even items sold directly to businesses—such as industrial equipment—are often advertised in the daily newspapers. Consumer goods are often advertised on radio and television. Billboards are frequently used in Venezuela, as are hand-distributed leaflets. Direct marketing by mail is hampered by deficiencies in the Venezuelan postal system; this is also a problem for mail delivery of goods. However, direct marketing via phone is growing rapidly.

It is vital that all materials be printed in Spanish. While some high-level executives will know English, their staff speak only Spanish. There is a shortage of trained technical personnel in the Venezuelan business community. Because of this, after-sale support for your product or service is vital. Venezuelan managers may request that their technical staff be trained in the country where the product originates; for a US product, they may want their staff trained in the United States.

LEGAL AFFAIRS IN VENEZUELA

Venezuela is a constant source of copyright violations. It is estimated that 70% of the video games sold in Venezuela are counterfeit.

The United States of America and Venezuela are currently battling over oil. US regulations now require reformulation of gasoline products to reduce pollution. US oil producers were given a grace period to switch to the production of reformulated gas. However, foreign producers (such as Venezuela) received no grace period. Venezuela accused the US of using unfair trade tactics and filed a complaint under the General Agreement on Trade and Tariffs (GATT). The World Trade Organization ruled in favor of Venezuela, but the US filed an appeal. The results are still pending as of this writing.

LEADING BUSINESSES IN VENEZUELA

The following businesses are some of the largest employers in Venezuela:

Aerovias Venezolanas SA
Caracas.
Airline. 4,000 employees.

CA Distribuidora de Alimentos
Caracas.
Grocery stores. 6,000 employees.
CA la Electricidad de Caracas Saica-Saca
Caracas.
Electric services. 5,300 employees.
CA Nacional Telefonos de Venezuela
Caracas.
Telephone services. 22,517 employees.
CA Metro de Caracas
Caracas.
Local and suburban transit. 5,800 employees.
Ceveceria Polar del Centro
Caracas.
Malt beverages. 6,000 employees.
Compania Anonima de Administracion y Fomento Electrico
Caracas.
Electric services. 14,000 employees.
Corporacion Venezolana de Transporte Silva CA
Caracas.
Freight transportation. 333,333 employees.
Corpoven SA
Caracas.
Crude petroleum and natural gas. 12,000 employees.
CVG Aluminios del Caroni SA
Caracas.
Aluminum foundries. 4,226 employees.
CVG Siderurgica del Orinoco CA
Caracas.
Primal metal products. 12,200 employees.
Instituto Postal Telegrafico de Venezuela DE
Caracas.
Direct mail advertising services. 5,000 employees.

Lagoven SA

Caracas.

Oil and gas exploration services. 14,532 employees.

Maraven SA

Caracas.

Crude petroleum and natural gas. 11,277 employees.

Muebleria Casa Abelardo SRL

Los Teques.

Furniture stores. 20,000 employees.

Petroleos de Venezuela SA

Caracas.

Holding companies. 49,218 employees.

The following are some of the largest newspaper publishers in Venezuela:

Corporacion Seremil SA

Caracas.

Newspapers and periodicals. 300 employees.

Edinter Corporacion SA

Caracas.

Newspapers and periodicals. 145 employees.

VENEZUELAN GEOGRAPHY

VENEZUELA

Maracaibo •   Caracas •

Ciudad Guayana •

VENEZUELA

FLAG AND MAP OF VENEZUELA

Francisco de Miranda, a Venezuelan native, liberated this entire part of South America. He selected the colors of the Venezuelan flag—yellow, blue, and red. The blue represents the sea, which separates South America from Spain. The red stands for the blood of freedom fighters. And the yellow was chosen to represent the new nations (perhaps in the hope that they would find gold). The flag also boasts an arc of seven white stars, representing Venezuela's seven provinces. Except for the white stars, the Venezuelan flag uses the same color scheme as neighboring countries Ecuador and Colombia.

VENEZUELAN HISTORY

Before 1498: Various Amerindian tribes live in Venezuela, including the Caribs on the coast. They do not build great cities like the Inca to the west, so we know little of them.

1498: Christopher Columbus becomes the first European to reach Venezuela. He names it Tierra de Gracia (the Land of Grace).

1499: Spanish Explorer Alonso de Ojeda gives Venezuela its present name. The Amerindian houses (built on stilts above shallow water) reminds him of the city of Venice. Venezuela means "Little Venice." (Some attribute the naming of Venezuela to mapmaker Amerigo Vespucci, who sailed with de Ojeda on this journey.)

1523: After years of fighting the fierce native Caribs, the Spanish manage to found their first mainland outpost at Cumaná. Exploration of the interior begins, but no gold is found.

1527–46: Needing money, the Spanish King Charles I grants his rights to Venezuela to his creditors, the German banking company Wesler. The Weslers spend almost two decades trying to make a profit out of Venezuela, and fail. Venezuela reverts to the Spanish Crown. For lack of anything else, the Spanish turn to agriculture.

1567: Caracas (full name Santiago de León de Caracas) is established by Diego de Losada. Caracas was the name of the local Indian tribe, now extinct. The town is sacked by English privateer Sir Francis Drake in 1595.

1717: Authority over Venezuela is transferred from the Viceroyalty of Peru to the new Viceroyalty of New Granada (Virreynato de la Nueva Granada), with its seat in Bogotá, Colombia.

1728: Spanish King Philip V grants all rights to Venezuelan agriculture to a Basque syndicate. Cocoa becomes Venezuela's cash crop, and the syndicate imports African slaves to farm it. The syndicate's monopoly is abolished in 1785, but slave importation continues for sugar and indigo plantations. By 1800, black slaves make up 60% of the Venezuelan population.

1797: The British occupy the island of Trinidad, off Venezuela's coast. To further their own economic interests, the British smuggle weapons to anti-Spanish Venezuelans, notably the creoles (Venezuelan-born whites, who are discriminated against by the Spanish).

1806: Supported by the British, Francisco Miranda of Caracas leads a force of rebels who demand independence for Venezuela. But the expected popular uprising does not appear. The black slave and poor mestizo populations are indifferent; they find Venezuelan overlords just as oppressive as Spanish ones. The *llaneros* (cowboys and ranchers) are openly hostile; they dislike the urban creoles and remain Royalists. The British are forced to evacuate Miranda's troops.

1810: The creole city leaders of Caracas decide that, since Napoleon Bonaparte has deposed the King of Spain, they will rule themselves "in the name of the deposed King Ferdinand VII." This soon evolves into a full-fledged independence movement.

1811: Francisco Miranda returns from exile in England. He becomes dictator of an independent Republic of Venezuela. But the untalented Miranda fails to gain control of other Venezuelan cities. By 1812, Royalist forces from Valencia (a city which contested

Caracas' position as capital of Venezuela) capture Miranda and regain control of the country.

1813: A former aide to Miranda, Simón Bolívar, a native of Venezuela, leads a rebel army from Colombia and defeats the Venezuelan Royalists. El Libertador (as he is known) becomes dictator of the Republic of Venezuela, but his ambitions are much larger.

1814: Bolívar is defeated by a force of Royalist llaneros. Bolívar flees to exile in Haiti. He successfully invades Venezuela in 1817 and forms the third Republic of Venezuela.

1819: Bolívar leaves Venezuela to attack Spanish troops in New Granada (Colombia). His associate, José Antonio Páez completes the conquest of Venezuela. By the time the Spanish are driven out of South America, Venezuela has lost as much as one-quarter of its population.

1821–22: Under Bolívar's leadership, Venezuela and Colombia are united. Eventually, he becomes president of the Confederation of Gran Colombia, which unites Venezuela, Ecuador, Colombia, and Panama. But Bolívar fails in his attempt to add Peru and Bolivia to Gran Colombia. Separatist forces begin to tear the Confederation apart. In 1828 Bolívar dismisses his vice president and rules as dictator, an unpopular move.

1830: Bolívar resigns as dictator. His opponents manage to get him banned from Venezuela. He dies shortly after in poverty in Colombia. Venezuela and Ecuador leave Gran Colombia. José Antonio Páez becomes the first president of the newly independent Venezuela, which has its capital at Caracas. Leadership in Venezuela comes into the hands of the "Conservative Oligarchy."

1846: With the support of Páez, José Tadeo Monagas becomes president. In 1848, he defies his Conservative backers and allies himself with what will become the Liberal Party. Reforms are instituted.

1854: Slavery is abolished in Venezuela under the Liberals. Venezuela soon slips into civil war, and peace is not restored until 1870.

1899: After another civil war and a boundary dispute with British Guiana, General Cipriano Castro seizes power as dictator.

1902–3: After Venezuela refuses to pay its foreign debt, European warships blockade Venezuelan ports. Invoking the Monroe Doctrine, the USA secures an end to the blockade.

1908: The brutal General Juan Vicente Gómez replaces Cipriano Castro as dictator. Gómez rules for the next 27 years.

1920: Massive petroleum reserves are discovered in Venezuela. Oil revenues make Gómez and his children wealthy (although he never married, he acknowledged fathering more than 80 children!). Foreign investment in Venezuela booms, and by 1928 Venezuela becomes the world's biggest exporter of oil.

1948: Venezuela's first democratically elected president, novelist Rómulo Gallegos takes office. He is accused of being a Communist, and a military coup removes him after nine months in office. Major Marcos Pérez Jiménez rules as dictator. He supports the USA in the Cold War, and oil wealth allows him to embark on a massive public works program. His rule lasts 10 years.

1959: Democracy returns with the election of Venezuela's second freely-elected president, Rómulo Betancourt. He completes his full five-year term, surviving attacks from both left and right (including an attempted military coup and a guerrilla insurgency from Communist Cuba).

1964: Raúl Leoni succeeds Betancourt as president. Venezuela celebrates its first transfer of power from one elected government to another.

1969: Rafael Caldera is elected president and serves until 1974. He initiates the establishment of a comprehensive welfare system for Venezuelans, which is paid for by oil exports.

1974: Venezuela, as a member of OPEC (the Organization of Petroleum Exporting Countries), profits from a quadrupling of oil prices.

1983: Slumping oil prices hurt the Venezuelan economy. Venezuela's currency, the *bolivar*, is devalued.

1989: The man who nationalized Venezuela's oil industry in the 1970s, Carlos Andres Perez, is elected president. His policies fail to improve Venezuela's faltering economy.

1992: The government survives two coup attempts by members of the Venezuelan military.

1993: President Carlos Andres Perez is indicted for corruption. He resigns, and Senator Ramon Jose Velasquez is appointed interim president until elections are held in December, when former President Rafael Caldera is elected.

1994: Venezuela's banks suffer a banking crisis. The Venezuelan government eventually takes over 16 major banks.

1996: Although he himself created Venezuela's welfare state during his first term (1969–74), President Caldera approves a massive austerity program. These economic reforms meet the approval of the International Monetary Fund, which awards Venezuela $1.4 billion US in credit.

1997: Within two months, Venezuela is subjected to three major oil spills that will cost millions of dollars to clean up. All three tankers ran aground in the channel that connects the Caribbean to Lake Maracaibo, but the Caldera Administration claims to lack the funds to dredge the channel.

VENEZUELAN BEHAVIOR

Why are Venezuelans the way they are?

Venezuela is a wealthy nation, with vast reserves of oil, coal, and bauxite. The country even has vast potential for hydroelectric generation. Despite these multitudinous resources, Venezuela grew to depend on income from a single source: oil. With oil revenues, the country built up a generous welfare system that made it the envy of its neighbors. But when the price of oil dropped in 1983, the country could no longer afford generous welfare benefits and price supports.

The oil boom had given Venezuelans rising expectations. The subsequent oil bust forced Venezuelans to cut back drastically. Initially, many Venezuelans refused to believe in their reduced circumstances and continued to spend as if oil dollars were still pouring in. It is difficult to convince people whose lives keep getting better that soon things will get much worse. When the realization came, Venezuelans were outraged, blaming their leaders. In the 1990s, Venezuela suffered from strikes, riots, and unsuccessful coup attempts.

Today, most Venezuelans are unhappy with their government and pessimistic about the future. Unfortunately, Venezuela does not have a long tradition of good government. In the past, Venezuela's many dictators enriched themselves at Venezuela's expense. The elected governments that followed had problems with corruption.

Infrastructure development was ignored, and the country failed to build an effective school system. Today, Venezuela cannot afford to dredge its seaways, even though the export of oil depends upon navigable passages for oil tankers. The country is struggling to build enough schools for its growing population.

Agriculture, once neglected, has been bolstered by farm subsidies. But even with these subsidies—which may have to be cut— fertile Venezuela is still a net importer of food. All of these difficulties can be traced to poor leadership.

VENEZUELA AND THE UNITED STATES OF AMERICA

Venezuela has a closer relationship with the USA than many countries in Latin America.

Historically, the USA invoked the Monroe Doctrine more than once to protect Venezuela from European incursion. The Venezuelan Boundary Dispute of 1887 occurred when the United Kingdom's colony of British Guiana extended its territorial claims westward. (Gold had been discovered in this region.) Venezuela broke off relations with the UK and asked the USA to intervene.

The UK rejected repeated offers of arbitration from the USA. By 1895, the Administration of US President Grover Cleveland appointed a commission to delineate the boundary, and invoked the Monroe Doctrine to enforce it. For a time the USA and the UK threatened to go to war. But pro-USA sentiment and the outbreak of the Boer War in South Africa convinced the UK to back down. An international commission in 1899 gave most of the disputed land to British Guiana, but Venezuela remained grateful to the USA.

The USA invoked the Monroe Doctrine yet again in 1903. Venezuela dictator Cipriano Castro refused to allow Venezuela to pay its foreign debt. In response, European warships began blocking Venezuelan harbors beginning in 1902. Once again, threats from the USA forced the Europeans to back down, and the blockade was lifted.

In more recent times, oil-rich Venezuelans came to the USA in droves. The oil money which flowed after the OPEC price hikes of 1973–74 brought Venezuelans one of the highest standards of living in Latin America. Even middle-class Venezuelans could afford shopping trips to Florida. So many Venezuelans bought homes around Miami that it the area became known as "Venezuela's 21st state."

The economic dislocations of the 1990s have put Florida homes out of the reach of the majority of Venezuelans, but the USA still remains the playground of the wealthy.

What's unusual about Venezuela's Táchira Province?

Táchira Province has the dubious honor of giving Venezuela most of its military dictators, including Cipriano Castro, Juan Vicente Gómez, the two succeeding dictators and Major Marcos Pérez Jiménez.

How do Venezuelans dress?

Clothes make the man (and woman) in Venezuela. Dress is considered an important indicator of a person's status. Conservative-but-stylish business attire is expected.

HOW CAN I FIND MORE INFORMATION ABOUT VENEZUELA?

Here are a few resources to start with:

Getting Through Customs' Web site at **http://www. getcustoms.com** tracks current holidays in Venezuela. They also post Cultural I.Q. Quizzes, gift-giving guidelines, a demo of the PASSPORT database, and further international information. Telephone: (610) 353-9894; fax (610) 353-6994.

Embassy of the Republic of Venezuela
1099 30th Street NW
Washington, DC 20007
Telephone: (202) 342-2214

The Venezuelan Embassy in Washington D.C. maintains a Web site at: **http://venezuela.mit.edu/embassy**.

The Venezuelan Consulate General in New York City has a Web site at: **http://www.panix.com/~vzla-ny/**.

Venezuelan Tourism Association
Box 3010
Sausalito, CA 94966
Telephone: (800) 331-0100 or (415) 331-0100

Venezuela on the Internet—Internet Resources about Venezuela and its culture, businesses, government, and economy. Venezuela en Internet (English/Español).
http://www.latinworld.com/countries/venezuela/

Venezuelan Chamber of Commerce of Florida—to promote the interests of its members and foster culture, trade and investment ties between Venezuela and the United States.
http://ourworld.compuserve.com/homepages/ Venezuela/

The International Academy at Santa Barbara at **http://www.iasb.org/cwl** publishes *Current World Leaders,* an excellent resource for data on political leaders and parties in Venezuela. Telephone (800) 530-2682 or (805) 965-5010 for subscription information.

The Bureau of Consular Affairs at **http://travel.state.gov** can give you detailed information on obtaining passports, visa requirements, and consular affairs bulletins.

The Center for Disease Control at **http://www.cdc.gov/** provides valuable medical information, as well as information on any outbreaks of virulent infections in Venezuela.

Like all Web sites, the preceding Internet addresses are subject to change, and there is no guarantee that they will continue to provide the data we list here.

Gift Giving in Latin America

The building of relationships in Latin America is a prerequisite for success in business.

By and large, Latin Americans do business with people they like. An executive in the United States may be required to deal with the lowest bidder, or need to produce some other documentation to justify the selection of a business partner. In Latin America, an executive needs no more than a gut instinct to justify his or her decision.

Once you establish a favorable first impression, the relationship is built more on a social than business basis. Time becomes the most important ingredient towards building successful partnerships. A foreign businessperson who never has lunch or dinner with a Latin executive will rarely establish a strong relationship. Every opportunity to build rapport should be taken advantage of, especially invitations to social events such as parties and celebrations.

Gift giving can be part of establishing successful business relationships.

It is easier to list the types of items that should NOT be given:

- *Knives or scissors.* Blades represent the severing of a friendship.

- *Carved elephants.* Some Latin Americans have an entire folklore about elephants. One should own three elephants—one bought, one found, and one given. They all must have their trunks curved upward; if the trunks curve down, all the household's luck will "run down the trunk." All three elephants should face the front door.

- *Yellow flowers.* Mexicans use them in their "Day of the Dead" festivities, so they are associated with death. In other areas, yellow roses have negative connotations.

- *Handkerchiefs.* These are associated with weeping and sorrow.

- *Items wrapped in black or purple paper.* These colors are symbolic of Holy Week (Semana Santa) processions.

The gift you select, the label, the color, and quality of the wrapping paper, the message with the gift, the timing of the presentation—all speak reams about you as a long-term business contact and reliable friend.

WHERE CAN I FIND THE PERFECT GIFT?

Many corporate gift-giving services exist to serve clients who need, for example, 50 presents for a delegation arriving from China next month. But not many retailers know the cultural significance of each gift. If you have time, corroborate the selection of the present with a representative from the country's embassy, or at least with a native of the country. Getting Through Customs will soon offer an online shoppng section at our Web site that will list appropriate presents for different situations in countries around the world. Culturally correct gifts for everything from introductory visits to Japan, to contract closings in Costa Rica will be offered. The option to review, select, and order the perfect presents online is a convenient and logical way to prepare for international travels—or to host international visitors. Check for the "Shop" or "Gift-Giving" button on our Web site at http://www.getcustoms.com or contact us at (610) 353-9894 or fax: (610) 353-6994.

APPENDIX 2

Christian Holidays in Latin America

Because of the predominance of Christians and Catholics in Latin America, we have included a brief explanation of their major religious holidays.

CHRISTIAN HOLIDAYS

Christians, in all their various forms, still constitute the largest religious group in the world. There are about 1,928 million Christians. The following constitute the major Christian holidays:

THE EPIPHANY

Also called the Feast of the Three Kings or the Feast of Lights (re: the Enlightenment of Baptism), or the Twelfth Day, is usually celebrated on January 6.

The commemoration of the Visit of the Magi (Three Wise Men) to Jesus' birthplace, or, the Baptism of Jesus, or the Twelfth Day After Christmas.

ASH WEDNESDAY

The official start of Lent, celebrated by the placing of ashes on the forehead. (The ashes are made from the previous year's Palm Sunday fronds.) While placing the ashes, the priest intones, "Remember, man, that you are dust, and to dust you shall return."

(Lent is the Forty Days of Sacrifice and Fasting in preparation for Easter.)

PALM SUNDAY (THE SUNDAY PRECEDING EASTER)

Celebrates Christ's final entry into Jerusalem, during which his path was decorated with palm fronds.

HOLY THURSDAY

Commemorates the day upon which Christ washed the feet of His apostles and celebrated His Last Supper.

GOOD FRIDAY

Commemorates the day of Christ's death on the cross.

HOLY SATURDAY

Commemorates the day Christ rested in His tomb. The final day of Lent.

EASTER

Celebrates the day of Christ's resurrection.

THE ASCENSION

Christ's final appearance to His apostles forty days after His resurrection. The Ascension of Christ into Heaven.

PENTECOST SUNDAY

Celebrated 50 days after Easter, this commemorates the disciples receiving the Holy Spirit. (This date is also Whit Sunday in some Protestant churches. Additionally, it is Shavuot, the Feast of Harvest, in Judaism.)

TRINITY SUNDAY

Observed the Sunday after Pentecost, or eight weeks after Easter. A celebration of the three aspects of God: the Father, the Son (Jesus Christ), and the Holy Spirit.

CORPUS CHRISTI

Observed on the Thursday after Trinity Sunday. A celebration of the Eucharist, which becomes the Body of Christ during each Mass.

THE ASSUMPTION

The Virgin Mary's ascension into heaven.

ALL SAINTS' DAY

A festival honoring all Christian Saints.

ALL SOULS' DAY

A special day of prayer for the dead.

THE FIRST DAY OF ADVENT

Advent consists of the four weeks before Christmas (November 27 to December 24). Advent marks the beginning of the church year, and prepares for the commemoration of the birth of Christ.

IMMACULATE CONCEPTION

Celebrates the conception of Mary, the Mother of Jesus Christ. Mary was never tainted with original sin—to which all other mortals are subject. (Not to be confused with the Virgin Mary's conception of the birth of Jesus Christ.)

CHRISTMAS (DECEMBER 25)

The commemoration of the birth of Jesus Christ.

ST. STEPHEN'S DAY (DECEMBER 26)

Saint Stephen was a Hellenistic Jew of the 1st century A.D. He became the first Christian martyr. This is not a particularly important Catholic holiday, but it is celebrated in many countries to make Christmas a two-day holiday.

Current holidays for each country are available online at **http://www.getcustoms.com**.